NEW HAMPSHIRE HIKING

NEW HAMPSHIRE HIKING

First Edition

Michael Lanza

AVALON
TRAVEL

FOGHORN OUTDOORS NEW HAMPSHIRE HIKING

First Edition

Michael Lanza

Printing History
1st edition—April 2005
5 4 3 2 1

Avalon Travel Publishing
An Imprint of
Avalon Publishing Group, Inc.

ISBN: 1-56691-935-5
ISSN: 1553-6106

Editor and Series Manager: Ellie Behrstock
Acquisitions Editor: Rebecca Browning
Copy Editors: Donna Leverenz
Graphics Coordinator: Deborah Dutcher
Production Coordinator: Darren Alessi
Cover and Interior Designer: Darren Alessi
Map Editors: Olivia Solís, Naomi Adler Dancis, Kat Smith, Kevin Anglin
Cartographers: Kat Kalamaras, Mike Morgenfeld
Proofreader: Kay Elliott
Indexers: Ellie Behrstock, Kay Elliott

Front cover photo: Grafton County, White Mountains, © Laurence Parent

Printed in the USA by Malloy, Inc.

About the Author

An avid four-season hiker, backpacker, climber, skier, and road and mountain biker, Michael Lanza first fell in love with hiking and the outdoors in New Hampshire's White Mountains 20 years ago. For years, he spent weekend after weekend hiking in the Whites, then branched out all over New England. During the year that he researched and wrote the first edition of *Foghorn Outdoors New England Hiking,* he figures he hiked 1,200 miles, covering all six New England states. He's now hiked and climbed extensively in the West and Northeast and as far afield as Nepal, but still returns regularly to New England to hike.

Michael is the Northwest Editor of *Backpacker* magazine and writes a monthly column and other articles for *AMC Outdoors* magazine. His work has also appeared in *National Geographic Adventure, Outside,* and other publications. He is also the author of *Foghorn Outdoors New England Hiking, Foghorn Outdoors Maine Hiking, Foghorn Outdoors Massachusetts Hiking,* and *Foghorn Outdoors Vermont Hiking.*

During the mid-1990s Michael syndicated a weekly column about outdoor activities in about 20 daily newspapers throughout New England and co-hosted a call-in show about the outdoors on New Hampshire Public Radio. A native of Leominster, Massachusetts, Michael has a B.S. in photojournalism from Syracuse University and spent 10 years as a reporter and editor at various Massachusetts and New Hampshire newspapers. When he's not hiking the trails of New England, he can be found in Boise, Idaho, with his wife, Penny Beach, and their son, Nate, and daughter, Alex.

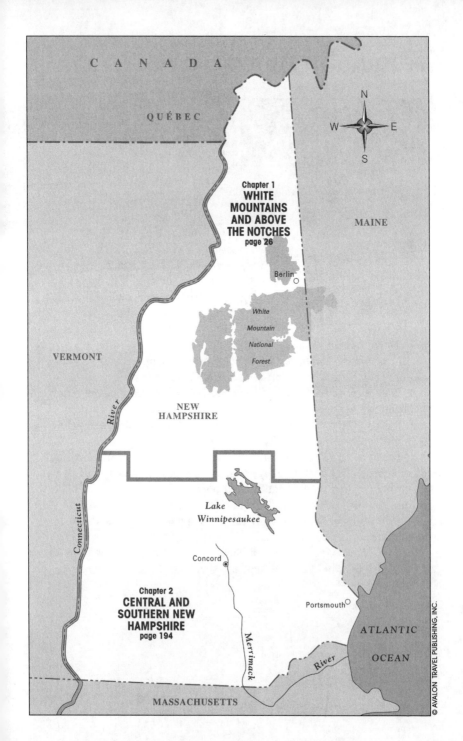

© MICHAEL LANZA

Contents

Chapter 1—White Mountains and Above the Notches.

Including:
- Crawford Notch State Park
- Dixville Notch State Park
- Echo Lake State Park
- Franconia Notch State Park
- Nash Stream State Forest
- White Mountain National Forest

Chapter 2—Central and Southern New Hampshire.

Including:
- Bear Brook State Park
- Cardigan State Park
- Great Bay National Estuarine Research Reserve
- Monadnock State Park
- Mount Sunapee State Park
- Odiorne Point State Park
- Pisgah State Park
- Winslow State Park

Resources

Index

Our Commitment

We are committed to making *Foghorn Outdoors New Hampshire Hiking* the most accurate and enjoyable hiking guide to the state. With this first edition you can rest assured that every hiking trail in this book has been carefully reviewed and is accompanied by the most up-to-date information. Be aware that with the passing of time some of the fees listed herein may have changed, and trails may have closed unexpectedly. If you have a specific need or concern, it's best to call the location ahead of time.

If you would like to comment on the book, whether it's to suggest a trail we overlooked, or to let us know about any noteworthy experience—good or bad—that occurred while using *Foghorn Outdoors New Hampshire Hiking* as your guide, we would appreciate hearing from you. Please address correspondence to:

Foghorn Outdoors New Hampshire Hiking, first edition
Avalon Travel Publishing
1400 65th Street, Suite 250
Emeryville, CA 94608

email: atpfeedback@avalonpub.com
If you send us an email, please put "New Hampshire Hiking" in the subject line.

How to Use This Book

Foghorn Outdoors New Hampshire Hiking is divided into two chapters, based on major regions of the state. Regional maps show the location of all the hikes in that chapter.

For White Mountains and Above the Notches: see pages 23–189
For Central and Southern New Hampshire: see pages 191–228

There are two ways to search for the perfect hike:
1. If you know the name of the specific trail you want to hike, or the name of the surrounding geographical area or nearby feature (town, national or state park, or forest, mountain, lake, river, etc.), look it up in the index and turn to the corresponding page.
2. If you want to find out about hiking possibilities in a particular part of the state, turn to the map at the beginning of that chapter. You can then determine the area where you would like to hike and identify which hikes are available; then turn to the corresponding numbers for those hikes in the chapter.

Trail Names, Distances, and Times

Each trail in this book has a number, name, mileage information, and estimated completion time. The trail's number allows you to find it easily on the corresponding chapter map. The name is either the actual trail name (as listed on signposts and maps) or a name I've given to a series of trails or a loop trail. In the latter cases, the name is taken from the major destination or focal point of the hike.

Most mileage listings are precise, though a few are very good estimates. All mileages and approximate times refer to round-trip travel unless specifically noted as one-way. In the case of one-way hikes, a car or bike shuttle is advised.

The estimated time is based on how long I feel an average adult in moderate physical condition would take to complete the hike. Actual times can vary widely, especially on longer hikes.

What the Ratings Mean

Every hike in this book has been rated on a scale of 1 to 10 for its overall quality and on a scale of 1 to 10 for difficulty.

The quality rating is based largely on scenic qualities, although it also takes into account how crowded a trail is and whether or not you see or hear civilization.

The difficulty rating is calculated based on the following scale:

10 —The hike entails all of the following qualities: climbs 3,000+ feet in elevation, covers at least seven miles, and has rugged and steep terrain with some exposure.

9 —The hike entails at least two of the following qualities: climbs 2,500+ feet in elevation, covers at least seven miles, and/or has rugged and steep terrain with some exposure.

8 —The hike entails one or more of the following qualities: climbs 2,000+ feet in elevation, covers at least seven miles, or has rugged and steep terrain with possible exposure.

7 —The hike entails at least two of the following qualities: climbs 1,500+ feet in elevation, covers at least five miles, and/or has steep and rugged sections.

6 —The hike entails one of the following qualities: climbs 1,500+ feet in elevation, covers at least five miles, or has steep and rugged sections.

5 —The hike covers at least four miles and either climbs 1,000+ feet in elevation or has steep, rugged sections.

4 —The hike entails one of the following qualities: climbs 1,000+ feet in elevation, covers at least four miles, or has steep, rugged sections.

3 —The hike has some hills—though not more than 1,000 feet of elevation gain—and covers at least three miles.

2 —The hike either has some hills—though not more than 1,000 feet of elevation gain—or covers at least three miles.

1 —The trail is relatively flat and less than three miles.

Hike Descriptions

The description for each listing is intended to give you some idea of what kind of terrain to expect, what you might see, and how to follow the hike from beginning to end. I've sometimes added a special note about the hike or a suggestion on how to combine it with a nearby hike or expand upon your outing in some other way.

There are a couple of terms used throughout the book that reflect the land usage history in the region. Forest roads are generally dirt or gravel roads maintained by the land manager and are typically not open to motor vehicles except those of the manager. Woods roads, or "old woods roads," are abandoned thoroughfares—many were formerly public routes between colonial communities—now heavily overgrown, but recognizable as a wide path. Their condition can vary greatly.

User Groups

I have designated a list of user groups permitted on each trail, including hikers, bicyclists, dogs, horses, hunters, cross-country skiers, snowshoers, and wheelchair users.

While this book is intended primarily as a hiking guide, it includes some trails that are mediocre hikes yet excellent mountain biking or cross-country skiing routes. The snowshoe reference is intended as a guide for beginners; experienced snowshoers know that many of New Hampshire's bigger mountains can be climbed on snowshoes in winter, but this book indicates when snowshoeing a trail may require advanced winter hiking skills. As always, the individual must make the final judgment regarding safety issues in winter.

Wheelchair accessibility is indicated when stated by the land or facility manager, but concerned persons should call to find out if their specific needs will be met.

The hunting reference is included to remind hikers to be aware of the hunting season when hiking, and that they may be sharing a trail with hunters, in which case they should take the necessary precautions (wearing a bright color, preferably fluorescent orange) to avoid an accident in the woods. Hunting is a popular sport in New Hampshire and throughout New England. The hunting season generally extends from fall into early winter. The state department of fish and game and state parks and forests offices can provide you with actual dates (see Resources in the back of the book for contact information).

Access and Fees

This section provides information on trail access, entrance fees, parking, and hours of operation.

Maps

Information on how to obtain maps for a trail and environs is provided for each hike listing. When several maps are mentioned, you might want to ask the seller about a map's detail, weatherproofness, range, and scale when deciding which one to obtain. Consider also which maps will cover other hikes that interest you. Prices are usually indicative of quality and detail. I've also listed the appropriate United States Geologic Survey (USGS) map or maps covering that area. Be advised that many USGS maps do not show trails or forest roads, and that trail locations may not be accurate if the map has not been updated recently. New Hampshire is covered by the standard 7.5-minute series maps (scale 1:24,000). An index map also covers New Hampshire/Vermont, showing the 7.5-minute and 15-minute maps.

See Resources in the back of the book for map sources. To order individual USGS maps or the New England index maps, write to USGS Map Sales, Federal Center, Box 25286, Denver, CO 80225.

Directions
This section provides mile-by-mile driving directions to the trailhead from the nearest major town.

Contact
Most of the hikes in this book list at least one contact agency, trail club, or organization for additional information. Many hikes will give you a sample of something bigger—a long-distance trail or public land. Use the contact information to explore beyond what is found in these pages. And remember to support the organizations listed here that maintain the trails you hike.

© MICHAEL LANZA

Author's Note

Dear fellow hiker,

I have a single black-and-white photograph from what was probably my first hike up a mountain. It shows two friends and me—young, dressed in flannel shirts and jeans—standing on a rocky New England summit. In the distance, clouds blot out much of the sky. The wind lifts our hair and fills our shirts; it appears to be a cool day in early autumn.

I no longer recall what peak we hiked, only that the hike had been the idea of one of my friends; I was tagging along on an outing that seemed like something I might enjoy. In fact, my recollection of the entire day amounts to little more than a lingering sense of the emotions it generated for me— kind of an artifact of memory, like an arrowhead dug up somewhere.

I was perhaps 18 or 20 years old, and standing on top of that little mountain struck me as quite possibly the most intense and wonderful thing I'd ever done.

Of course, at that age most people have limited experience with things intense and wonderful. But I found that as my fascination with high places grew, so did the inspiration that began on that first summit.

I have since done much hiking all over New Hampshire and the rest of New England and taken my thirst for that feeling to bigger mountains out West—hiking, backpacking, and climbing in the Sierra Nevada, the Cascades and Olympics, the Tetons and Wind River Range, the Rockies from Colorado to Alberta, and Alaska. My work allows me to spend many days and nights every year in wild country.

When asked to write *Foghorn Outdoors New England Hiking,* I realized I would spend a summer hiking trails I had not yet visited but which belong in a guide this comprehensive. While I expected to sorely miss the West, where I'd been spending summers hiking and climbing, instead I found myself enjoying a reunion of sorts with my hiking roots. I finally got to many places that had been on my checklist for some time. And, to my surprise, the hikes I relished most were those I had known the least about, those scattered trails that for various reasons attract relatively few hikers.

Foghorn Outdoors New Hampshire Hiking is the product of many days on the trail and a reflection of many personal memories. As you use it to explore New Hampshire's trails, I urge you to walk lightly, to do your part to help preserve these fragile places, and to venture beyond the popular, well-beaten paths to lesser-known destinations.

I also invite you to let me know about any inaccuracies by writing to my publisher, Avalon Travel Publishing, at the following address:

Foghorn Outdoors New Hampshire Hiking, Avalon Travel Publishing, 1400 65th Street, Suite 250, Emeryville, CA 94608.

I hope this book helps you find the same kind of experiences I have enjoyed in these mountains and forests—to discover your own arrowhead.

—Michael Lanza

New Hampshire Overview

New Hampshire is home to what is probably the most popular destination in New England among serious hikers: the White Mountain National Forest. It covers nearly 800,000 acres and pushes numerous summits and ridges far above tree line, with 48 summits higher than 4,000 feet. Smaller mountains and hills scattered around the state reward hikers with sweeping views that demand less driving and hiking time than the big peaks up north.

The state manages 206 state parks and forests from the coast to the remote and wild North Country. The Appalachian Trail (AT) extends for 161 miles through New Hampshire, from the Connecticut River in Hanover to the Mahoosuc Range on the Maine border.

Northern New Hampshire, referred to in this book as the White Mountains and Above the Notches, harbors the state's best-known, most scenically spectacular, and most challenging hiking. Steep, rocky trails—even on the lower mountains—frequently lead to rocky, open summits with long views. Hikers travel from all over the country to see New Hampshire's trails during the late-September to mid-October foliage peak.

In the southern part of the Granite State, lower hills, many of them in state parks, have excellent hiking that's less well known and less crowded. Two long-distance trails in southern New Hampshire—the 21-mile Wapack Trail and the 50-mile Monadnock-Sunapee Greenway—offer scenic hiking over hills that see far fewer boots than the popular corners of the Whites. While mostly wooded, these trails have occasional long views, or lead to craggy summits with excellent views, or simply provide quiet refuge from the workaday world for a hike, run, mountain bike ride, or cross-country ski or snowshoe tour.

The Appalachian Trail

Perhaps the most famous hiking trail in the world, the Appalachian Trail (AT) runs 2,174 miles from Springer Mountain in Georgia to Mount Katahdin in Maine, along the spine of the Appalachian Mountains in 14 states.

About 161 miles of the Appalachian Trail passes through New Hampshire, from Hanover on the Connecticut River, across the White Mountains, to the Mahoosuc Range on the Maine border. The Granite State's portion of the Appalachian Trail is widely regarded as the trail's most consistently spectacular and rugged long stretch.

A few hundred people hike the entire Appalachian Trail end to end every year, but countless thousands take shorter backpacking trips and day hikes somewhere along the Appalachian Trail. Well maintained by various hiking clubs that assume responsibility for different sections, the trail is well marked with signs and white blazes on trees and rocks, or cairns above tree line. Shelters and campsites are spaced out along the Appalachian Trail so that backpackers have choices of where to spend each night, but those shelters can fill up during the busy season of summer and early fall, especially on weekends.

The prime hiking season for the Appalachian Trail in New Hampshire generally runs from June through October.

Hiking Tips

Climate

With New Hampshire's biggest peaks in the north and smaller hills and flatlands in the south, as well as an ocean moderating the Seacoast climate, the state's fair-weather hikers can find a trail to explore virtually year-round. But the wildly varied character of hiking opportunities here also demands some basic knowledge of and preparation for hitting the trails.

New Hampshire's prime hiking season stretches for several months from spring through fall. September is often the best month for hiking, with dry, comfortable days, cool nights, and few bugs. Fall foliage colors peak anywhere from mid-September to early October. The period from mid-October into November offers cool days, cold nights, no bugs, few people, and often little snow.

The ocean generally keeps the Seacoast a little warmer in winter and cooler in summer than inland areas. Otherwise, any time of year, average temperatures typically grow cooler as you gain elevation or move northward. In general, summer high temperatures range 60–90°F with lows from 50°F to around freezing at higher elevations. Days are often humid in the forests and lower elevations and windy on the mountaintops. July and August see occasional thunderstorms, but July through September are the driest months.

Black flies, or mayflies, emerge by late April or early May and pester hikers until late June or early July, while mosquitoes come out in late spring and dissipate (but do not disappear) by midsummer.

In the higher peaks, high-elevation snow disappears and alpine wildflowers bloom in late spring; by late October, wintry winds start blowing and snow starts flying (though it can snow above 4,000 feet in any month of the year). Spring trails are muddy at low elevations—some are closed to hiking during the April–May "mud season"—and buried under deep, slushy snow up high, requiring snowshoes. Winter conditions set in by mid-November and can become very severe, even life-threatening. Going above tree line in winter is considered a mountaineering experience by many (though these mountains lack glacier travel and high altitude), so be prepared for harsh cold and strong winds.

In the smaller hills and flatlands of southern New Hampshire, the snow-free hiking season often begins by late spring and lasts into late autumn. Some of these trails are even occasionally free of snow during the winter, or offer opportunities for snowshoeing or cross-country skiing in woods protected from strong winds, with warmer temperatures than you'll find on

Cross-Country Skiing and Snowshoeing

Many hikes in this book are great for cross-country skiing or snowshoeing in winter. But added precaution is needed. Days are short and the temperature may start to plummet by mid-afternoon, so carry the right clothing and don't overestimate how far you can travel in winter. Depending on snow conditions and your own fitness level and experience with either snowshoes or skis, a winter outing can take much longer than anticipated—and certainly much longer than a trip of similar distance on groomed trails at a cross-country ski resort. Breaking your own trail through fresh snow can also be very exhausting—take turns leading, and conserve energy by following the leader's tracks, which also serve as a good trail to return on.

The proper clothing becomes essential in winter, especially the farther you wander from roads. Wear a base layer that wicks moisture from your skin and dries quickly (synthetics or wool, not cotton), middle layers that insulate and do not retain moisture, and a windproof shell that breathes well and is waterproof or water-resistant (the latter type of garment usually breathes much better than something that's completely waterproof). Size boots to fit over a thin, synthetic liner sock and a thicker, heavyweight synthetic-blend sock. For your hands, often the most versatile system consists of gloves and/or mittens that also can be layered, with an outer layer that's water- and windproof and preferably also breathable.

Most importantly, don't overdress: Remove layers if you're sweating heavily. Avoid becoming wet with perspiration, which can lead to you cooling too much. Drink plenty of fluids and eat snacks frequently to maintain your energy level; feeling tired or cold on a winter outing may be an indication of dehydration or hunger.

As long as you're safe, cautious, and aware, winter is a great time to explore New England's trails. Have fun out there.

the bigger peaks up north. Seacoast trails rarely get snow, though they can get occasional heavy snowfall and be icy.

For more information about weather-related trail conditions, refer to the individual hike listings.

Basic Hiking Safety

Few of us would consider hiking a high-risk activity. But like any physical activity, it does pose certain risks, and it's up to us to minimize them. For starters, make sure your physical condition is adequate to your objective— the quickest route to injury is overextending either your skills or your physical abilities. You wouldn't presume that you could rock climb a 1,000-foot cliff if you've never climbed before; don't assume you're ready for one of New Hampshire's hardest hikes if you've never—or not very recently—done anything nearly as difficult.

Build up your fitness level by gradually increasing your workouts and the

First-Aid Checklist

Although you're probably at greater risk of injury while driving to the trailhead than you are on the trail, it's wise to carry a compact and lightweight first-aid kit for emergencies in the backcountry, where an ambulance and hospital are often hours, rather than minutes, away. Many are available at outdoor gear retailers. Or prepare your own first-aid kit with attention to the type of trip, the destination, and the needs of people hiking (for example, children or persons with medical conditions). Pack everything into a thick, clear plastic resealable bag. And remember, merely carrying a first-aid kit does not make you safe; knowing how to use what's in it does.

A basic first-aid kit consists of:

- ❑ 2 large cravats
- ❑ 2 large gauze pads
- ❑ 4 four-inch-square gauze pads
- ❑ 1 six-inch Ace bandage
- ❑ roll of one-inch athletic tape
- ❑ several one-inch adhesive bandages
- ❑ several alcohol wipes
- ❑ safety pins
- ❑ tube of povidone iodine ointment (for wound care)
- ❑ Moleskin or Spenco Second Skin (for blisters)
- ❑ knife or scissors
- ❑ paper and pencil
- ❑ aspirin or an anti-inflammatory medication
- ❑ SAM splint (a versatile and lightweight splinting device available at many drug stores)
- ❑ blank SOAP note form

length of your hikes. Beyond strengthening muscles, you must strengthen the soft connective tissue in joints like knees and ankles that are too easily strained and take weeks or months to heal from injury. Staying active in a variety of activities—hiking, running, bicycling, Nordic skiing, etc.—helps develop good overall fitness and decreases the likelihood of an overuse injury. Most importantly, stretch muscles before and after a workout to reduce the chance of injury.

New Hampshire's most rugged trails—and even parts of its more moderate paths—can be very rocky and steep. Uneven terrain is often a major contributor to falls resulting in serious, acute injury. Most of us have a fairly reliable self-preservation instinct—and you should trust it. If something strikes you as dangerous or beyond your abilities, don't try it, or simply wait until you think you're ready for it.

An injury far from a road also means it may be hours before the victim reaches a hospital. Basic training in wilderness first aid is beneficial to anyone who frequents the mountains, even recreational hikers. New England happens to have two highly respected sources for such training, and the basic course requires just one weekend. Contact SOLO (Conway, NH; 603/447-6711, website: www.soloschools.com) or Wilderness Medical Associates (Bryant Pond, ME; 888/945-3633, website: www.wildmed.com) for information.

Clothing and Gear

Much could be written about how to outfit oneself for hiking in New Hampshire, with its significant range of elevations and weather, alpine zones, huge seasonal temperature swings, and fairly wet climate. But in the simplest of terms, you should select your clothing and equipment based on:

- the season and the immediate weather forecast
- the amount of time you plan to be out (a couple of hours, a full day, more than one day)
- the distance you'll be wandering from major roads
- the elevation you will hike to
- the abilities of your hiking companions

At lower elevations amid the protection of trees or on a warm day, you may elect to bring no extra clothing for an hour-long outing, or no more than a light jacket for a few hours or more. The exception to this is in the Seacoast region, where hikes are more exposed to cool wind. But higher elevations, especially above tree line, get much colder than the valleys—about three degrees Fahrenheit per thousand feet—and winds can grow much stronger. Many a White Mountains hiker has departed from a valley basking in summer-like weather and reached a summit wracked by wintry winds and lying under a carpet of fresh snow, even during the summer months. Insulating layers, a jacket that protects against wind and precipitation, a warm hat, and gloves are always a good idea when climbing New England's highest peaks.

The most important piece of gear may be well-fitting, comfortable, supportive shoes or boots. Finding the right footwear requires trying on various models and walking around in them in the store before deciding. Everyone's feet are different, and shoes or boots that feel great on your friend won't necessarily fit you well. Deciding how heavy your footwear should be depends on variables like how often you hike, whether you easily injure feet or ankles, and how much weight you'll carry. Generally, I recommend hiking in the most lightweight footwear that you find comfortable and adequately supportive.

Above all, use good judgment and proceed with caution. When you're not sure, take the extra layer of clothing, just in case.

Foot Care

At an Appalachian Mountain Club seminar on winter backpacking that I attended years ago, one instructor told us that, besides the brain, "Your feet are the most important part of your body." Hurt any other body part and you might conceivably still make it home under your own power. Hurt your feet, and you're in trouble.

Take care of your feet. Wear clean socks that wick moisture from your skin while staying dry. If you anticipate your socks getting wet from perspiration or water, bring extra socks; on a multiday trip, have dry socks for each day, or at least change socks every other day. Make sure your shoes or boots fit properly, are laced properly, and are broken in if they require it. Wear the appropriate footwear for the type of hiking you plan to do.

Whenever I stop for a short rest on the trail—even if only for a few minutes—I sit down, pull off my boots and socks, and let them and my feet dry out. When backpacking, wash your feet at the end of the day. If you feel any hot spots developing, intervene before they progress into blisters. A slightly red or tender hot spot can be protected from developing into a blister with an adhesive bandage, tape, or a square of moleskin.

If a blister has formed, clean the area around it thoroughly to avoid infection. Sterilize a needle or knife in a flame, then pop and drain the blister to promote faster healing. Put an antiseptic ointment on the blister. Cut a piece of moleskin or Second Skin (both of which have a soft side and a sticky side with a peel-off backing) large enough to overlap the blistered area. Cut a hole as large as the blister out of the center of the moleskin, then place the moleskin over the blister so that the blister is visible through the hole. If done properly, you should be able to walk without aggravating the blister.

Water and Food

Streams and brooks run everywhere in New Hampshire. If you're out for more than a day in the backcountry, finding water is rarely a problem (except on ridgetops and summits). But protozoans and bacteria occur in backcountry water sources, and campers do not always maintain an appropriate distance between their messes and the stream. Assume you should always treat water from backcountry sources, whether by using a filter or iodine tablets, boiling, or another proven method. Day hikers will usually find it more convenient to simply carry enough water from home for the hike.

Most of us require about two liters of water per day when we're not active. Like any physical activity, hiking increases your body's fluid needs by a factor of two or more. On a hot, sticky summer day, or even on a cold, dry winter day (when the air draws moisture from your body even though you may not be perspiring), you'll need even more water than you would on a cool autumn afternoon. A good rule of thumb for an all-day hike is two liters of water per person, but that could even leave you mildly dehydrated, so carry a third liter if you think you may need it. Dehydration can lead to other, more serious problems, like heat exhaustion, hypothermia, frostbite, and injury. If you're well hydrated, you will urinate frequently and your urine will be clear. The darker your urine, the greater your level of dehydration. If you feel thirsty, dehydration has already commenced. In short: Drink a lot.

Similarly, your body burns a phenomenal amount of calories walking up and down a mountain. Feed it frequently. Carbohydrates like bread, chocolate, dried fruit, fig bars, snack bars, fresh vegetables, and energy bars provide a source of quick energy. Fats contain about twice the calories per pound than carbs or protein, and provide the slow-burning fuel that keeps you going all day and warm through the night if you're sleeping outside; sate your need for fats by eating cheese, chocolate, canned meats or fish, pepperoni, sausage, or nuts.

Animals

The remarkable recovery of New Hampshire's mountains and forests during the past century from the abuses of the logging industry has spawned a boom in the populations of many wild animals, from increased numbers of black bears and moose to the triumphant return of the bald eagle. For the most part, you don't have to worry for your safety in the backcountry. In years of hiking, I've never encountered a bear on the trail, though I've seen scat and other signs of their presence.

Still, a few sensible precautions are in order. If you're camping in the backcountry, know how to hang or store your food properly to keep it

 Moose

If you don't see moose in New Hampshire, it's not their fault. The Granite State's *Alces alces* population has exploded in the past 20 years; estimates put their numbers near 10,000.

The largest members of the deer family, moose may measure six feet tall at the shoulder, and the largest antlers on record spanned 81 inches—as broad as many NBA forwards are tall. Look for them at dusk and dawn, grazing in low, wet forest and ponds—and be careful driving after dark, when the big ungulates occasionally cause mutually deadly collisions. For roadside viewing, drive the Kancamagus Highway and the stretch of NH-3 north of Pittsburg known as "Moose Alley."

from bears and smaller animals like mice, which are more likely to be a problem. If you're fortunate enough to see a moose or bear, you certainly should never approach either. These creatures are wild and unpredictable, and a moose can weigh several hundred pounds and put the hurt on a much smaller human.

The greatest danger posed by moose and other wildlife is that of hitting one while driving on dark back roads at night; hundreds of collisions occur in Maine and New Hampshire every year, often wrecking vehicles and injuring people. At night, drive more slowly than you would during daylight.

Low-Impact Practices

Many of New Hampshire's trails receive heavy use, making it imperative that we all understand how to minimize our physical impact on the land. The nonprofit organization Leave No Trace (LNT) advocates a set of principles for low-impact backcountry use that are summarized in these basic guidelines:

• Plan ahead and prepare
• Travel and camp on durable surfaces
• Dispose of waste properly
• Leave what you find
• Minimize campfire impact
• Respect wildlife
• Be considerate of other visitors

Below are more-specific recommendations that apply to many backcountry areas:

• Choose a campsite at least 200 feet from trails and water sources, unless you're using a designated site. Make sure your site bears no evidence of your stay when you leave.
• Avoid building campfires; cook with a backpacking stove.
• Carry out everything you carry in.
• Do not leave any food behind, even buried, as animals will dig it up. Learn how to hang food appropriately to keep it from bears. Black bears have spread their range over much of New England in recent years, and problems have arisen in isolated backcountry areas where human use is heavy.
• Bury human waste beneath six inches of soil at least 200 feet from any water source. Burn and bury, or carry out, used toilet paper.
• Even biodegradable soap is harmful to the environment, so simply wash your cooking gear with water away from any streams or ponds.

Hiking Blazes

New England's forests abound with blazes—slashes of paint on trees used to mark trails. Sometimes the color of blazes seems random and unrelated to other trails in the same area, but most major trails and trail systems are blazed consistently. The Appalachian Trail bears white blazes for its entire length, including its 161 miles within New Hampshire. Most side trails connecting to the Appalachian Trail are blazed with blue paint. Although not all trails are well blazed, popular and well-maintained trails usually are—you'll see a colored slash of paint at frequent intervals at about eye level on tree trunks. Double slashes are sometimes used to indicate a sharp turn in the trail. Trails are blazed in both directions, so whenever you suspect you may have lost the trail, turn around to see whether you can find a blaze facing in the opposite direction; if so, you'll know you're still on the trail.

Above tree line, trails may be marked either with blazes painted on rock or with cairns, which are piles of stone constructed at regular intervals.

- Avoid trails that are very muddy in spring; that's when they are most susceptible to erosion.
- And last but not least, know and follow any regulations for the area you will be visiting.

LNT offers more in-depth guidelines for low-impact camping and hiking on its website, www.lnt.org. You can also contact them by mail or phone: Leave No Trace Inc., P.O. Box 997, Boulder, CO 80306; 303/442-8222 or 800/332-4100, website: www.lnt.org.

Trail Etiquette

One of the great things about hiking—at least for as long as I've been hiking—has always been the quality of the people you meet on the trail. Hikers generally do not need an explanation of the value of courtesy, and I hope that will always ring true.

Personally, I yield the trail to others whether I'm going uphill or down. All trail users should yield to horses by stepping aside for the safety of everyone present. Likewise, horseback riders should, whenever possible, avoid situations where their animals are forced to push past hikers on very narrow trails. Mountain bikers should yield to hikers, announce their approach, and pass non-bikers slowly. During hunting season, non-hunters should wear blaze orange, or an equally bright, conspicuous color. Most of the hunters I meet are responsible and friendly and deserve like treatment.

Many of us enjoy the woods and mountains for the quiet, and we should keep that in mind on the trail, at summits, or backcountry campsites. Many of us share the belief that things like cell phones, radios, CD players,

Peak Bagging

In the Northeast, peak bagging—the practice of ticking off established lists of peaks, often over a period of many years—is a cultural phenomenon.

The best-known list is the New Hampshire 4,000-footers, 48 White Mountains summits that top that landmark elevation, from the loftiest, 6,288-foot Mount Washington, down to number 48, 4,003-foot Mount Tecumseh above Waterville Valley. Since the Appalachian Mountain Club's Four Thousand Footer Committee (FTFC) formed in 1957, establishing the official list (then 46 peaks), more than 7,000 people have registered with the FTFC as finishing—although undoubtedly thousands more have ticked off the list without notifying the committee.

Some who succeed in these arenas move on to the New England 4,000-footers (67 peaks), the New England Hundred Highest, and the Northeast 111, comprising all 4,000-footers in New England and New York—a list originally numbering 111 (so the name has stuck), but now at 115 since four peaks were discovered in recent years to top 4,000 feet. An obsessive few get esoteric—ticking off the lists in winter, from every compass direction, or in every month of the year (known as "48 by 12").

and hand-held personal computers do not belong in the mountains; if you must use them, use discretion.

This region has seen some conflict between hikers and mountain bikers, but it's important to remember that solutions to those issues are never reached through hostility and rudeness. Much more is accomplished when we begin from a foundation of mutual respect and courtesy. After all, we're all interested in preserving and enjoying our trails.

Large groups have a disproportionate impact on backcountry campsites and on the experience of other people. Be aware of and respect any restrictions on group size. Even where no regulation exists, keep your group size to no more than 10 people.

Dogs can create unnecessary friction in the backcountry. Dog owners should respect any regulations and not presume that strangers are eager to meet their pet. Keep your pet under physical control whenever other people are approaching.

Best Hikes in New Hampshire

Can't decide where to hike this weekend? Here are my picks for the best hikes in several categories:

Top Trails for Fall Foliage Viewing

Zealand Notch, White Mountains and Above the Notches, page 94. The notch blazes in color when the foliage peaks.

Welch and Dickey, White Mountains and Above the Notches, page 175. This relatively easy hike offers plenty of rest stops and viewpoints to take in the sights.

Mount Chocorua via any trail, White Mountains and Above the Notches, pages 183 and 184. Hikers who complete this steep ascent are rewarded with superb forest views, including a gorgeous array of fiery colors in the autumn.

Squam Mountains, Central and Southern New Hampshire, page 200. This popular hike features year-round lake views and a great seasonal show.

Mount Monadnock via any trail, Central and Southern New Hampshire, pages 221 and 222. Bring kids on this trek for crisp autumn air and a colorful view.

Top Hikes to Waterfalls

Glen Ellis Falls, White Mountains and Above the Notches, page 89. Visit in springtime, when heavy water flows make this 70-foot cascade even more spectacular.

Ethan Pond/Thoreau Falls, White Mountains and Above the Notches, page 105. This 10.4-mile trek has two spur trails, leading to the double pleasures of Ripley Falls and Thoreau Falls.

Mounts Lincoln and Lafayette, White Mountains and Above the Notches, page 133. The dramatic Cloudland Falls is the highlight of this 8.8-mile hike, but you'll also see other cascades and brooks.

Arethusa Falls and Frankenstein Cliff, White Mountains and Above the Notches, page 150. You'll pass several pools and cascades on this moderate hike, including the tallest falls in the state.

Ripley Falls, White Mountains and Above the Notches, page 151. The typical route to this 100-foot cascade is an easy, one-mile walk.

Top Hikes to Lakes and Swimming Holes

Mounts Adams and Madison: the Air Line, White Mountains and Above the Notches, page 47. It's not deep enough for a swim, but little Star

a hiker overlooking King Ravine on Mount Adams

Lake, near Madison Springs Hut, is arguably the most beautiful alpine tarn in the Whites.

Carter Notch, Wildcat River Trail, White Mountains and Above the Notches, page 86. Tiny ponds reflect towering cliffs in this dramatic axe-cut between the Carter Range and Wildcat Mountain.

Emerald Pool, White Mountains and Above the Notches, page 118. The name says it all—a beautiful spot reached by an easy walk.

Lonesome Lake, White Mountains and Above the Notches, page 125. This popular backcountry spot has a killer view across the water to Franconia Ridge.

Greeley Ponds North, White Mountains and Above the Notches, page 165. A sandy beach at the upper pond's north end is a great spot for a swim and nap.

Top Hikes Under Five Miles

Square Ledge, White Mountains and Above the Notches, page 80. Visible from Pinkham Notch and just a short climb above it, this ledge has one of the best lower-elevation views of Mount Washington.

Mount Willard, White Mountains and Above the Notches, page 108. It doesn't take much effort to reach the superb viewpoints from the cliffs of this mount—the trail rises less than 1,000 feet in about three miles.

Welch and Dickey, White Mountains and Above the Notches, page 175. With its relatively gentle grade, this hike is a good choice for those seeking summit-top views without putting in a long day's work.

Mount Cardigan: West Side Loop, Central and Southern New Hampshire, page 204. Beloved by many, Mount Cardigan is easily ascended via this steady climb.

Mount Monadnock via any trail, Central and Southern New Hampshire, pages 221 and 222. This popular mount, designated a National Natural Landmark, can be ascended via either of two trails, each topping out at about 4.5 miles.

Top Hikes for Children

Sabbaday Falls, White Mountains and Above the Notches, page 171. Less than a mile from the parking lot, the cascading falls here drop through a narrow gorge to the delight of young and old alike.

Welch and Dickey, White Mountains and Above the Notches, page 175. Young leaf-collectors will enjoy this hike during the peak of foliage season.

Mount Chocorua via any trail, White Mountains and Above the Notches, pages 183 and 184. Young adventurers will be challenged and thrilled by this difficult hike—and reaching the summit is an accomplishment for hikers of any age.

Mount Cardigan: East Side Loop, Central and Southern New Hampshire, page 205. With expansive views and steep sections of trail, this is a popular pick for older children looking for the next level of adventure.

Mount Monadnock via any trail, Central and Southern New Hampshire, pages 221 and 222. Designated a National Natural Landmark, this is a regional favorite—and a great choice for older kids looking for a chance to top a summit.

Top Easy and Scenic Walks

Lost Pond, White Mountains and Above the Notches, page 87. Minutes from the roadside in Pinkham Notch, this placid little pond offers a nice foreground for Mount Washington.

Mount Willard, White Mountains and Above the Notches, page 108. The view of Crawford Notch from these ledges atop towering cliffs is widely considered one of the best in the Whites for the relatively minor effort required to get there.

Sabbaday Falls, White Mountains and Above the Notches, page 171. A gravel trail, just under a mile long, follows a babbling brook to this lovely cascade.

Holt's Ledge, Central and Southern New Hampshire, page 197. A gentle climb of barely more than a mile on the Appalachian Trail reaches this ledge with views of Smarts Mountain and Mounts Cube, Cardigan, Kearsarge, and Ascutney.

Beaver Brook, Central and Southern New Hampshire, page 227. This chunk of conservation has a great trail system for hiking, snowshoeing, and cross-country skiing.

Top Easy Backpacking Hikes

Kilkenny Loop, White Mountains and Above the Notches, page 38. One of the least-traveled portions of the White Mountains, this hike makes a good overnight trip for those seeking peace and quiet.

Mahoosuc Range: Gentian Pond, White Mountains and Above the Notches, page 44. With great views at dusk, the shelter at Gentian Pond is a fine place to rest your feet for the night.

Mounts Washington and Monroe: Crawford Path, White Mountains and Above the Notches, page 76. Okay, it's not "easy," but it's one of the easier overnight trips in the Whites, especially staying at Lakes of the Clouds Hut.

Carter Notch: Wildcat River Trail, White Mountains and Above the Notches, page 86. Just 4.3 miles one-way and 1,500 feet uphill to Carter Notch Hut, this is a good overnight outing for beginners or kids.

Pemigewasset Wilderness Traverse, White Mountains and Above the Notches, page 146. This crossing of the Northeast's largest wilderness area sticks primarily to wooded valleys, with no big elevation gain or loss.

Top Difficult Backpacking Hikes

Presidential Range Traverse, White Mountains and Above the Notches, page 61. The biggest hills in New England, carpeted with boulders, wildflowers blooming in summer, and the best views in the region.

The Carter-Moriah Range, White Mountains and Above the Notches, page 64. A challenging traverse, but good training for harder ranges like the Presidentials.

Zealand Notch/Twins Loop, White Mountains and Above the Notches, page 96. From beautiful Zealand Notch to rugged North and South Twin mountains, here's a two-day outing that's as scenic as it is tough.

Franconia Notch Loop, White Mountains and Above the Notches, page 136. See all of the second-most famous ridge in the Whites in an overnight trip.

a backpacker on Franconia Ridge

© MICHAEL LANZA

Twins–Bonds Traverse, White Mountains and Above the Notches, page 143. One of the most remote backpacking trips in New England, and one of the author's favorites.

Top Summit Hikes

Mount Adams via any trail, White Mountains and Above the Notches, pages 49 and 52. With top marks for both scenic beauty and trail difficulty, Mount Adams' lofty summit tops out at a whopping 5,799 feet.

Mount Madison via any trail, White Mountains and Above the Notches, page 53. Some of the most strenuous hikes in the region, the trails up Mount Madison rise up 4,000 feet of elevation.

Mount Lafayette via any trail, White Mountains and Above the Notches, pages 120 and 131. The highest peak in the Northeast outside the Presidentials, this rocky mountain boasts some of the best views in New England.

Mount Chocorua via any trail, White Mountains and Above the Notches, pages 183 and 184. Diminutive compared to other peaks in the White Mountains, the views from this 3,500-foot summit are still striking.

Mount Monadnock via any trail, Central and Southern New Hampshire, pages 221 and 222. No wonder this little mountain was designated a National Natural Landmark, given its big area above tree line with views to distant hills and mountains.

Top Hikes for Solitude and Remoteness

Diamond Peaks, White Mountains and Above the Notches, page 30. Up in a little-traveled portion of New Hampshire, this mixed-use trail is rarely busy.

Sugarloaf Mountain, White Mountains and Above the Notches, page 33. A mid-sized peak in one of the least-crowded parts of New Hampshire, this 3.5-mile hike has some steeply inclined sections.

North Percy Peak, White Mountains and Above the Notches, page 34. More accessible than Sugarloaf Mountain, yet still a good choice for those seeking peace and quiet.

Mount Isolation, White Mountains and Above the Notches, page 114. The name says it all; this peak lies so far from pavement that you'll see few hikers.

Pemigewasset Wilderness Traverse, White Mountains and Above the Notches, page 146. A relatively easy route through valleys and flat areas, this traverse cuts through a federally designated wilderness area.

Top Hikes to Mountain Ridges

Mounts Adams and Madison: the Air Line, White Mountains and Above the Notches, page 47. Few trails are as airy and scenic as this steady climb to the saddle between Adams and Madison.

Mount Jefferson: Ridge of the Caps, White Mountains and Above the Notches, page 59. The shortest route from trailhead to 5,000-foot peak in the region, this 6.6-mile trek incorporates the dramatic Castellated Ridge.

Presidential Range Traverse, White Mountains and Above the Notches, page 61. A multiday trek with 15 continuous ridge-top miles above the tree line.

The Baldies Loop, White Mountains and Above the Notches, page 116. On this grueling 10-mile trek, four miles are on open ridge that afford spectacular views.

Mounts Lincoln and Lafayette, White Mountains and Above the Notches, page 133. Hikers flock here in summertime to enjoy the ridgeline views on this 8.8-mile hike.

Top Hikes for Rugged Mountain Terrain

Mount Adams: King Ravine, White Mountains and Above the Notches, page 49. A brutal but sensational hike up New England's second-highest peak.

Mount Madison: Madison Gulf and Webster Trails, White Mountains and Above the Notches, page 53. Gaining 4,000 feet in elevation over 11.5 miles, this trail will test even the most experienced hikers.

Mount Washington: Huntington Ravine and the Alpine Garden, White Mountains and Above the Notches, page 67. Another super-tough White Mountains trail: This one should only be attempted in summer and early fall due to the possibility of slippery ice formations in the colder months.

Mount Washington: Tuckerman Ravine, White Mountains and Above the Notches, page 72. For those hardy souls looking to top New England's tallest mountain, this is the standard route.

Mount Tripyramid, White Mountains and Above the Notches, page 173. A chance for experienced trekkers to hit three summits in one long day.

looking down the North Slide of Mount Tripyramid

© MICHAEL LANZA

Top Hikes to Watch the Sunrise

Table Rock, Dixville Notch, White Mountains and Above the Notches, page 31. You may share this out-of-the-way ledge high above Dixville Notch with only the sound of a moose calling in the early morning.

Mount Jefferson: Ridge of the Caps, White Mountains and Above the Notches, page 59. The shortest route to a 5,000-foot peak in the Whites affords a chance to hustle up there for dawn without a ridiculously early start.

Mount Washington: Ammonoosuc Ravine/Jewell Trail, White Mountains and Above the Notches, page 74. Want to catch sunrise from the highest peak in the Northeast? Go easy on yourself and spend the night before at nearby Lakes of the Clouds Hut.

Twins–Bonds Traverse, White Mountains and Above the Notches, page 143. Take your pick—the five summits on this trek allow you numerous chances to catch a stellar sunrise.

Mount Cardigan: West Side Loop, Central and Southern New Hampshire, page 204. Just 1.5 miles from the trailhead, this summit has a 360-degree panorama stretching from the White Mountains to the Green Mountains and the hills of southern New Hampshire.

Top Hikes to Watch the Sunset

Mounts Adams and Madison: the Air Line, White Mountains and Above the Notches, page 47. Spend the night at nearby Madison Springs Hut and you could watch the sunset over the Whites from either summit.

Presidential Range Traverse, White Mountains and Above the Notches, page 61. You'll have your choice of nine prime peaks for sunset viewing as you traverse this deservedly acclaimed route.

The Carter–Moriah Range, White Mountains and Above the Notches, page 64. Before turning in for the night at the Imp Mountain campsite, watch the setting sun from a ledge just below the shelter.

Mounts Flume and Liberty, White Mountains and Above the Notches, page 141. Overnighting at Liberty Spring campsite makes for a short post-sunset hike back to your tent after watching the sun drop behind from Moosilauke and the Kinsmans from Mount Liberty's summit.

Great Bay National Estuarine Research Reserve: Sandy Point Trail, Central and Southern New Hampshire, page 216. This easy boardwalk trail is a great pick for abundant birdlife and can't-fail sunsets.

Chapter 1

© MICHAEL LANZA

White Mountains and Above the Notches

White Mountains and Above the Notches

When hikers and backpackers think of New Hampshire, they usually think of the White Mountains. With numerous summits that reach above tree line within a national forest encompassing about 800,000 acres and 1,200 trail miles, the Whites are the most spectacular range east of the Rockies.

Besides encompassing the classic and popular Presidential Range—which has seven summits higher than 5,000 feet—this chapter's 82 hikes will take you to more obscure peaks throughout the White Mountains and in New Hampshire's sprawling, wild northern woods, "above the notches." Several hikes in this chapter lie along the new 162-mile Cohos Trail, which stretches from U.S. 302 to the Canadian border.

The southern Whites feature trails from the heights of Franconia Ridge and Mount Moosilauke to spectacular Zealand and Crawford Notches and the peaks around Waterville Valley, and from the largest federal wilderness in the Northeast (the Pemigewasset) to some of New England's most impressive waterfalls; this huge area of the White Mountains is a treasure trove of classic hiking. And I-93 makes much of the southern Whites more accessible to population centers than the northern Whites.

Some of these hikes (Mounts Lincoln and Lafayette, Mount Chocorua, Zealand Notch, Mount Moosilauke) are among the most popular in New England, and it's common to see crowds of hikers on them on nice weekends in summer and fall—and even in winter. Others (Mount Tripyramid and Mounts Flume and Liberty) are much less trampled. Some of the lower peaks (Welch and Dickey, The Moats, Cathedral Ledge, Mount Willard) in this chapter offer the best views per ounce of sweat that you'll find anywhere in New England, while other peaks (Flume and Tripyramid) rank among the region's most rugged and difficult.

Hikes to the bigger peaks of the Whites often entail more than 3,000 or even 4,000 feet of elevation gain, at least several miles round-trip, very rugged terrain, and the possibility of severe weather year-round. You should be well prepared any time of year, and shouldn't go in winter without the right equipment and training.

Along the Appalachian Trail, dogs must be kept under control, and horses, bikes, hunting, and firearms are prohibited. Cross-country skiing and snowshoeing are allowed, though the trail is often too rugged for skiing.

Keep group sizes to no more than 10 people in any federal wilderness area in the White Mountain National Forest (a good guideline to follow in nonwilderness areas as well, because large groups disproportionately affect the land and the experience of other hikers); contact the White Mountain National Forest (see Resources appendix) for information on permits for larger groups.

In the White Mountain National Forest, fires are prohibited above timberline, and camping is prohibited within 0.25 mile of any hut or shelter except at authorized tent sites. Camping is permitted above timberline only where there exists a base of at least two feet of snow. Timberline is defined as that elevation at which trees are less than eight feet tall, and is often indicated by trailside signs. Stay on the trail in the alpine zone (the area above timberline) to avoid damaging fragile alpine vegetation.

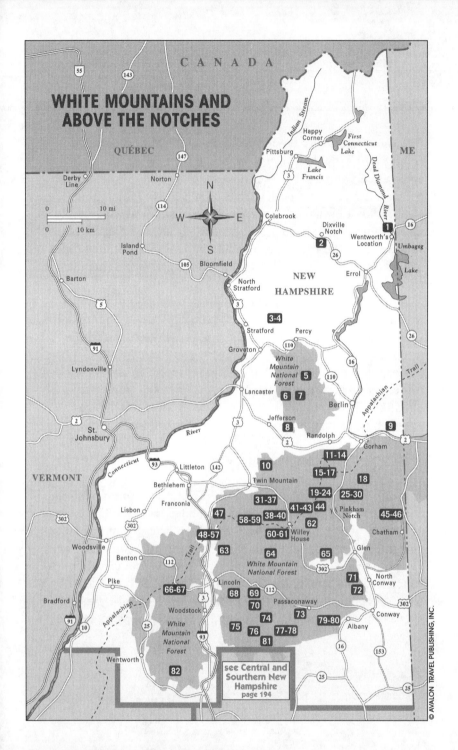

WHITE MOUNTAINS AND ABOVE THE NOTCHES

Contents

1 DIAMOND PEAKS

near Wentworth's Location in the Second College Grant

Total distance: 7 miles round-trip   **Hiking time:** 4.5 hours

Difficulty: 6   **Rating:** 8

Here's a wild, seven-mile hike in the North Country—way north of the White Mountains—that's too far from anything approaching civilization to ever become popular. You can mountain bike or cross-country ski the 2.5 miles of flat road to the trailhead to give this little adventure a mixed flavor. The hike up Diamond Peaks climbs about 600 feet.

About 0.2 mile past the Mount Dustan Store in the Wentworth's Location village center, turn left at a small cemetery onto Dead Diamond Road. Remember how far north you are—this road will be snow covered from mid-autumn well into spring and may be a mud bog until July. Follow it for 2.5 miles to the Management Center. The yellow-blazed trail up the Diamond Peaks begins at a sign on the right (east) side of the road, across from the Management Center. It rises gently through the woods at first (easy skiing, but bikes are prohibited), then makes a short but steep ascent up the rocky hillside. You pass a short spur trail on the left, marked by a sign, which leads to Alice Ledge, with a good view of the Dead Diamond River Valley. The grade becomes moderate again until the final push up to the first of the three Diamond Peaks. The trail ascends the ridge along the top of tall cliffs, with several good views of the valley below and the wooded hills across the valley. Just below the first peak's wooded summit is an open ledge overlooking the precipitous cliffs. The trail ends atop the tall cliffs of the second peak. Follow the same route back.

User Groups

Hikers, snowshoers, and dogs. No wheelchair facilities. This trail may be difficult to ski and is not suitable for horses. Bikes are prohibited. Hunting is allowed in season.

Access and Fees

The hike is on private land in the state's far north, within the Second College Grant, a township of nearly 27,000 acres owned by Dartmouth College in Hanover. The college uses gates to control access. A permit from the Outdoor Programs Office at Dartmouth College is required to park within the grant and is available only to persons affiliated with the college or its Outing Club. However, day use by the public is allowed, provided you park outside the grant.

Maps

The Outdoor Programs Office at Dartmouth College sells a waterproof contour trail map of the Second College Grant for $2. To obtain a topographic area map, request Wilsons Mills from USGS Map Sales, Federal Center, Box 25286, Denver, CO 80225, 888/ASK-USGS (888/275-8747), website: http://mapping.usgs.gov.

Directions

From the junction of Routes 16 and 26 in Errol, follow Route 16 north into Wentworth's Location. Stop and ask about parking at the Mount Dustan Store in the village center. Or park at the turnout along Route 16 about 0.2 mile past the store (about 75 yards beyond a small cemetery and Dead Diamond Road).

Contact

Dartmouth College Outdoor Programs Office, 119 Robinson Hall, Dartmouth College, Hanover, NH 03755, 603/646-2834, website: www.dartmouth.edu/~doc.

2 TABLE ROCK, DIXVILLE NOTCH
in Dixville Notch State Park

Total distance: 0.7 miles round-trip   **Hiking time:** 1.5 hours

Difficulty: 4   **Rating:** 10

Scrambling up the steep, rocky trail to Table Rock, I was stopped by an odd sound piercing the silence. Hearing it again, I realized the source—a bull moose. In late September, the bellowing of a moose in rut is not an unusual sound in the North Country. Vibrant fall foliage, however, is an unusual sight by this late in autumn: Winter arrives sooner here than in the White Mountains farther south. This hike is along the new, 162-mile Cohos Trail, which stretches from the southern Presidential Range to the Canadian border; full completion of the trail is anticipated in 2004 or 2005.

From the road, the trail climbs very steeply over difficult, rocky ground for 0.3 mile to the clifftops flanking the notch. Turn right, walk uphill another 40 feet or so, and then walk the long gangplank of Table Rock. This giant buttress of shattered rock thrusting far out from the main cliff face presents a rare perch hundreds of feet above the floor of one of New Hampshire's wildest notches. The precipitous drops off either side of the narrow walkway make it a rather unnerving adventure. With the notch so far from population centers, you may have this place to yourself, as I did.

Although you can link other trails in the notch on a five-mile loop, this hike descends the way you came—arguably more difficult and dangerous than the ascent, because of the steepness and frequently wet rock.

There is now also a five-mile loop hike around Dixville Notch. Although I have not done it myself, Kim Nilsen of the Cohos Trail Association tells me it was "made possible by the completion of the Three Brothers Trail by students in the North Country Trailmaster program. They reopened an old trail along the south side of the notch going east-bound all the way down to Huntington Falls and out to the picnic area near the Whittemore graveyard next to Route 26 east of the notch. This new trail makes it possible to swing over Route 26 to the Sanguinary Mountain Trail to a number of cliffs (very good views) on the north side of the notch and out to the perch high above the Balsams. Then the trail descends steeply down to the junction of Route 26 and The Balsams resort driveway."

Table Rock, Dixville Notch

User Groups

Hikers only. No wheelchair facilities. This trail would be very difficult to snowshoe and is not suitable for bikes, dogs, horses, or skis. Hunting is allowed in season.

Access and Fees

Parking and access are free.

Maps

For information, a guidebook, and maps to the Cohos Trail, contact the Cohos Trail Association. For a topographic area map, request Dixville Notch from USGS Map Sales, Federal Center, Box 25286, Denver, CO 80225, 888/ASK-USGS (888/275-8747), website: http://mapping.usgs.gov.

Directions

Park in the ample turnout along Route 26 in Dixville Notch, immediately west of the highest point of the road in the notch, where a sign marks the Dixville Notch Heritage Trail start (behind the state park sign).

Contact

New Hampshire Division of Parks and Recreation, P.O. Box 1856, Concord, NH 03302-1856, 603/271-3254. Cohos Trail Association, 252 Westmoreland Road, Spofford, NH 03462, 603/363-8902, website: www.cohostrail.org.

3 SUGARLOAF MOUNTAIN
in Nash Stream State Forest

Total distance: 3.5 miles round-trip   **Hiking time:** 2.5 hours

Difficulty: 6   **Rating:** 9

The 39,601-acre Nash Stream State Forest in New Hampshire's quiet North Country offers some of the most remote and lonely hiking in the Granite State—and on some sizable hills, no less. Were 3,701-foot Sugarloaf just a few hundred feet taller, peak-baggers would flock here. As it is, the state forest sees few visitors. I stood alone on this summit one afternoon in late September, enjoying a panorama of peaks stretching into Vermont, Maine, and Quebec. In fact, Sugarloaf fronts a large range of peaks that are virtually unknown to many hikers and that nearly rival in size the Pilot Range of the northern White Mountain National Forest to the south. This 3.5-mile hike ascends about 2,100 feet in elevation. This hike is along the new, 162-mile Cohos Trail, which stretches from the southern Presidential Range to the Canadian border; full completion of it is anticipated in 2004 or 2005.

From the parking area, follow the old jeep road past a cabin. Within 0.3 mile, a snowmobile trail diverges left, but continue straight ahead. The road ascends steeply without pause—a real calf-burner. But I felt I had no right to complain about its difficulty after seeing moose tracks following the same trail upward; he was carrying a lot more weight than I was. (I also found the angle perfect for letting my momentum carry me in a run on the descent.) The upper part of the trail eases somewhat, passing an excellent spring and skirting left around a major blowdown just before reaching the craggy summit, about 1.7 miles from the trailhead. Hike back the same way.

User Groups

Hikers, snowshoers, and dogs. Dogs must be leashed. No wheelchair facilities. This trail is not suitable for bikes, horses, or skis. Hunting is allowed in season.

Access and Fees

Parking and access are free. Nash Stream Road is typically open from Memorial Day to early November, depending on weather, and can be cross-country skied in winter.

Maps

An oversized locator map is posted along the entrance road. For information, a guidebook, and maps for the Cohos Trail, contact the Cohos Trail Association. For topographic area maps, request Tinkerville, Blue Mountain, Stratford, and Percy Peaks from USGS Map Sales, Federal Center, Box 25286, Denver, CO 80225, 888/ASK-USGS (888/275-8747), website: http://mapping.usgs.gov.

Directions

From Route 110, 2.6 miles east of the junction of Route 110 and U.S. 3 in Groveton and 4.3 miles west of the Stark Union Church in Stark, turn north on Emerson Road. Drive 2.2 miles and turn left onto the dirt Nash Stream Road. Continue 0.5 mile to an open area with an oversized locator map posted on a sign. From the map, follow Nash Stream Road another 4.6 miles, bear left, and continue 3.2 miles. Drive over a bridge and another 100 feet to a parking area on the left.

Contact

New Hampshire Division of Forests and Lands, P.O. Box 1856, Concord, NH 03302-1856, 603/271-3456. New Hampshire Division of Parks and Recreation, Bureau of Trails, P.O. Box 1856, Concord, NH 03302-1856, 603/271-3254. Cohos Trail Association, 252 Westmoreland Road, Spofford, NH 03462, 603/363-8902, website: www.cohostrail.org.

4 NORTH PERCY PEAK
in Nash Stream State Forest

Total distance: 4 miles round-trip   **Hiking time:** 3 hours

Difficulty: 8   **Rating:** 9

More accessible than Sugarloaf Mountain, which is also located in the sprawling, 39,601-acre Nash Stream State Forest, the 3,418-foot, scrub-covered summit of North Percy Peak offers long views in every direction. The orange-blazed Percy Peaks Trail climbs through hardwoods to the base of a partially overgrown path up a rockslide. The trail, once called the Slide Trail, used to run straight up the slide and exposed slabs.

These were dangerously slick when wet and the trail was closed following the death of a hiker 30 years ago; this old trail has since been rerouted. The Percy Peaks Trail now angles southeast away from the slabs, rounds the peak to a col between North Percy and South Percy, and then runs at a steep angle up vast southern slabs near the summit. Remember where the trail reenters the woods at the tree line: The trail is only sporadically blazed and marked with cairns above tree line, and the landscape of scrub brush quickly becomes ubiquitous. Lose your way back to the trail and you'll be bushwhacking through viciously dense subalpine vegetation, or you'll find yourself at the brink of a cliff with nowhere to go but back. The vertical ascent is about 2,200 feet. This hike is along the new, 162-mile Cohos Trail, which stretches from the southern Presidential Range to the Canadian border; full completion of it is anticipated in 2004 or 2005.

North Percy can now be approached from two other trails that have been opened in the past two years as part of the long-distance Cohos Trail. A mile north of the Percy Peaks Trail trailhead at Long Mountain Brook begins the Percy Loop Trail. Follow yellow blazes that rise moderately up the northeast flank of North Percy, first on an ancient logging road and then on a new trail. The trail eventually rounds the peak to the col where it meets the Percy Peak Trail coming up from the other side of the mountain. These two trails now make it possible, with a one-mile walk on the dirt Nash Stream Road—which connects the Percy Loop and Percy Peaks Trails—to make a complete circuit around North Percy Peak.

North Percy may also be approached from the south on the newly rebuilt Old Summer Club Trail, which was originally marked nearly 100 years ago. To reach the trail, one must park at the state parking lot at Christine Lake in Percy hamlet. Walk out of the parking lot and turn left. Take the first right into the woods and pass the gate. Walk 0.4 mile and turn left onto an old logging road. Follow the road a mile easily uphill until it crosses the Jimmy Cole Brook Road—a gated, grassy road. The Old Summer Club Trail begins on the north side of the road, passes a massive boulder, and ascends gradually at first and then moderately steeply. In 0.25 mile it passes a side spur trail that leads to the fine cliffs of Victor Head 20 minutes up the trail.

The Old Summer Club Trail, marked with yellow blazes, passes two branches of Jimmy Cole Brook and begins a moderate uphill pull to a granite rib that takes some hand- and footwork to scale. Walk the rib northwest into the col between North and South Percy Peaks. Turn right at the junction with the South Percy Trail and walk 300 feet north to the Percy Peaks Trail. Turn right and make your way to the summit of North Percy.

User Groups

Hikers, snowshoers, and dogs. Dogs must be leashed. No wheelchair facilities. This trail is not suitable for bikes, horses, or skis. Hunting is allowed in season.

Access and Fees

Parking and access are free. Nash Stream Road is typically open from Memorial Day to early November, depending on weather, and can be cross-country skied in winter.

Maps

An oversized locator map is posted along the entrance road. For information, a guidebook, and maps for the Cohos Trail, contact the Cohos Trail Association. For topographic area maps, request Tinkerville, Blue Mountain, Stratford, and Percy Peaks from USGS Map Sales, Federal Center, Box 25286, Denver, CO 80225, 888/ASK-USGS (888/275-8747), website: http://mapping.usgs.gov.

Directions

From Route 110, 2.6 miles east of the junction of Route 110 and U.S. 3 in Groveton, and 4.3 miles west of the Stark Union Church in Stark, turn north on Emerson Road. Drive 2.2 miles and turn left onto the dirt Nash Stream Road. Continue 0.5 mile to an open area with an oversized locator map posted on a sign. From the map, follow the Nash Stream Road another 2.2 miles to a turnout on the right.

Contact

New Hampshire Division of Forests and Lands, P.O. Box 1856, Concord, NH 03302-1856, 603/271-3456. New Hampshire Division of Parks and Recreation, Bureau of Trails, P.O. Box 1856, Concord, NH 03302-1856, 603/271-3254. Cohos Trail Association, 252 Westmoreland Road, Spofford, NH 03462, 603/363-8902, website: www.cohostrail.org.

5 ROGERS LEDGE

in the northern White Mountain National Forest east of Lancaster and west of Berlin

Total distance: 10 miles round-trip   **Hiking time:** 6 hours

Difficulty: 7   **Rating:** 8

This 10-mile, fairly easy hike passes through a relatively untrammeled area of the White Mountain National Forest before reaching Rogers Ledge and its beautiful mountain views. From the parking lot, follow the Mill Brook Trail 3.8 easy miles to the Kilkenny Ridge Trail. Turn right (north) and walk this easy stretch of the Kilkenny 0.6 mile to Rogers Ledge. At 2,945 feet, this high ledge overlooks the Presidentials to the south, the Pilot Range to the southwest, and Berlin and the Mahoosuc Range to the east. After enjoying the view, follow the same route back. The elevation gain from the trailhead to Rogers Ledge is about 1,500 feet.

User Groups

Hikers, snowshoers, and dogs. No wheelchair facilities. This trail may be difficult to ski and is not suitable for bikes or horses. Hunting is allowed in season.

Access and Fees

No backcountry permit is needed, but a permit is required for day use or overnight parking at any White Mountain National Forest trailhead, as indicated by signs posted at most trailheads. Permits are available at several area stores and from the national forest at a cost of $5 for seven consecutive days or $20 per year. A $3 one-day permit can be purchased at self-service stations at national forest trailheads, but the permit is good only for the trailhead at which it's purchased. The entrance gate to the U.S. Fish Hatchery on York Pond Road is closed 4 P.M.–8 A.M., but not locked; close and pin the gate again after passing through if it is closed when you arrive. There is a backcountry campsite with a pit toilet on the Kilkenny Ridge Trail, 0.1 mile north of the Mill Brook Trail junction.

Maps

For a contour map of hiking trails, get the *Carter Range-Evans Notch/ North Country-Mahoosuc* map, $7.95 in waterproof Tyvek, available in many stores and from the Appalachian Mountain Club, 800/262-4455, website: www.outdoors.org; or the *Trail Map and Guide to the White Mountain National Forest* for $7.95 from the DeLorme Publishing Company, 800/642-0970. For topographic area maps, request West Milan, Milan, Pliny Range, and Berlin from USGS Map Sales, Federal Center, Box 25286, Denver, CO 80225, 888/ASK-USGS (888/275-8747), website: http://mapping.usgs.gov.

Directions

From the junction of Routes 16 and 110 in Berlin, drive north on Route 110 for about seven miles and turn left onto York Pond Road at a sign for the U.S. Fish Hatchery. Follow the paved road to the hatchery and then follow the Mill Brook Trail signs to a small parking area at the end of a short dirt road behind the hatchery office.

Contact

White Mountain National Forest Supervisor, 719 North Main Street, Laconia, NH 03246, 603/528-8721, TDD for hearing impaired 603/528-8722, website: www.fs.fed.us/r9/white. New Hampshire Division of Parks and Recreation, Bureau of Trails, P.O. Box 1856, Concord, NH 03302-1856, 603/271-3254.

6 KILKENNY LOOP
in the northern White Mountain National Forest east of
Lancaster and west of Berlin

Total distance: 18.5 miles one-way **Hiking time:** 2 days

Difficulty: 8 **Rating:** 9

Imagine, in a national forest as heavily used as the White Mountains, hiking a trail of pine-needle duff and moss that actually gives softly like a cushion underfoot. Or taking a two-day backpacking trip during the height of the foliage season and seeing just a few other people. That was the experience two friends and I had on a traverse of the Pilot Range, much of it on the Kilkenny Ridge Trail. Located within the national forest's northernmost reaches, the Pilot Range is far removed from population centers and boasts no giant peaks to attract hikers. Instead, you revel in the solitude and quiet in a forest not yet loved to death, passing a mountain pond and impressive, if sporadic, views. This hike includes side trips to Rogers Ledge and the Horn, perhaps the two best views in the range.

Previously Kilkenny Traverse began at the fish hatchery and ended at the Heath's Gate trailhead, but Heath's Gate is on private land and has since been closed to the public. The hike described here instead loops back to the York Pond Road about two miles from where you begin the hike; you can either shuttle vehicles or use one vehicle and just walk two miles of road. This hike's distance includes the two miles of walking down York Pond Road. The cumulative elevation gained on this two-day trip is about 4,000 feet.

Follow the gently rising Mill Brook Trail 3.8 miles to the Kilkenny Ridge Trail, passing through an extensive area of birch forest. Drop your packs and turn right (north) for the side trip of 1.2 miles to Rogers Ledge, an open ledge atop cliffs with sweeping views south to the Presidentials, southwest to the unfolding Pilot Range, and southeast to Berlin's smokestacks and the Mahoosuc Range beyond. Double back to your packs and hike southwest on the Kilkenny Ridge Trail for 2.1 miles, much of it an easy walk, with a moderate hill climb just before you reach Unknown

Pond and the intersection with the Unknown Pond Trail. Turn right at the pond, walk the trail paralleling its shore for less than 0.1 mile, and then turn left with the Kilkenny Ridge Trail. It climbs fairly steeply, gaining several hundred feet in elevation over 1.7 miles to a side trail leading left (east) 0.3 mile to the craggy, 3,905-foot summit of the Horn, with expansive views in every direction. Reaching the very summit of the Horn requires a little hand and foot scrambling, but it's not difficult.

Back on the Kilkenny Ridge Trail, continue southwest over the wooded summit of the Bulge (3,920 feet) and on to the highest point on the ridge, 4,170-foot Mount Cabot, 2.8 miles from Unknown Pond. Cabot's summit is wooded, with no views, but a mile farther down the Kilkenny Ridge Trail lies Bunnell Rock, with a wide view to the south. From Cabot's summit, the Kilkenny Ridge Trail coincides with the Mount Cabot Trail for 1.4 miles; where they split, bear left (east) with the Kilkenny Ridge Trail and follow it for another 0.3 mile to the Bunnell Notch Trail. They coincide for 0.1 mile; where they split, stay left (east) on the Bunnell Notch Trail for another 2.6 miles. Turn left on the York Pond Trail and follow it 0.2 mile back to York Pond Road, which you can walk down about two miles to the fish hatchery and the Mill Brook trailhead.

User Groups
Hikers, snowshoers, and dogs. No wheelchair facilities. This trail is not suitable for bikes, horses, or skis. Hunting is allowed in season.

Access and Fees
No backcountry permit is needed, but a permit is required for day use or overnight parking at any White Mountain National Forest trailhead, as indicated by signs posted at most trailheads. Permits are available at several area stores and from the national forest at a cost of $5 for seven consecutive days or $20 per year. A $3 one-day permit can be purchased at self-service stations at national forest trailheads, but the permit is good only for the trailhead at which it's purchased. The U.S. Fish Hatchery entrance gate on York Pond Road is closed 4 P.M.–8 A.M., but not locked; close and pin the gate again after passing through if it is closed when you arrive. There are two backcountry campsites with pit toilets on the Kilkenny Ridge Trail, 0.1 mile north of the Mill Brook Trail junction, the other at Unknown Pond, and a cabin with bunks on the Kilkenny Trail 0.4 mile south of the Mount Cabot summit.

Maps
For a map of hiking trails, get the *Carter Range-Evans Notch/North Country-Mahoosuc* map, $7.95 in waterproof Tyvek, available in many stores and

from the Appalachian Mountain Club, 800/262-4455, website: www.out-doors.org; or the *Trail Map and Guide to the White Mountain National Forest* for $7.95 from the DeLorme Publishing Company, 800/642-0970. For topographic area maps, request West Milan, Milan, Pliny Range, and Berlin from USGS Map Sales, Federal Center, Box 25286, Denver, CO 80225, 888/ASK-USGS (888/275-8747), website: http://mapping.usgs.gov.

Directions

You can either shuttle vehicles to either end of this hike or use one vehicle and hike two miles of road at the end of the trip. From the junction of Routes 16 and 110 in Berlin, drive north on Route 110 for about seven miles and turn left onto York Pond Road at the U.S. Fish Hatchery sign. Follow the paved road to the hatchery and then follow signs for the Mill Brook Trail to a small parking area at the end of a short dirt road behind the hatchery office. The hike begins there and ends at the York Pond Trail, which begins two miles farther down York Pond Road.

Contact

White Mountain National Forest Supervisor, 719 North Main Street, Laconia, NH 03246, 603/528-8721, TDD for the hearing impaired 603/528-8722, website: www.fs.fed.us/r9/white.

---

7 MOUNT CABOT

in the northern White Mountain National Forest east of Lancaster and west of Berlin

Total distance: 11.5 miles round-trip

Hiking time: 7 hours

Difficulty: 9

Rating: 8

Although Mount Cabot (4,170 feet) has a wooded summit with no views, it attracts hikers for its status as one of New Hampshire's 48 official 4,000-footers. Still, there are hardly the crowds up here that are found on peaks of comparable size to the south. And Bunnell Rock, an open ledge along this hike, offers a broad view of this corner of the Pilot Range. In previous editions of this book, the hike up Cabot was described from the Heath's Gate trailhead, but Heath's Gate is on private land and has since been closed to the public. The hike described here reaches the summits of Cabot and The Horn—which has the best view on this loop—and takes in Unknown Pond, making it actually a more scenic (though longer) hike than the one I'd described in earlier editions. This hike gains nearly 3,000 feet over its course.

Follow the York Pond Trail for 0.2 mile, then bear right onto the Bunnell Notch Trail and follow it for 2.6 miles, to where it meets the Kilkenny Ridge Trail (the Bunnell Notch Trail may not be blazed, making it challenging to follow in winter but not difficult when there's no snow). The Bunnell Notch Trail generally follows the north side of the stream all the way to the junction with the Kilkenny Ridge Trail at the height of land in the col. Bear right onto the two trails, which coincide for 0.1 mile. Where they split, stay to the right on the Kilkenny Ridge Trail for another 0.3 mile, to where it joins the Mount Cabot Trail. Turn right, and follow the Kilkenny Ridge/Mount Cabot Trail uphill—passing the great view from Bunnell Rock along the way—for 1.4 miles to the wooded summit of Mount Cabot. The Kilkenny Ridge Trail continues northward past Cabot's summit, bouncing up and down along a wooded ridge. It passes over the 3,920-foot summit of the Bulge, and, 1.1 miles from Cabot's summit, reaches a side path that leads 0.3 mile to the craggy, 3,905-foot summit of the Horn, which is reached by an easy scramble and offers great views of the Whites. Backtrack to the Kilkenny Ridge Trail, turn right (north), and descend, steeply at times, for 1.7 miles to Unknown Pond. Turn right (southeast), following the pond's shoreline briefly; where the Kilkenny Ridge Trail swings left (northeast), continue straight ahead on the Unknown Pond Trail, descending 3.3 miles to York Pond Road. Turn right and walk a short distance up the road to the York Pond Trail and your vehicle.

User Groups

Hikers, snowshoers, and dogs. No wheelchair facilities. This trail is not suitable for bikes, horses, or skis. Hunting is allowed in season.

Access and Fees

No backcountry permit is needed, but a permit is required for day use or overnight parking at any White Mountain National Forest trailhead, as indicated by signs posted at most trailheads. Permits are available at several area stores and from the national forest at a cost of $5 for seven consecutive days or $20 per year. A $3 one-day permit can be purchased at self-service stations at national forest trailheads, but the permit is good only for the trailhead at which it's purchased. The U.S. Fish Hatchery entrance gate on York Pond Road is closed 4 P.M.–8 A.M., but not locked; close and pin the gate again after passing through if it is closed when you arrive. The York Pond Road has been plowed all the way to its end in recent winters, but check first with the White Mountain National Forest. There is a cabin with bunks on the Kilkenny Ridge Trail 0.4 mile south of the Mount Cabot summit.

Maps

For a contour map of hiking trails, get the *Carter Range–Evans Notch/ North Country–Mahoosuc* map, $7.95 in waterproof Tyvek, available in many stores and from the Appalachian Mountain Club, 800/262-4455, website: www.outdoors.org; or the *Trail Map and Guide to the White Mountain National Forest* for $7.95 from the DeLorme Publishing Company, 800/642-0970. For topographic area maps, request Pliny Range and Stark from USGS Map Sales, Federal Center, Box 25286, Denver, CO 80225, 888/ASK-USGS (888/275-8747), website: http://mapping.usgs.gov.

Directions

From the junction of Routes 16 and 110 in Berlin, drive north on Route 110 for about seven miles and turn left onto York Pond Road at the U.S. Fish Hatchery sign. Follow the paved road to the hatchery and then continue about two miles farther to a small parking area on the right, just before the end of York Pond Road. The York Pond Trail begins at the end of the road.

Contact

White Mountain National Forest Supervisor, 719 North Main Street, Laconia, NH 03246, 603/528-8721, TDD for the hearing impaired 603/528-8722, website: www.fs.fed.us/r9/white.

---

8 MOUNTS STARR KING AND WAUMBEK

in the White Mountain National Forest near Jefferson

Total distance: 7.2 miles round-trip   **Hiking time:** 4.5 hours

Difficulty: 8   **Rating:** 7

Just a 20-minute drive from the popular peaks of the Presidential Range, this underappreciated hike sees much less foot traffic. A friend and I hiked the trail one winter day when the clouds were building up around the northern Presidentials just to the southeast, and we had clear weather on Starr King and Waumbek (elevation 4,006 feet). Plus, we saw no one else. While the trail has no terribly steep sections, the climb to Starr King gains about 2,400 feet in elevation, and continuing to Waumbek adds another 200 feet of ascent.

Ascending steadily but at a moderate grade, the trail leads 2.6 miles to the Starr King top and a sweeping view of the Whites, from the Presidential Range (southeast) to the Pemigewasset Wilderness peaks (south) and Franconia Ridge (southwest). Ed Hawkins, an avid hiker in New Hampshire, tells me he has counted more than 30 4,000-foot peaks visible from this outlook. The trail continues another mile on easy terrain to the summit of one of New Hampshire's least-visited 4,000-footers, Mount Waumbek. This route is a good introduction to winter hiking because the trail is almost completely in the woods and protected. Low trees obstruct the view from Waumbek for most of the year, but when there's snow on the ground, you get some views similar to those from Starr King. Watch for signs and arrows indicating turns in the trail early on. It's sporadically blazed but not too difficult to follow. At the edge of an open area on Starr King's summit sits a fireplace from a former shelter. On Waumbek's summit, the Kilkenny Ridge Trail leads east and north into the Pilot Range, toward Mount Cabot, Unknown Pond, and Rogers Ledge. This hike descends the same way you came.

User Groups

Hikers, snowshoers, and dogs. No wheelchair facilities. This trail is not suitable for bikes, horses, or skis. Hunting is allowed in season.

Access and Fees

No backcountry permit is needed, but a permit is required for day use or overnight parking at any White Mountain National Forest trailhead, as indicated by signs posted at most trailheads. Permits are available at several area stores and from the national forest at a cost of $5 for seven consecutive days or $20 per year. A $3 one-day permit can be purchased at self-service stations at national forest trailheads, but the permit is good only for the trailhead at which it's purchased.

Maps

For a contour map of hiking trails, get the *Carter Range-Evans Notch/ North Country-Mahoosuc* map, $7.95 in waterproof Tyvek, available in many stores and from the Appalachian Mountain Club, 800/262-4455, website: www.outdoors.org; or the *Randolph Valley and the Northern Peaks* map, available for $5 in waterproof Tyvek from the Randolph Mountain Club. For a topographic area map, request Pliny Range from USGS Map Sales, Federal Center, Box 25286, Denver, CO 80225, 888/ASK-USGS (888/275-8747), website: http://mapping.usgs.gov.

Directions

From the junction of Route 115A and U.S. 2 in Jefferson, follow U.S. 2 east for 0.2 mile. Turn left up a narrow road at a sign for the Starr King Trail. The road ends in about 0.1 mile at a small parking area at the trailhead. (The road is not maintained in winter; park at the Jefferson swimming pool on U.S. 2 near the town center, a short walk from the trailhead.)

Contact

White Mountain National Forest Supervisor, 719 North Main Street, Laconia, NH 03246, 603/528-8721, TDD for the hearing impaired 603/528-8722, website: www.fs.fed.us/r9/white. Randolph Mountain Club, P.O. Box 279, Randolph, NH 03581, website: www.randolphmountainclub.org.

9 MAHOOSUC RANGE: GENTIAN POND
in Shelburne

Total distance: 7 miles round-trip   **Hiking time:** 4 hours

Difficulty: 6   **Rating:** 8

While Gentian Pond may seem an unlikely destination for a hike, it's actually a picturesque big puddle tucked into an evergreen woods amid the steep and rugged Mahoosucs. The thing to do is load up a backpack for two or three days and stay in the shelter at Gentian Pond—the dusk view southward to the Androscoggin Valley and the Carter-Moriah Range is fantastic. The shelter is a good base for exploring this end of the Mahoosucs. A friend and I once spent three days in March here and saw no one else—and the shelter's register showed only a handful of visitors all winter. Expect more hiker traffic during the warmer months, of course, but not the level you'd see on many of the popular White Mountains trails. Go in June to see hundreds of rare white and pink lady's slippers in bloom along the trail. The hike climbs about 800 feet uphill.

The Austin Brook Trail follows old logging roads for more than two miles. After narrowing to a hiking trail, it skirts the edge of a swampy area, and then gains much of its elevation in the last 0.5-mile push up to the shelter, where it meets the Mahoosuc Trail, which is also the Appalachian Trail. To return to your vehicle, follow the Austin Brook Trail back out.

User Groups

Hikers, snowshoers, and dogs. No wheelchair facilities. This trail could be skied easily for the first two miles along logging roads, but it grows more difficult where the trail narrows and would be very difficult for its steep final half mile. This trail is not suitable for bikes or horses. Hunting is allowed in season.

Access and Fees

Parking and access are free. The Mahoosuc Range is on private property, not within the White Mountain National Forest. Camping is only allowed at shelters and designated camping areas.

Maps

For a contour map of hiking trails, get the *Carter Range-Evans Notch/ North Country-Mahoosuc* map, $7.95 in waterproof Tyvek, available in many stores and from the Appalachian Mountain Club, 800/262-4455, website: www.outdoors.org; or map 7 in the *Map and Guide to the Appalachian Trail in New Hampshire and Vermont,* an eight-map set and guidebook for $19.95 ($14.95 for the maps alone) from the Appalachian Trail Conference. For a topographic area map, request Shelburne from USGS Map Sales, Federal Center, Box 25286, Denver, CO 80225, 888/ASK-USGS (888/275-8747), website: http://mapping.usgs.gov.

Directions

In Shelburne Village, which lies between Gorham and Gilead, Maine, turn off U.S. 2 onto Meadow Road, crossing the Androscoggin River. At North Road, turn left. Immediately on the right you'll see an old logging road that leads to the Austin Brook Trail; there may be limited roadside parking here. The trail begins 0.5 mile farther west on North Road, where there is some additional parking.

Contact

Appalachian Mountain Club Pinkham Notch Visitor Center, P.O. Box 298, Gorham, NH 03581, 603/466-2721, website: www.outdoors.org. Appalachian Trail Conference, P.O. Box 807, Harpers Ferry, WV 25425, 304/535-6331, website: www.appalachiantrail.org. New Hampshire Division of Parks and Recreation, Bureau of Trails, P.O. Box 1856, Concord, NH 03302-1856, 603/271-3254.

---

10 CHERRY MOUNTAIN: OWL'S HEAD TRAIL
in the White Mountain National Forest south of Jefferson

Total distance: 3.8 miles round-trip   **Hiking time:** 3.5 hours

Difficulty: 6   **Rating:** 9

On the broad, open ledges of the Owl's Head on Cherry Mountain, you get an expansive view of the Presidential Range—and maybe a little solitude to boot in this quiet corner of the White Mountains. I stood up here alone one cool, windy autumn day, not seeing another person until I passed two hikers on my way back down again. The trail ascends less than 2,000 feet in elevation.

From the parking lot, the Owl's Head Trail enters a thin strip of woods, crosses a small brook, and emerges immediately into a cleared area. Head straight across the clearing to a post marker that reads "Path." Watch for orange blazes. Follow a wide double track for about 300 feet past the post, watching closely for where the trail enters the woods to the right (a spot I easily overlooked). The trail has been relocated a bit in this area in recent years, so keep an eye out for signs of recent trail work and brush clearing. The hiking is fairly easy at first, crossing some logged areas—watch for cairns and trail markers. It then begins climbing at a moderate grade. Thanks to work done by the Randolph Mountain Club, the trail no longer ascends the steep, loose, former rockslide path, so it's much easier. About 1.8 miles from the road, the trail crests the Cherry Mountain ridge; walk a relatively flat 0.1 mile to the ledges. To the south, the trail continues on to Mount Martha, 0.8 mile farther, where there is a good view. Return along the same route.

This hike is along the new, 162-mile Cohos Trail, which stretches from the southern Presidential Range to the Canadian border; full completion of the trail is anticipated in 2004 or 2005.

User Groups

Hikers and dogs. No wheelchair facilities. This trail may be difficult to snowshoe and is not suitable for bikes, horses, or skis. Hunting is allowed in season.

Access and Fees

No backcountry permit is needed, but a permit is required for day use or overnight parking at any White Mountain National Forest trailhead, as indicated by signs posted at most trailheads. Permits are available at several area stores and from the national forest at a cost of $5 for seven consecutive days or $20 per year. A $3 one-day permit can be purchased at self-service stations at national forest trailheads, but the permit is good only for the trailhead at which it's purchased.

Maps

Maps covering this area's hiking trails include the *Franconia–Pemigewasset Range* map, for $7.95 in waterproof Tyvek, available in many stores and from the Appalachian Mountain Club, 800/262-4455, website: www.outdoors.org; the *Randolph Valley and the Northern Peaks* map, available for $5 in waterproof Tyvek from the Randolph Mountain Club; and the *Trail Map and Guide to the White Mountain National Forest* for $7.95 from the DeLorme Publishing Company, 800/642-0970. For information, a guidebook, and maps to the Cohos Trail, contact the Cohos Trail Association. For topographic area maps, request Bethlehem and Mount Washington from USGS Map Sales, Federal Center, Box 25286, Denver, CO 80225, 888/ASK-USGS (888/275-8747), website: http://mapping.usgs.gov.

Directions

The trailhead parking area is on Route 115, 5.8 miles north of the junction of Route 115 and U.S. 3 and four miles south of the junction of Route 115 and U.S. 2.

Contact

White Mountain National Forest Supervisor, 719 North Main Street, Laconia, NH 03246, 603/528-8721, TDD for the hearing impaired 603/528-8722, website: www.fs.fed.us/r9/white. Randolph Mountain Club, P.O. Box 279, Randolph, NH 03581, website: www.randolphmountainclub.org. Cohos Trail Association, 252 Westmoreland Road, Spofford, NH 03462, 603/363-8902, website: www.cohostrail.org.

11 MOUNTS ADAMS AND MADISON: THE AIR LINE
in the White Mountain National Forest south of Randolph

Total distance: 9.5 miles round-trip   **Hiking time:** 8 hours

Difficulty: 10   **Rating:** 10

This is the most direct route to the second-highest peak summit in New England—5,799-foot Mount Adams—though not necessarily the fastest. It follows Adams's spectacular Durand Ridge, giving hikers extended views from atop high cliffs, down into King Ravine, southwest across the prominent ridges on the northern flanks of Mounts Adams and Jefferson, and north across the Randolph Valley to the Pilot Range peaks. Some scrambling is necessary, and you need to be comfortable with exposure—there's an interesting little foot ledge traverse that can get your heart pumping. This route allows a fit hiker blessed with good weather the option of hitting both Adams and Madison in a day. The vertical ascent to Adams is nearly 4,500 feet, and Madison adds about another 500 feet. If the weather turns bad, descend the Valley Way, which enters the woods more quickly than other trails. On this hike, the Appalachian Trail coincides with the Osgood Trail up Mount Madison and with the Gulfside Trail, which this hike crosses on Mount Adams.

From the parking lot at Appalachia, the Air Line makes a 4.3-mile beeline to Adams's summit, with the final 1.5 miles above the trees. Descend via the Air Line—or go for Madison's summit (5,366 feet). To reach Madison from Adams's summit, either backtrack 0.8 mile on the Air Line to the Air Line cutoff leading 0.2 mile toward the Madison hut, or take a

at Emerald Bluff above Castle Ravine, Mount Adams

somewhat more difficult but very scenic option: the less-traveled, mile-long Star Lake Trail, which descends southeast from Adams's summit, then swings northeast and traverses the steep northeast face of Adams. It passes beautiful Star Lake on the way to the hut. From the hut, follow the Osgood Trail 0.5 mile to Madison's summit, then descend north via the Watson Path, Scar Trail, and the Valley Way back to Appalachia. If you descend the Valley Way, be sure to take the side paths that parallel it past Tama Fall and Gordon Fall, which are marked by signs not far from the trailhead and do not add any appreciable distance to this hike.

User Groups

Hikers and dogs. No wheelchair facilities. This trail should not be attempted in winter except by hikers experienced in mountaineering and prepared for severe winter weather, and is not suitable for bikes, horses, or skis. Hunting is allowed in season.

Access and Fees

Parking and access are free.

Maps

Several maps cover this area's hiking trails, including the *Presidential Range* map, for $7.95 in waterproof Tyvek, available in many stores and from the Appalachian Mountain Club, 800/262-4455, website: www.outdoors.org; the

Randolph Valley and the Northern Peaks map, available for $5 in waterproof Tyvek from the Randolph Mountain Club; map 2 in the *Map and Guide to the Appalachian Trail in New Hampshire and Vermont,* an eight-map set and guidebook available for $19.95 ($14.95 for the maps alone) from the Appalachian Trail Conference; and the *Trail Map and Guide to the White Mountain National Forest* for $7.95 from the DeLorme Publishing Company, 800/642-0970. For a topographic area map, request Mount Washington from USGS Map Sales, Federal Center, Box 25286, Denver, CO 80225, 888/ASK-USGS (888/275-8747), website: http://mapping.usgs.gov.

Directions

Park in the large lot at the Appalachia Trailhead on U.S. 2 in Randolph, 2.1 miles west of the northern junction of U.S. 2 and Route 16 in Gorham, and 7.1 miles east of the junction of U.S. 2 and Route 115. The Air Line begins there.

Contact

White Mountain National Forest Supervisor, 719 North Main Street, Laconia, NH 03246, 603/528-8721, TDD for the hearing impaired 603/528-8722, website: www.fs.fed.us/r9/white. Appalachian Trail Conference, 799 Washington Street, P.O. Box 807, Harpers Ferry, WV 25425-0807, 304/535-6331, website: www.appalachiantrail.org. The Appalachian Mountain Club Pinkham Notch Visitor Center has up-to-date weather and trail information about the Whites; call 603/466-2725. Randolph Mountain Club, P.O. Box 279, Randolph, NH 03581, website: www.randolphmountainclub.org.

12 MOUNT ADAMS: KING RAVINE

in the White Mountain National Forest south of Randolph

Total distance: 8.8 miles round-trip   **Hiking time:** 8 hours

Difficulty: 10   **Rating:** 10

This route through King Ravine is one of the most difficult and spectacular hikes in the White Mountains, and an adventurous way up the second-highest peak in New England: 5,799-foot Mount Adams. Besides involving hard scrambling over boulders and up the talus of a very steep ravine headwall, you will gain nearly 4,400 feet in elevation from the trailhead to Adams's summit. I hiked this on a banner June day with my friend Larry from Seattle, who's climbed all over Washington's Cascades and Olympics and was making his first trip to New England. At one point, he turned to me and gushed, "Mike, I love trails like this."

From the Appalachia parking lot, pick up the Air Line trail and follow it for 0.8 mile, ascending steadily but at an easy grade through mixed deciduous forest, and then bear right on the Short Line. Follow that trail for 1.9 miles—it coincides for nearly a half mile with the Randolph Path—until it joins the King Ravine Trail. The Short Line parallels Cold Brook, which drops through numerous cascades, drawing near the brook in spots—though much of the trail is separated from the brook by forest too dense to bushwhack through. Immediately after you turn onto the King Ravine Trail, a sign marks Mossy Fall on the right, a five-foot-tall waterfall that drops into a shallow pool. The forest here is dense but low, and you start getting views of the ravine walls towering high overhead. Beyond Mossy Fall, the trail grows much steeper, weaving amid massive boulders that have tumbled off the ravine cliffs over the eons. Scrambling atop one of these boulders offers an unforgettable view of King Ravine; the cabin visible on the western wall is Crag Camp, managed by the Randolph Mountain Club.

Just past the junction with the Chemin des Dames at 2.1 miles—a trail that scales the steep ravine wall to the left, or east, to join the Air Line atop the ridge—the King Ravine Trail divides. To the left is an easier route known as the Elevated, which skirts most of the boulders that the route to the right passes through and offers more ravine views. To the right, the Subway will have you crawling through boulder caves, at times removing your pack to squeeze through narrow passages. The two trails rejoin within about 200 yards. The Great Gully Trail diverges right soon afterward, and then the King Ravine Trail offers another choice of options: to the left, the main trail; to the right, a side loop through the Ice Caves, where ice tends to linger year-round. Again, these two paths rejoin within a short distance, then the trail emerges completely from the trees and reaches the base of the King Ravine headwall, 0.7 mile past the Short Line trail junction. The King Ravine Trail grows its steepest up the headwall, basically following a talus slope. Over 0.5 mile, the trail gains 1,100 feet in elevation, and footing is tricky on the sometimes loose rocks.

Atop the headwall, the trail passes between rocky crags at a spot called the Gateway. On the other side, 1.2 miles past the Short Line junction, turn right on the Air Line and follow it for 0.6 mile over treeless alpine terrain to the Adams summit. On the way down, you have the option of bagging the Mount Madison summit as well. (See Mounts Adams and Madison: the Air Line, and other Mount Adams hike descriptions in this chapter for more on the summit views.) Descend the Air Line; it's 4.3 miles back to the trailhead.

User Groups
Hikers and dogs. No wheelchair facilities. This trail should not be attempted in winter except by hikers experienced in mountaineering and prepared

for severe winter weather, and is not suitable for bikes, horses, or skis. Hunting is allowed in season.

Access and Fees
Parking and access are free.

Maps
Several maps cover this area's hiking trails, including the *Presidential Range* map, for $7.95 in waterproof Tyvek, available in many stores and from the Appalachian Mountain Club, 800/262-4455, website: www.outdoors.org; the *Randolph Valley and the Northern Peaks* map, available for $5 in waterproof Tyvek from the Randolph Mountain Club; map 2 in the *Map and Guide to the Appalachian Trail in New Hampshire and Vermont*, an eight-map set and guidebook available for $19.95 ($14.95 for the maps alone) from the Appalachian Trail Conference; and the *Trail Map and Guide to the White Mountain National Forest* for $7.95 from the DeLorme Publishing Company, 800/642-0970. For a topographic area map, request Mount Washington from USGS Map Sales, Federal Center, Box 25286, Denver, CO 80225, 888/ASK-USGS (888/275-8747), website: http://mapping.usgs.gov.

Directions
Park in the large lot at the Appalachia trailhead on U.S. 2 in Randolph, 2.1 miles west of the northern junction of U.S. 2 and Route 16 in Gorham, and 7.1 miles east of the junction of U.S. 2 and Route 115. The Air Line begins there.

Contact
White Mountain National Forest Supervisor, 719 North Main Street, Laconia, NH 03246, 603/528-8721, TDD for the hearing impaired 603/528-8722, website: www.fs.fed.us/r9/white. Appalachian Trail Conference, 799 Washington Street, P.O. Box 807, Harpers Ferry, WV 25425-0807, 304/535-6331, website: www.appalachiantrail.org. The Appalachian Mountain Club Pinkham Notch Visitor Center has up-to-date weather and trail information about the Whites; call 603/466-2725. Randolph Mountain Club, P.O. Box 279, Randolph, NH 03581, website: www.randolphmountainclub.org.

13 MOUNT ADAMS: LOWE'S PATH

in the White Mountain National Forest south of Randolph

Total distance: 9.5 miles round-trip   **Hiking time:** 8 hours

Difficulty: 9   **Rating:** 10

This is the easiest route to the Mount Adams summit, which at 5,799 feet is the second-highest peak in New England and one of the most interesting. I've hiked it several times, in summer, fall, and winter, and have never gotten bored with this mountain. The trail has moderate grades and is well protected until timberline, but the last 1.5 miles are above the trees. It's also the oldest trail coming out of the Randolph Valley, cut in 1875–1876.

Lowe's Path ascends gently at first, making several crossings of brooks through an area often wet and muddy. After 2.5 miles you reach the Log Cabin, a Randolph Mountain Club shelter where a caretaker collects the $5 per person nightly fee. About 0.7 mile farther, at timberline, a trail branching left leads 0.1 mile to the RMC's Gray Knob cabin, which is winterized and costs $10 per night per person. This trail junction offers the first sweeping views, with the Mount Jefferson Castellated Ridge thrusting its craggy teeth skyward and much of the White Mountains visible on a clear day. From here, Lowe's Path cuts through some krummholz (the dense stands of stunted and twisted conifers that grow at timberline) and then ascends the barren talus, where it can be tricky to find the cairns. Nearly a mile from the Gray Knob Trail, you scramble over the rock mound known as Adams 4, then hike the final 0.7-mile stretch to the 5,799-foot summit to be rewarded with some of the best views in these mountains. To the south are Mounts Jefferson, Clay, and Washington, and to the north lies Madison. This crescent-shaped ridge nearly encloses the largest glacial cirque in the region, the Great Gulf.

User Groups

Hikers and dogs. No wheelchair facilities. This trail should not be attempted in winter except by hikers experienced in mountaineering and prepared for severe winter weather, and is not suitable for bikes, horses, or skis. Hunting is allowed in season.

Access and Fees

Access is free. There is a parking fee of $2 per day per vehicle at Lowe's Store parking lot.

Maps

Several maps cover this area's hiking trails, including the *Presidential Range* map, for $7.95 in waterproof Tyvek, available in many stores and from the Appalachian Mountain Club, 800/262-4455, website: www.outdoors.org; the *Randolph Valley and the Northern Peaks* map, available for $5 in waterproof Tyvek from the Randolph Mountain Club; map 2 in the *Map and Guide to the Appalachian Trail in New Hampshire and Vermont,* an eight-map set and guidebook available for $19.95 ($14.95 for the maps alone) from the Appalachian Trail Conference; and the *Trail Map and Guide to the White Mountain National Forest* for $7.95 from the DeLorme Publishing Company, 800/642-0970. For a topographic area map, request Mount Washington from USGS Map Sales, Federal Center, Box 25286, Denver, CO 80225, 888/ASK-USGS (888/275-8747), website: http://mapping.usgs.gov.

Directions

Park at Lowe's Store and gas station on U.S. 2, five miles east of the junction with Route 115 and 8.4 miles west of the north junction of U.S. 2 and Route 16 in Gorham. Cross U.S. 2, walking to the right (west), and turn up a dirt driveway that leads about 50 yards to Lowe's Path (on the right).

Contact

White Mountain National Forest Supervisor, 719 North Main Street, Laconia, NH 03246, 603/528-8721, TDD for the hearing impaired 603/528-8722, website: www.fs.fed.us/r9/white. Appalachian Trail Conference, 799 Washington Street, P.O. Box 807, Harpers Ferry, WV 25425-0807, 304/535-6331, website: www.appalachiantrail.org. The Appalachian Mountain Club Pinkham Notch Visitor Center has up-to-date weather and trail information about the Whites; call 603/466-2725. Randolph Mountain Club, P.O. Box 279, Randolph, NH 03581, website: www.randolphmountainclub.org.

14 MOUNT MADISON: MADISON GULF AND WEBSTER TRAILS

in the White Mountain National Forest south of Randolph

Total distance: 11.5 miles round-trip   **Hiking time:** 10 hours

Difficulty: 10   **Rating:** 10

The Madison headwall ascent on the Madison Gulf Trail is without question one of the most difficult hikes I have ever done in the White Mountains. At 11.5 miles and 4,000 feet of elevation gain, this hike also represents one of the most strenuous days you could spend in these parts. But it also rates as one of the wildest hikes in these mountains—and you may well see no other

hikers in fresh October snow on Mount Madison

hikers on the trail. On this hike, the Appalachian Trail coincides with the Madison Gulf Trail south of the Osgood Trail junction, and with the Osgood Trail from Madison hut over the Madison summit to the Daniel Webster (scout) Trail.

From the parking area, follow the Great Gulf Link Trail a flat mile to the Great Gulf Trail. Turn right and continue about three easy miles (passing the Osgood Trail junction in less than two miles); soon after a jog left in the trail, turn right (north) onto the Madison Gulf Trail. You are in the Great Gulf, the enormous glacial cirque nearly enclosed by the high peaks of the northern Presidentials, which loom around you. The Madison Gulf Trail grows increasingly steep, following Parapet Brook through a dense forest for about two miles to the base of the formidable headwall. Moss-covered glacial-erratic boulders fill the streambed; one huge boulder has a tall tree growing atop it. You cross a lush, boggy area along a shelf at the headwall's base, then attack the main headwall, which involves scrambling over steep, exposed rock ledges that can be hazardous in wet weather.

After a strenuous mile, the trail reaches the flat saddle between Mounts Madison and Adams, where you find the Appalachian Mountain Club's Madison hut and Star Lake, a beautiful little tarn and one of the few true alpine ponds in the Whites. From the hut, turn right (east) on the Osgood Trail leading to Madison's ridgelike summit (elevation 5,366 feet). Continue over the summit and down the open Osgood Ridge for 0.5 mile. The Daniel Webster Trail branches left (northeast) at Osgood Junction, heading diagonally down a vast talus slope to the woods, leading another 3.5 miles to the campground road in Dolly Copp. Turn right and walk 0.2 mile down the road to your car.

User Groups

Hikers and dogs. No wheelchair facilities. This trail should not be attempted in winter except by hikers experienced in mountaineering and prepared for severe winter weather, and is not suitable for bikes, horses, or skis. Hunting is allowed in season.

Access and Fees

No backcountry permit is needed, but a permit is required for day use or overnight parking at any White Mountain National Forest trailhead, as indicated by signs posted at most trailheads. Permits are available at several area stores and from the national forest at a cost of $5 for seven consecutive days or $20 per year. A $3 one-day permit can be purchased at self-service stations at national forest trailheads, but the permit is good only for the trailhead at which it's purchased.

Maps

Several maps cover this area's hiking trails, including the *Presidential Range* map, for $7.95 in waterproof Tyvek, available in many stores and from the Appalachian Mountain Club, 800/262-4455, website: www.outdoors.org; the *Randolph Valley and the Northern Peaks* map, available for $5 in waterproof Tyvek from the Randolph Mountain Club; map 2 in the *Map and Guide to the Appalachian Trail in New Hampshire and Vermont,* an eight-map set and guidebook available for $19.95 ($14.95 for the maps alone) from the Appalachian Trail Conference; and the *Trail Map and Guide to the White Mountain National Forest* for $7.95 from the DeLorme Publishing Company, 800/642-0970. For a topographic area map, request Mount Washington from USGS Map Sales, Federal Center, Box 25286, Denver, CO 80225, 888/ASK-USGS (888/275-8747), website: http://mapping.usgs.gov.

Directions

From Gorham, drive south on Route 16 to the U.S. Forest Service's Dolly Copp Campground (entrance on right), which is operated on a first-come, first-served basis. From Pinkham Notch, drive north on Route 16; the campground will be on your left. Drive to the end of the campground road and park in the dirt lot at the start of the Great Gulf Link Trail. About a quarter mile before the parking lot, you pass the start of the Daniel Webster (scout) Trail, which is where you will end this hike.

Contact

White Mountain National Forest Supervisor, 719 North Main Street, Laconia, NH 03246, 603/528-8721, TDD for the hearing impaired 603/528-8722, website: www.fs.fed.us/r9/white. Appalachian Trail Conference, 799 Washington Street, P.O. Box 807, Harpers Ferry, WV 25425-0807, 304/535-6331, website: www.appalachiantrail.org. The Appalachian Mountain Club Pinkham Notch Visitor Center has up-to-date weather and trail information about the Whites; call 603/466-2725. Randolph Mountain Club, P.O. Box 279, Randolph, NH 03581, website: www.randolphmountainclub.org.

15 MOUNT JEFFERSON: THE CASTELLATED RIDGE
in the White Mountain National Forest south of Bowman

Total distance: 10 miles round-trip   **Hiking time:** 9 hours

Difficulty: 10   **Rating:** 10

The stretch of the Castle Trail above timberline ranks among the most spectacular ridge walks in New England—but you work hard getting there, climbing some 4,200 feet on this 10-mile round-tripper. The Castellated Ridge narrows to a rocky spine jutting above the krummholz (the dense stands of stunted and twisted conifers that grow at timberline), with long, sharp drops off either side. The ridge acquired its name from the three castles, or towers, of barren rock you scramble over and around, which are visible from a distance. This can be a dangerous place in nasty weather. A friend and I once backpacked in early October as far as the first castle only to turn back in the face of ice, snow, and a looming whiteout—then returned a week later to hike the ridge in shorts and T-shirts. On a clear day, from Jefferson's summit (5,716 feet), you can see almost all of the Whites and all the way to Vermont's Green Mountains. I've even caught glimpses of New York's Adirondacks, beyond the Green Mountains, on super clear days. You also walk briefly on the Appalachian Trail where it coincides with the Gulfside Trail north of Jefferson's summit.

From the parking area, follow the dirt driveway to the right for about 150 yards until you reach a somewhat hidden marker on the right where the Castle Trail enters the woods. In the first half mile there's a bridgeless crossing of the Israel River, which can be difficult at high water. The hiking is fairly easy at first. Approximately one mile beyond the stream crossing, the trail passes the junction with the Israel Ridge Path on the left, on which you will return. The last certain water source is located at a brook a

a hiker in fresh snow on Mount Jefferson

short distance up that path. The trail ascends the ridge, growing steep and passing through an interesting subalpine forest before reaching the junction with the Link at 3.5 miles out.

The Castle Trail requires scrambling from this point, reaching the first castle 0.25 mile past the Link junction. Continue up the ridge to the vast talus field covering the upper flanks of Mount Jefferson, watching carefully for cairns. The trail follows a direct line to the summit, where twin rock mounds are separated by a short distance; the first you encounter, farther west, is the true summit, five miles from the trailhead.

Descend to the trail junction between the two summits, walk north on the Jefferson Loop Trail toward Mount Adams for 0.4 mile, and then continue on the Gulfside Trail for another 0.2 mile into Edmands Col. Bear left onto the Randolph Path, which leads to the right (northeast) around the Castle Ravine headwall 0.7 mile from Edmands Col to the Israel Ridge Path. The trails coincide briefly, then split; stay to the left on the Israel Ridge Path, continuing nearly a half mile to just beyond the Perch Path junction, where the Emerald Trail diverges left. If you have time, make the worthwhile 20-minute detour on the Emerald Trail out to Emerald Bluff, which offers a stunning view of Castle Ravine. The Israel Ridge Path continues down into the woods, eventually rejoining the Castle Trail 2.4 miles below the Perch Path junction. Turn right and continue to the trailhead parking area, 1.3 miles ahead.

User Groups

Hikers and dogs. No wheelchair facilities. This trail should not be attempted in winter except by hikers experienced in mountaineering and prepared for severe winter weather, and is not suitable for bikes, horses, or skis. Hunting is allowed in season.

Access and Fees

No backcountry permit is needed, but a permit is required for day use or overnight parking at any White Mountain National Forest trailhead, as indicated by signs posted at most trailheads. Permits are available at several area stores and from the national forest at a cost of $5 for seven consecutive days or $20 per year. A $3 one-day permit can be purchased at self-service stations at national forest trailheads, but the permit is good only for the trailhead at which it's purchased.

Maps

Several maps cover this area's hiking trails, including the *Presidential Range* map, for $7.95 in waterproof Tyvek, available in many stores and from the Appalachian Mountain Club, 800/262-4455, website: www.outdoors.org; the *Randolph Valley and the Northern Peaks* map, available for $5 in waterproof Tyvek from the Randolph Mountain Club; map 2 in the *Map and Guide to the Appalachian Trail in New Hampshire and Vermont,* an eight-map set and guidebook available for $19.95 ($14.95 for the maps alone) from the Appalachian Trail Conference; and the *Trail Map and Guide to the White Mountain National Forest* for $7.95 from the DeLorme Publishing Company, 800/642-0970. For a topographic area map, request Mount Washington from USGS Map Sales, Federal Center, Box 25286, Denver, CO 80225, 888/ASK-USGS (888/275-8747), website: http://mapping.usgs.gov.

Directions

The parking area is on the south side of U.S. 2 in Randolph, 4.1 miles east of the junction of U.S. 2 and Route 115.

Contact

White Mountain National Forest Supervisor, 719 North Main Street, Laconia, NH 03246, 603/528-8721, TDD for the hearing impaired 603/528-8722, website: www.fs.fed.us/r9/white. Appalachian Trail Conference, 799 Washington Street, P.O. Box 807, Harpers Ferry, WV 25425-0807, 304/535-6331, website: www.appalachiantrail.org. The Appalachian Mountain Club's Pinkham Notch Visitor Center has up-to-date reports on weather in the Presidential Range; call 603/466-2721. Randolph Mountain Club, P.O. Box 279, Randolph, NH 03581, website: www.randolphmountainclub.org.

16 MOUNT JEFFERSON: RIDGE OF THE CAPS

in the White Mountain National Forest south of Jefferson

Total distance: 6.6 miles round-trip   **Hiking time:** 5 hours

Difficulty: 8   **Rating:** 10

Beginning at an elevation of 3,008 feet, the highest trailhead accessed by a public road in the White Mountains, the Caps Ridge Trail provides the shortest route from a trailhead to a 5,000-foot summit in these mountains: five miles round-trip if you go up and down the Caps Ridge Trail. This hike extends the distance to 6.6 miles to make a loop and incorporate the spectacular Castellated Ridge. Despite the relatively short distance compared to other Presidential Range hikes, all of this loop's trails are rugged. Though its 2,700 feet of elevation gain does not compare with most other routes up Presidential Range summits, this hike is fairly strenuous. See the next hike's trail notes for more information about the views from the Castellated Ridge and Mount Jefferson's summit.

Follow the Caps Ridge Trail, which rises steadily through conifer forest; at mile one, an open ledge offers sweeping views to the Ridge of the Caps above, the Castellated Ridge to the north, and the southern Presidentials to the south. You may also see the black smoke from the cog railway chugging up Mount Washington. The potholes in the granite on the ledge were left by glaciers in the last Ice Age. Continue up the Caps Ridge Trail, immediately passing the junction with the Link trail, on which this route returns. The Caps Ridge Trail soon emerges from the woods and zigzags up the craggy ridge, with excellent views of most of the Whites. When the ridge becomes less distinct in a sprawling talus slope, you are near Jefferson's summit, a pile of rocks rising to 5,716 feet above the ocean.

For a five-mile total hike, descend the way you came. To continue on this hike, descend the other side of Jefferson's summit cone, follow the summit loop trail northward just a few steps, and then turn left (northwest) onto the Castle Trail. Follow its cairns, descending at a moderate angle over the vast boulder fields of Jefferson, to the prominent Castellated Ridge. The trail follows close to the ridge crest, passing the three distinct stone castles along it. At 1.5 miles below the summit, turn left (south) on the Link, which wends a rugged—and in spots heavily eroded—path through dense forest for 1.6 miles back to the Caps Ridge Trail. Turn right (west) and descend a mile back to the trailhead.

User Groups

Hikers and dogs. No wheelchair facilities. This trail is not accessible in winter and is not suitable for bikes or horses. Hunting is allowed in season.

Access and Fees

No backcountry permit is needed, but a permit is required for day use or overnight parking at any White Mountain National Forest trailhead; signs indicating so are posted at most of them. Permits are available at several area stores and from the national forest at a cost of $5 for seven consecutive days or $20 per year. A $3 one-day permit can be purchased at self-service stations at national forest trailheads, but the permit is good only for the trailhead at which it's purchased.

Maps

Several maps cover this area's hiking trails, including the *Presidential Range* map, for $7.95 in waterproof Tyvek, available in many stores and from the Appalachian Mountain Club, 800/262-4455, website: www.outdoors.org; the *Randolph Valley and the Northern Peaks* map, available for $5 in waterproof Tyvek from the Randolph Mountain Club; map 2 in the *Map and Guide to the Appalachian Trail in New Hampshire and Vermont,* an eight-map set and guidebook available for $19.95 ($14.95 for the maps alone) from the Appalachian Trail Conference; and the *Trail Map and Guide to the White Mountain National Forest* for $7.95 from the DeLorme Publishing Company, 800/642-0970. For a topographic area map, request Mount Washington from USGS Map Sales, Federal Center, Box 25286, Denver, CO 80225, 888/ASK-USGS (888/275-8747), website: http://mapping.usgs.gov.

Directions

The hike begins from the Caps Ridge Trail parking lot at the height of land in Jefferson Notch. From U.S. 2 in Jefferson, turn south onto Valley Road and follow it more than a mile. Then turn left onto the gravel Jefferson Notch Road and continue on it for about four miles to the trailhead. From U.S. 302 in Bretton Woods, turn onto the Base Road at a sign for the Mount Washington Cog Railway and drive 5.6 miles. Then turn left on Jefferson Notch Road and follow it to Jefferson Notch. Or from U.S. 302 in Crawford Notch, 0.2 mile north of the visitor information center, turn onto Mount Clinton Road. Follow it 3.7 miles, cross Base Road, and continue straight ahead onto Jefferson Notch Road.

Contact

White Mountain National Forest Supervisor, 719 North Main Street, Laconia, NH 03246, 603/528-8721, TDD for the hearing impaired 603/528-8722, website: www.fs.fed.us/r9/white. Appalachian Trail Conference, 799 Washington Street, P.O. Box 807, Harpers Ferry, WV 25425-0807, 304/535-6331, website: www.appalachiantrail.org. The Appalachian Mountain Club's Pinkham Notch Visitor Center has up-to-date reports on weather in the Presidential Range; call 603/466-2721. Randolph Mountain Club, P.O. Box 279, Randolph, NH 03581, website: www.randolphmountainclub.org.

17 PRESIDENTIAL RANGE TRAVERSE
in the White Mountain National Forest between Gorham and Crawford Notch

Total distance: 20 miles one-way   **Hiking time:** 2.5 days

Difficulty: 9   **Rating:** 10

This is the premier backpacking trek in New England—in fact, nowhere else east of the Rockies can you hike a 15-mile ridge entirely above timberline. The route hits nine summits, seven of them higher than 5,000 feet—including New England's highest, 6,288-foot Mount Washington—and each with its own unique character. From the junction of the Osgood and Daniel Webster Trails to the junction of the Crawford Path and the Webster Cliffs Trail, this hike coincides with the Appalachian Trail. The route covers some very rugged terrain and is quite strenuous, with a cumulative vertical ascent of well more than 8,000 feet. The task is complicated by the fact that the odds of having three straight days of good weather in these peaks may be only slightly better than those of winning the lottery. Finding appropriate campsites can be difficult, too, because of the prohibition against camping above timberline (see detailed White Mountain National Forest regulations at the beginning of this chapter). Skipping the side paths to summits and staying on the Gulfside Trail, Westside Trail, and Crawford Path will reduce the distance slightly and the elevation gain significantly. Masochistic types have been known to attempt this traverse in a single day, a feat known in some circles as the Death March (two friends and I attempted it once, only to have to descend from Washington when gray clouds abruptly smothered the mountain, leaving us in a pea-soup fog). A winter traverse of the Presidentials is a mountaineering challenge considered by many to be good training for Alaskan peaks in summer.

My route here deviates a bit from the more common approach to this traverse—Lowe's Path (see Mount Adams: Lowe's Path listing in this chapter)—incorporating two scenic trails that see fewer hikers. The first, the Daniel Webster (scout) Trail, begins at the Dolly Copp Campground road and ascends moderately through the woods to a vast, open talus slope where the climbing grows steeper. Upon reaching Osgood Ridge, you're treated to a stunning view of the Great Gulf Wilderness and the peaks of the northern Presidentials. Follow the Osgood Trail to the top of Mount Madison, 4.1 miles from the trailhead, its 5,366-foot summit a narrow ridge of boulders. Continue over the summit on the Osgood Trail 0.5 mile down to Madison hut and turn left for the Star Lake Trail, a less-traveled footpath that passes the beautiful little tarn named Star Lake and winds a mile up the steep east side of 5,799-foot Mount Adams, the second-highest peak in New England. Adams has five distinct summits, several ridges and ravines, and excellent views. Descend via Lowe's Path nearly a half mile over an expansive talus field to the giant cairn at Thunderstorm Junction, where several trails meet.

From here, you can descend the Spur Trail a mile to the Randolph Mountain Club's Crag Camp cabin, or follow Lowe's Path for 1.3 miles to the Gray Knob cabin. To continue on, turn left (southwest) onto the Gulfside Trail (which follows the ridge to Mount Washington while avoiding the summits). At 0.6 mile south of Thunderstorm Junction, you pass the Israel Ridge Path branching to the right toward the RMC's Perch camping area (one mile away via Israel Ridge, Randolph Path, and the Perch Path). From Edmands Col (the saddle 1.3 miles south of Thunderstorm Junction and 0.6 mile north of the Mount Jefferson summit), hike 0.2 mile southwest and bear right onto the Jefferson Loop Trail, climbing 0.4 mile to Mount Jefferson's top. Of its two summits, the westernmost (to your right from this direction) is the highest at 5,716 feet. The other summit is 11 feet lower.

Continue between the two summits on the loop trail and rejoin the Gulfside Trail. About a half mile farther, after dipping down through Sphinx Col, bear left onto the Mount Clay Loop Trail. On a day when you see two dozen hikers on Jefferson, you may have Clay to yourself. This is probably because Clay is considered a shoulder of Mount Washington rather than a distinct peak. Yet, on Clay's broad 5,533-foot summit, you can observe abundant alpine wildflowers (particularly in the second half of June) and peer down the sheer headwall of the Great Gulf. The Clay Loop rejoins the Gulfside in 1.2 miles, and then it's another mile to the roof of New England, Washington's 6,288-foot summit, finishing via the Crawford Path. The summit has a visitors center with a cafeteria and bathrooms—which many hikers consider as much of a blemish on the mountain as the cog railway, which belches black smoke carrying tourists up and down Washington's west slope.

From the summit, turn southwest onto the Crawford Path and follow it 1.4 miles down to Lakes of the Clouds, the location of another Appalachian Mountain Club hut. Just south of the hut, bear right off the Crawford onto the Mount Monroe Loop Trail for the steep 0.5-mile climb to its

5,372-foot summit (a great place to catch the sunset if you're staying at the Lakes hut). The Monroe Loop rejoins the Crawford Path southbound 0.3 mile past the summit. The Crawford then traverses the bump on the ridge known as Mount Franklin (5,001 feet), also not considered a distinct summit. About two miles south of the Lakes hut, bear right for the loop over 4,760-foot Mount Eisenhower. A mile south of Eisenhower, follow the Webster Cliffs Trail 0.1 mile to the 4,312-foot summit of Mount Pierce, then double back and turn left on the Crawford Path, descending nearly three miles. Just before reaching U.S. 302 in Crawford Notch, turn right onto the Crawford Connector path leading 0.2 mile to the parking area on the Mount Clinton Road.

User Groups

Hikers and dogs. No wheelchair facilities. This hike should not be attempted in winter except by hikers experienced in mountaineering and prepared for severe winter weather, and is not suitable for skis. Bikes, horses, and hunting are prohibited.

Access and Fees

No backcountry permit is needed, but a permit is required for day use or overnight parking at any White Mountain National Forest trailhead, as indicated by signs posted at most trailheads. Permits are available at several area stores and from the national forest at a cost of $5 for seven consecutive days or $20 per year. A $3 one-day permit can be purchased at self-service stations at national forest trailheads, but the permit is good only for the trailhead at which it's purchased. The Appalachian Mountain Club operates the Madison and Lakes of the Clouds huts, where a crew prepares meals and guests share bunkrooms and bathrooms. The Randolph Mountain Club operates two cabins on Mount Adams: Crag Camp (capacity 20) and the winterized Gray Knob (capacity 15), both of which cost $10 per person per night and are run on a first-come, first-served basis. The RMC also operates two open-sided shelters on Adams, the Perch (capacity eight, plus four tent platforms) and the Log Cabin (capacity 10), both of which cost $5 per night, with the fee collected by a caretaker. All shelters are open year-round.

Maps

Several maps cover this area's hiking trails, including the *Presidential Range* map, for $7.95 in waterproof Tyvek, available in many stores and from the Appalachian Mountain Club, 800/262-4455, website: www.outdoors.org; map 2 in the *Map and Guide to the Appalachian Trail in New Hampshire and Vermont,* an eight-map set and guidebook available for

$19.95 ($14.95 for the maps alone) from the Appalachian Trail Conference; and the *Trail Map and Guide to the White Mountain National Forest* for $7.95 from the DeLorme Publishing Company, 800/642-0970. For a topographic area map, request Mount Washington from USGS Map Sales, Federal Center, Box 25286, Denver, CO 80225, 888/ASK-USGS (888/275-8747), website: http://mapping.usgs.gov.

Directions

From Gorham, drive south on Route 16 to the U.S. Forest Service's Dolly Copp Campground (entrance on right), which is operated on a first-come, first-served basis. Drive to the end of the campground road to a dirt parking lot at the Great Gulf Link Trailhead. About a quarter mile before the parking lot is the start of the Daniel Webster (scout) Trail, which is where you begin this hike. Leave a second vehicle at the other end of this traverse, just off U.S. 302 in Crawford Notch State Park. The Crawford Path Trailhead parking area is on Mount Clinton Road, opposite the Crawford House site and just north of Saco Lake.

Contact

White Mountain National Forest Supervisor, 719 North Main Street, Laconia, NH 03246, 603/528-8721, TDD for the hearing impaired 603/528-8722, website: www.fs.fed.us/r9/white. Appalachian Trail Conference, 799 Washington Street, P.O. Box 807, Harpers Ferry, WV 25425-0807, 304/535-6331, website: www.appalachiantrail.org. The Appalachian Mountain Club Pinkham Notch Visitor Center has up-to-date weather and trail information about the Whites; call 603/466-2725.

18 THE CARTER-MORIAH RANGE

in the White Mountain National Forest between Pinkham Notch and Shelburne

Total distance: 20 miles one-way   **Hiking time:** 3 days

Difficulty: 4   **Rating:** 9

This section of the Appalachian Trail just might have you cursing one moment, uttering expressions of awe the next. This is a great three-day ridge walk on the Appalachian Trail, with excellent views of the Presidential Range to the west and the Wild River Valley to the east. The cumulative elevation gained on this 20-mile hike is more than 6,700 feet.

From the Appalachian Mountain Club Visitor Center, follow the Lost Pond Trail to the Wildcat Ridge Trail; turn left (east), and you will soon begin the steep climb to the ridge, passing over open ledges with commanding views of Mount Washington—a good destination for a short day hike. The first of Wildcat's five summits that you'll encounter—Peak E, 4,041 feet high—is a 3.8-mile round-trip hike of about three hours. The trail traverses the roller coaster Wildcat Ridge, up and down five humped summits with few views. Just beyond the final peak is a short spur trail to a view atop cliffs overlooking Carter Notch and the Carter Range that will make you eat all your nasty comments about this trail. Descend north a steep mile—including a traverse of about 25 feet across a loose, very steep rockslide area—turning right (east) onto the Nineteen-Mile Brook Trail for the final 0.2 mile into the notch and circling around the larger of two ponds there. Tent sites can be found near the junction of the Wildcat Ridge and Nineteen-Mile Brook Trails, or ask a caretaker at the Appalachian Mountain Club hut in Carter Notch about nearby sites.

From the notch, hike north, climbing steeply on the Carter-Moriah Trail, passing one ledge with a view of the entire notch from high above it. You'll pass a side trail leading to a good spring. A bit more than a mile from the notch, the trail passes over the highest point on this ridge, Carter Dome, at 4,832 feet. Unfortunately, trees block any views. The trail continues nearly a mile to the rocky summit of Mount Hight (4,675 feet)—the nicest summit in the range, with 360-degree views of the Presidentials and far into Maine to the east. From Hight, the Carter-Moriah Trail turns sharply left (west) a short distance, drops north down a steep slope into the forest for 0.5 mile to Zeta Pass, then continues north over the wooded summits of South Carter and Middle Carter (2.7 miles from Mount Hight). As the ridge ascends gradually again toward North Carter, you break into the alpine zone and some of the best views on this hike, particularly west to Mount Washington. From the viewless summit of North Carter, the trail drops several hundred feet over rock ledges that require scrambling, passes over the hump known as Imp Mountain, and reaches the spur trail to the Imp campsite in two miles. Check out the view at sunset from the ledge just below the shelter.

Continuing north on the Carter-Moriah Trail, you cross over some open ledges on Imp Mountain before the trail ascends steadily onto the open southern ledges of Mount Moriah two miles from the shelter. A short distance farther, the Carter-Moriah Trail peels off left toward the town of Gorham; this hike continues on the Appalachian Trail, which at this point coincides with the Kenduskeag Trail—but drop your pack and make the short detour on the Carter-Moriah for the rocky scramble up the spur trail to Moriah's summit. Backtrack to the Kenduskeag—an Abenaki word meaning "a pleasant walk"—and follow its often wet path 1.5 miles to the Rattle River Trail, where you'll turn left (north). The trail descends steeply at first, through a dense, damp forest, then levels out before reaching the Rattle River shelter in 2.5 miles. From there, it's less than two miles to a parking lot on U.S. 2 in Shelburne, the terminus of this traverse.

User Groups

Hikers and dogs. No wheelchair facilities. This trail should not be attempted in winter except by hikers experienced in mountaineering and prepared for severe winter weather, and is not suitable for skis. Bikes, horses, and hunting are prohibited.

Access and Fees

No backcountry permit is needed, but a permit is required for day use or overnight parking at any White Mountain National Forest trailhead, as indicated by signs posted at most trailheads. Permits are available at several area stores and from the national forest at a cost of $5 for seven consecutive days or $20 per year. A $3 one-day permit can be purchased at self-service stations at national forest trailheads, but the permit is good only for the trailhead at which it's purchased. Backcountry campsites along this route are scarce and camping is prohibited along much of the high ridge. Carry cash for camping overnight at the Appalachian Mountain Club hut in Carter Notch ($25 per person per night) or the Appalachian Mountain Club's Imp campsite ($8 per person per night).

Maps

For a contour map of hiking trails, obtain the *Carter Range–Evans Notch/North Country–Mahoosuc* map, $7.95 in waterproof Tyvek, available in many stores and from the Appalachian Mountain Club, 800/262-4455, website: www.outdoors.org; the *Trail Map and Guide to the White Mountain National Forest* for $7.95 from the DeLorme Publishing Company, 800/642-0970; or map 2 in the *Map and Guide to the Appalachian Trail in New Hampshire and Vermont,* an eight-map set and guidebook for $19.95 ($14.95 for the maps alone) from the Appalachian Trail Conference. For a topographic area map, request Carter Dome from USGS Map Sales, Federal Center, Box 25286, Denver, CO 80225, 888/ASK-USGS (888/275-8747), website: http://mapping.usgs.gov.

Directions

You will need to shuttle two vehicles for this traverse. Leave one at the hike's terminus, a parking area where the Appalachian Trail crosses U.S. 2, 3.6 miles east of the southern junction of U.S. 2 and Route 16 in Shelburne. The hike begins at the Appalachian Mountain Club Visitor Center on Route 16 in Pinkham Notch at the base of Mount Washington, 12 miles south of the junction with U.S. 2 in Gorham and about eight miles north of Jackson.

Contact

White Mountain National Forest Supervisor, 719 North Main Street, Laconia, NH 03246, 603/528-8721, TDD for the hearing impaired 603/528-8722, website: www.fs.fed.us/r9/white. Appalachian Trail Conference, 799 Washington Street, P.O. Box 807, Harpers Ferry, WV 25425-0807, 304/535-6331, website: www.appalachiantrail.org.

---

19 MOUNT WASHINGTON: HUNTINGTON RAVINE AND THE ALPINE GARDEN

in the White Mountain National Forest in Pinkham Notch

Total distance: 8 miles round-trip

Hiking time: 8 hours

Difficulty: 10

Rating: 10

Discard all your preconceived notions of hard trails. Huntington Ravine has earned a reputation as the most difficult regular hiking trail in the White Mountains for good reason. The trail ascends the ravine headwall, involving very exposed scrambling up steep slabs of rock with significant fall potential. Inexperienced scramblers should shy away from this route, and persons carrying a heavy pack may want to consider another way up the mountain. The ravine is strictly a summer and early fall hike, and even in those seasons snow can fall, treacherous ice can form, or the steep rock slabs may be slick with water. I've hiked this trail in good August weather, but had to turn back from a technical rock climb up another section of Huntington's headwall when sleet fell in September. The headwall, the Alpine Garden, and the top of the Lion Head all lie above tree line and are exposed to the weather. From late fall through early spring, the headwall is draped with ice and snow, and is a prized destination for experienced ice climbers. For hikers comfortable with exposure and rugged scrambling, Huntington Ravine has few equals. And this eight-mile loop, which climbs about 3,400 feet in elevation, will lead you through a variety of mountain terrain found on few other peaks east of the Rockies. I've deliberately avoided Washington's crowded summit with this hike, because the alternative to going to the summit, walking across the Alpine Garden, is such a treat. But the description below details how to reach the summit if that's your goal.

From the Appalachian Mountain Club Visitor Center, follow the wide

a hiker on Mount Washington's summit

Tuckerman Ravine Trail. Less than 1.5 miles up, the Huntington Ravine Trail diverges right (north); watch closely for it, because the sign may be partly hidden by trees, and the path is narrow and easily overlooked. This trail climbs steeply in spots, and you get fleeting glimpses of the ravine headwall above. Within 1.5 miles from the Tuckerman Ravine Trail, you reach a flat, open area on the Huntington Ravine floor—and your first sweeping view of the massive headwall, riven by several ominous gullies separating tall cliffs. Novice hikers can reach this point without any trouble, and the view of the ravine is worth it. Nearby is a first-aid cache bearing a plaque memorializing Albert Dow, a climber and mountain rescue volunteer killed by an avalanche in Huntington Ravine during a 1982 search for a pair of missing ice climbers.

The trail leads through a maze of giant boulders to the headwall base and then heads diagonally up the talus. On the headwall proper, the well-blazed trail ascends rock slabs, which may be wet, and sections of blocky boulders. Two miles from the Tuckerman Ravine Trail, you reach the top of the ravine and the broad tableland known as the Alpine Garden, where colorful wildflowers bloom from mid-June (which is a little early to attempt the headwall, so hike up the Lion Head Trail) through August.

By following the Huntington Ravine Trail 0.25 mile farther, you can pick up the Nelson Crag Trail for the final mile (or not quite a mile) to Washington's summit and then descend the Tuckerman Ravine and Lion Head Trails to rejoin this loop at the other side of the Alpine Garden—

adding two miles and about 800 feet of ascent to this hike. But this hike takes a finer route–free from the tourists who flock to the summit via the auto road or cog railway–crossing the Alpine Garden to the Lion Head. Turn left (south) onto the Alpine Garden Trail, which traverses the mile-wide, tundralike plain. In a short distance, you see to your left the top of a prominent cliff known as the Pinnacle, which is part of the Huntington Ravine headwall; the view from atop the Pinnacle merits the short detour, but take care to walk on rocks and not the fragile alpine vegetation. The sprawling boulder pile of the mountain's upper cone rises up on your right.

Once you're across the Alpine Garden, turn left (east) onto the Lion Head Trail. The flat trail follows the crest of a prominent buttress, above the cliffs that form the northern or right-hand wall of Tuckerman Ravine. There are numerous good views down into the ravine before the trail drops back into the woods again, descending steeply and eventually rejoining the Tuckerman Ravine Trail about two miles from the Appalachian Mountain Club Visitor Center. Turn left (east) and head down.

User Groups

Hikers only. No wheelchair facilities. This trail is not suitable for bikes, dogs, horses, or skis, and should not be attempted in winter except by hikers experienced in mountaineering and prepared for severe winter weather. Hunting is prohibited.

Access and Fees

No backcountry permit is needed, but a permit is required for day use or overnight parking at any White Mountain National Forest trailhead, as indicated by signs posted at most trailheads. Permits are available at several area stores and from the national forest at a cost of $5 for seven consecutive days or $20 per year. A $3 one-day permit can be purchased at self-service stations at national forest trailheads, but the permit is good only for the trailhead at which it's purchased.

Maps

For a map of hiking trails, get the *Presidential Range* map for $7.95 in waterproof Tyvek, available in many stores and from the Appalachian Mountain Club, 800/262-4455, website: www.outdoors.org; map 2 in the *Map and Guide to the Appalachian Trail in New Hampshire and Vermont,* an eight-map set and guidebook available for $19.95 ($14.95 for the maps alone) from the Appalachian Trail Conference; or the *Trail Map and Guide to the White Mountain National Forest* for $7.95 from the DeLorme Publishing Company, 800/642-0970. For a topographic area map, request Mount Washington from USGS Map Sales, Federal Center, Box 25286, Denver, CO 80225, 888/ASK-USGS (888/275-8747), website: http://mapping.usgs.gov.

Directions

The hike begins from the Appalachian Mountain Club Visitor Center on Route 16 in Pinkham Notch at the base of Mount Washington, 12 miles south of the junction of Route 16 and U.S. 2 in Gorham and about eight miles north of Jackson. The trailhead is behind the visitors center.

Contact

White Mountain National Forest Supervisor, 719 North Main Street, Laconia, NH 03246, 603/528-8721, TDD for the hearing impaired 603/528-8722, website: www.fs.fed.us/r9/white. Appalachian Trail Conference, 799 Washington Street, P.O. Box 807, Harpers Ferry, WV 25425-0807, 304/535-6331, website: www.appalachiantrail.org. The Appalachian Mountain Club's Pinkham Notch Visitor Center has up-to-date reports on weather in the Presidential Range; call 603/466-2721.

20 MOUNT WASHINGTON: THE LION HEAD

in the White Mountain National Forest in Pinkham Notch

Total distance: 8.2 miles round-trip   **Hiking time:** 7 hours

Difficulty: 9   **Rating:** 10

The preceding and following hikes both suggest the Lion Head Trail as a logical descent route off Mount Washington. But it's also a less-traveled route up New England's highest peak than the Tuckerman Ravine Trail in summer, and it's the standard route for a challenging winter ascent. The actual winter Lion Head Trail follows a different route than the summer trail to avoid avalanche hazard. Trail signs are posted in the appropriate places when each trail is opened or closed for the season. To check on the status of the changeover, call the Appalachian Mountain Club's Pinkham Notch Visitor Center. For more information about Mount Washington, see the trail notes for the preceding or following hikes.

From Pinkham Notch, pick up the wide Tuckerman Ravine Trail, follow it for 2.3 miles, and then turn right onto the Lion Head Trail. It soon begins steep switchbacks up the face of the Lion Head ridge, breaking out of the forest within 0.5 mile of the Tuckerman Ravine Trail junction for excellent views of Pinkham Notch and the Carter Range across the notch. Shortly after leaving the forest, the trail crests the Lion Head for much flatter walking across the Alpine Garden, a tundralike plateau that's one of the best places in these mountains to view alpine wildflowers from late spring well into summer, depending on how long the snow lingers. To your left, the ridge drops away abruptly into Tuckerman Ravine; straight ahead lies Washington's summit, still more than 1,200 feet higher.

At 1.1 miles from the Tuckerman Ravine Trail, the Lion Head Trail crosses the Alpine Garden Trail, and soon afterward begins climbing Mount Washington's summit cone. A half mile farther, turn right onto the Tuckerman Ravine Trail and follow it another 0.4 mile to Washington's summit. Descend the way you came.

User Groups

Hikers only. No wheelchair facilities. This trail is not suitable for bikes, dogs, horses, or skis, and should not be attempted in winter except by hikers experienced in mountaineering and prepared for severe winter weather. Hunting is prohibited.

Access and Fees

No backcountry permit is needed, but a permit is required for day use or overnight parking at any White Mountain National Forest trailhead, as indicated by signs posted at most trailheads. Permits are available at several area stores and from the national forest at a cost of $5 for seven consecutive days or $20 per year. A $3 one-day permit can be purchased at self-service stations at national forest trailheads, but the permit is good only for the trailhead at which it's purchased.

Maps

For a map of hiking trails, obtain the *Presidential Range* map for $7.95 in waterproof Tyvek, available in many stores and from the Appalachian Mountain Club, 800/262-4455, website: www.outdoors.org; map 2 in the *Map and Guide to the Appalachian Trail in New Hampshire and Vermont,* an eight-map set and guidebook available for $19.95 ($14.95 for the maps alone) from the Appalachian Trail Conference; or the *Trail Map and Guide to the White Mountain National Forest* for $7.95 from the DeLorme Publishing Company, 800/642-0970. For a topographic area map, request Mount Washington from USGS Map Sales, Federal Center, Box 25286, Denver, CO 80225, 888/ASK-USGS (888/275-8747), website: http://mapping.usgs.gov.

Directions

The hike begins from the Appalachian Mountain Club Visitor Center on Route 16 in Pinkham Notch at the base of Mount Washington, 12 miles south of the junction of Route 16 and U.S. 2 in Gorham and about eight miles north of Jackson. The trailhead is behind the visitors center.

Contact

White Mountain National Forest Supervisor, 719 North Main Street, Laconia, NH 03246, 603/528-8721, TDD for the hearing impaired 603/528-8722, website: www.fs.fed.us/r9/white. Appalachian Trail Conference, 799 Washington Street, P.O. Box 807, Harpers Ferry, WV 25425-0807, 304/535-6331, website: www.appalachiantrail.org. The Appalachian Mountain Club's Pinkham Notch Visitor Center has up-to-date reports on weather in the Presidential Range; call 603/466-2721.

21 MOUNT WASHINGTON: TUCKERMAN RAVINE

in the White Mountain National Forest in Pinkham Notch

Total distance: 8.4 miles round-trip   **Hiking time:** 7 hours

Difficulty: 10   **Rating:** 10

This trail is the standard route and most direct way up the 6,288-foot Mount Washington, the Northeast's highest peak, so it typically sees hundreds of hikers on nice weekends in summer and early autumn. It's also a busy place in spring, when skiers make the hike up into Tuckerman Ravine to ski its formidable headwall. Although the crowds can diminish the mountain experience, the ravine is spectacular, an ascent of the headwall is a serious challenge, and reaching Washington's summit is an accomplishment sought by many. This is the common route for first-time hikers of Washington. The trail on the ravine headwall is sometimes closed due to ice; check on weather and conditions at the visitors center. While hiking the headwall, watch out for rocks kicked loose by hikers above you and be careful not to dislodge any rocks yourself. When you pass over the Mount Washington summit, you'll be walking on the Appalachian Trail. The elevation gained on this hike is about 4,300 feet.

From behind the visitors center, the wide Tuckerman Ravine Trail ascends at a moderate grade, passing the short side path to Crystal Cascade within 0.5 mile. As you continue up the Tuckerman Ravine Trail, you'll pass intersections with several trails. At 2.5 miles the trail reaches the floor of the ravine, a worthwhile destination in itself; to the right is the Lion Head, and to the left the cliffs of Boott Spur. (From the Hermit Lake shelter, which is along the Tuckerman Ravine Trail, walk to the right less than 0.25 mile for a striking reflection of Boott Spur in Hermit Lake.) The trail then climbs the headwall, reaching its lip a mile from Hermit Lake, and follows rock cairns nearly another mile to the summit. Although many hikers descend Tuckerman's headwall, an easier way down is via the Lion Head Trail, which diverges left from the Tuckerman Ravine Trail just below the summit and then rejoins it 0.1 mile below Hermit Lake.

User Groups

Hikers only. No wheelchair facilities. This trail is not suitable for bikes, dogs, horses, or skis, and should not be attempted in winter except by hikers experienced in mountaineering and prepared for severe winter weather. Hunting is prohibited.

Access and Fees

No backcountry permit is needed, but a permit is required for day use or overnight parking at any White Mountain National Forest trailhead, as indicated by signs posted at most trailheads. Permits are available at several area stores and from the national forest at a cost of $5 for seven consecutive days or $20 per year. A $3 one-day permit can be purchased at self-service stations at national forest trailheads, but the permit is good only for the trailhead at which it's purchased.

Maps

Several maps cover this area's hiking trails, including the *Presidential Range* map for $7.95 in waterproof Tyvek, available in many stores and from the Appalachian Mountain Club, 800/262-4455, website: www.outdoors.org; map 2 in the *Map and Guide to the Appalachian Trail in New Hampshire and Vermont,* an eight-map set and guidebook available for $19.95 ($14.95 for the maps alone) from the Appalachian Trail Conference; and the *Trail Map and Guide to the White Mountain National Forest* for $7.95 from the DeLorme Publishing Company, 800/642-0970. For a topographic area map, request Mount Washington from USGS Map Sales, Federal Center, Box 25286, Denver, CO 80225, 888/ASK-USGS (888/275-8747), website: http://mapping.usgs.gov.

Directions

The hike begins from the Appalachian Mountain Club Visitor Center on Route 16 in Pinkham Notch, at the base of Mount Washington, 12 miles south of the junction of Route 16 and U.S. 2 in Gorham and about eight miles north of Jackson. The trailhead is behind the visitors center.

Contact

White Mountain National Forest Supervisor, 719 North Main Street, Laconia, NH 03246, 603/528-8721, TDD for the hearing impaired 603/528-8722, website: www.fs.fed.us/r9/white. Appalachian Trail Conference, 799

Washington Street, P.O. Box 807, Harpers Ferry, WV 25425-0807, 304/
535-6331, website: www.appalachiantrail.org. The Appalachian Mountain
Club's Pinkham Notch Visitor Center has up-to-date reports on weather in
the Presidential Range; call 603/466-2721.

22 MOUNT WASHINGTON: AMMONOOSUC RAVINE/JEWELL TRAIL

in the White Mountain National Forest north
of Crawford Notch

Total distance: 9.6 miles round-trip   **Hiking time:** 7.5 hours

Difficulty: 9   **Rating:** 10

Like any route up the Northeast's biggest hill, this hike offers great views
and rough terrain. Like most others, it is also a popular loop. And like any
other route to the 6,288-foot summit of Mount Washington, this one can
run you into some nasty weather. One September day not long ago I left
behind a sun-splashed valley and ventured up here, only to reach the Lakes
of the Clouds hut and find fog engulfing the mountain and a bitterly cold
wind raking across the alpine zone. Dressed warmly and waiting patiently,
I watched the clouds slowly dissipate under a warm sun—and made my
way to the summit. This hike traverses exposed ground from just below the
Lakes hut until you have descended more than a half mile down the Jewell
Trail. The Ammonoosuc Ravine Trail provides the most direct route—3.1
miles—to the Appalachian Mountain Club's Lakes of the Clouds hut, in
the saddle between Mounts Washington and Monroe. There are tricky
stretches on the ravine's steep upper headwall, which can be slick with
water, and several brook crossings, some of which would be impossible in
times of high water. This hike climbs about 3,800 feet in elevation.

From the parking lot, follow the Ammonoosuc Ravine Trail, which
climbs moderately, passing picturesque Gem Pool about two miles out. For
the next half mile, the trail makes a steep ascent of the headwall, passing
several cascades and pools and good views back into Ammonoosuc Ravine.
At three miles, you leave the last scrub vegetation behind and enter the
alpine zone; take care to walk on rocks and not the fragile plant life. From
the Lakes hut (reached at 3.1 miles), the detour south to the 5,384-foot
summit of Monroe adds a relatively easy one-mile round-trip and 360 feet
of climbing to this hike. From the Lakes hut to the junction of the Jewell
and Gulfside Trails, this hike follows the route of the Appalachian Trail.

To continue the hike, turn left (north) from the Lakes hut onto the
Crawford Path, which passes by the two tiny tarns that give the hut its

name and ascends more than 1,000 vertical feet over 1.4 miles to the top of Washington, where there is a visitors center, private weather observatory, and other buildings. Descend the Crawford Path from the summit for 0.2 mile and bear right onto the Gulfside Trail heading north. Follow it 1.4 miles, walking the crest of the exposed ridge, passing the loop trail up Mount Clay, to the Jewell Trail. (Making the loop hike over Mount Clay adds about two miles and a couple hundred feet of climbing to this hike, but you'll get great views from the top of Clay and a relatively secluded summit.) Turn left and descend the Jewell for 3.7 miles to the parking lot. It descends steep ground through several switchbacks at first, then proceeds at a more moderate grade.

User Groups

Hikers and dogs. No wheelchair facilities. This trail should not be attempted in winter except by hikers experienced in mountaineering and prepared for severe winter weather, and is not suitable for skis. Bikes, horses, and hunting are prohibited.

Access and Fees

No backcountry permit is needed, but a permit is required for day use or overnight parking at any White Mountain National Forest trailhead, as indicated by signs posted at most trailheads. Permits are available at several area stores and from the national forest at a cost of $5 for seven consecutive days or $20 per year. A $3 one-day permit can be purchased at self-service stations at national forest trailheads, but the pass is good only for the trailhead at which it's purchased. Mount Clinton Road is not maintained in winter. The Appalachian Mountain Club operates the Lakes of the Clouds hut, where a crew prepares meals and guests share bunkrooms and bathrooms; call 603/466-2727 for reservation and rate information.

Maps

For a map of hiking trails, obtain the *Presidential Range* map for $7.95 in waterproof Tyvek, available in many stores and from the Appalachian Mountain Club, 800/262-4455, website: www.outdoors.org; map 2 in the *Map and Guide to the Appalachian Trail in New Hampshire and Vermont,* an eight-map set and guidebook available for $19.95 ($14.95 for the maps alone) from the Appalachian Trail Conference; or the *Trail Map and Guide to the White Mountain National Forest* for $7.95 from the De-Lorme Publishing Company, 800/642-0970. For a topographic area map, request Mount Washington from USGS Map Sales, Federal Center, Box 25286, Denver, CO 80225, 888/ASK-USGS (888/275-8747), website: http://mapping.usgs.gov.

Directions

From the junction of U.S. 302 and U.S. 3 in Twin Mountain, drive east on U.S. 302 for 4.6 miles and turn left at signs for the Mount Washington Cog Railway. Continue 6.7 miles to a large parking lot on the right. Or from U.S. 302 in Crawford Notch, 0.2 mile north of the visitor information center, turn onto Mount Clinton Road (which is not maintained in winter). Follow it 3.7 miles and turn right. Continue 1.1 miles and turn right into the parking lot.

Contact

White Mountain National Forest Supervisor, 719 North Main Street, Laconia, NH 03246, 603/528-8721, TDD for the hearing impaired 603/528-8722, website: www.fs.fed.us/r9/white. Appalachian Trail Conference, 799 Washington Street, P.O. Box 807, Harpers Ferry, WV 25425-0807, 304/535-6331, website: www.appalachiantrail.org. The Appalachian Mountain Club's Pinkham Notch Visitor Center has up-to-date reports on weather in the Presidential Range; call 603/466-2721.

23 MOUNTS WASHINGTON AND MONROE: CRAWFORD PATH

in the White Mountain National Forest and
Crawford Notch State Park

Total distance: 16.4 miles round-trip　　　**Hiking time:** 11 hours

Difficulty: 9　　　**Rating:** 10

This is a hike typically covered in two days, with a stay at the Appalachian Mountain Club's Lakes of the Clouds hut, but the gentle nature of the Crawford Path allows very fit hikers to do this in a day. The southern ridge of the Presidentials is far less rugged than the northern ridge, yet the views surpass those of most hikes in New England. Another draw: the Lakes of the Clouds, which are among the few true alpine tarns in the White Mountains. The 5,372-foot Mount Monroe rolls like a wave south from the 6,288-foot Mount Washington—and if you do spend a night at the hut, make the short walk up onto Monroe to watch the sunset. Remember that weather changes quickly on these peaks and may even be radically different atop Washington than on the other summits. I once hiked up the Crawford Path in early September, leaving a valley enjoying 65-degree temperatures, to find fresh snow on Mount Pierce—and to hear that Washington's summit was being bombarded by 100 mph winds.

From the parking area, follow the Crawford Connector 0.2 mile to the Crawford Path, considered the oldest continuously maintained footpath in the country. (Nearby, a side path leads left for 0.4 mile over rough ground to Crawford Cliff, with a good view of Crawford Notch.) From the connector trail junction, the Crawford Path ascends steadily, passing a short side path in 0.4 mile that leads to Gibbs Falls. Less than three miles from U.S. 302, the trail emerges from the forest and meets the Webster Cliff Trail (turning right and walking about 150 yards south on that trail brings you to the 4,312-foot summit of Mount Pierce). From this point to Washington's summit, this hike follows the Appalachian Trail. Turn left, following the Crawford Path over more level ground, with views in all directions. A bit more than a mile from the Webster Cliffs Trail junction, the Mount Eisenhower loop trail diverges for the 0.4-mile climb to Eisenhower's 4,760-foot summit, then descends, steeply in spots, another 0.4 mile to rejoin the Crawford Path. Although bagging Eisenhower entails 300 feet of climbing and 0.2 mile more hiking than taking the Crawford Path around the summit, the view from its summit is worth the small effort. The Crawford Path continues to ascend at a very gentle grade until, six miles from U.S. 302, the Mount Monroe Loop branches left for its two summits (from this direction, the second, or northernmost, summit is the highest).

It's the same distance, 0.7 mile, via either the Crawford Path or the Monroe Loop to where the two trails meet again north of Monroe, but the Monroe Loop involves another 350 feet of elevation gain and is much more exposed. From the northern junction of the trails, the Crawford Path leads a flat 0.1 mile to the Lakes of the Clouds hut. From there, it's a steady climb for 1.4 miles over very rocky terrain up the barren summit cone of Washington to the roof of New England. Return via the same route.

User Groups

Hikers and dogs. No wheelchair facilities. This trail should not be attempted in winter except by hikers experienced in mountaineering and prepared for severe winter weather, and is not suitable for skis. Bikes, horses, and hunting are prohibited.

Access and Fees

No backcountry permit is needed, but a permit is required for day use or overnight parking at any White Mountain National Forest trailhead, as indicated by signs posted at most trailheads. Permits are available at several area stores and from the national forest at a cost of $5 for seven consecutive days or $20 per year. A $3 one-day permit can be purchased at self-service stations at national forest trailheads, but the pass is good only for the trailhead at which it's purchased. The Appalachian Mountain Club operates the Lakes of the Clouds hut in the saddle between the summits of

Washington and Monroe, where a crew prepares meals and guests share bunkrooms and bathrooms; call 603/466-2727 for reservation and rate information, or see the website: www.outdoors.org.

Maps

For a map of hiking trails, obtain the *Presidential Range* map for $7.95 in waterproof Tyvek, available in many stores and from the Appalachian Mountain Club, 800/262-4455, website: www.outdoors.org; map 2 in the *Map and Guide to the Appalachian Trail in New Hampshire and Vermont,* an eight-map set and guidebook available for $19.95 ($14.95 for the maps alone) from the Appalachian Trail Conference; or the *Trail Map and Guide to the White Mountain National Forest* for $7.95 from the DeLorme Publishing Company, 800/642-0970, website: www.DeLorme.com). For a topographic area map, request Mount Washington from USGS Map Sales, Federal Center, Box 25286, Denver, CO 80225, 888/ASK-USGS (888/275-8747), website: http://mapping.usgs.gov.

Directions

Drive on U.S. 302 into Crawford Notch. The trailhead parking area is 0.1 mile up Mount Clinton Road, which leaves U.S. 302 opposite the Crawford House site, just north of Saco Lake.

Contact

White Mountain National Forest Supervisor, 719 North Main Street, Laconia, NH 03246, 603/528-8721, TDD for the hearing impaired 603/528-8722, website: www.fs.fed.us/r9/white. Appalachian Trail Conference, 799 Washington Street, P.O. Box 807, Harpers Ferry, WV 25425-0807, 304/535-6331, website: www.appalachiantrail.org. The Appalachian Mountain Club's Pinkham Notch Visitor Center has up-to-date reports on weather in the Presidential Range; call 603/466-2721.

24 MOUNT WASHINGTON: BOOTT SPUR/ GULF OF SLIDES

in the White Mountain National Forest in Pinkham Notch

Total distance: 7.2 miles round-trip   **Hiking time:** 5 hours

Difficulty: 9   **Rating:** 10

The summit of 6,288-foot Mount Washington, with its commercial development and access by road and cog railway, is one of the least appealing features of this sprawling mountain—which is why I sometimes prefer a hike like this one, with its stiff climb onto a high shoulder of Washington and views down into two of its ravines. The ascent to the high point named Boott Spur is about 3,500 feet.

From the Appalachian Mountain Club Visitor Center, follow the Tuckerman Ravine Trail for nearly a half mile. Shortly after passing the side path to Crystal Cascade, turn left onto the Boott Spur Trail. In another 1.7 miles, a side path leads a short distance right to Ravine Outlook, high above Tuckerman Ravine. Return to the Boott Spur Trail, which emerges from the woods nearly two miles from the Tuckerman Ravine Trail and passes between the halves of Split Rock at 2.2 miles. It then ascends the open ridge known as Boott Spur, with excellent views down into Tuckerman Ravine. Although the grade is moderate, a few false summits along the steplike ridge deceive many hikers. Once atop the shoulder, three miles from the Tuckerman Ravine Trail, turn left (south) onto the Davis Path and follow it for 0.5 mile. Then turn left again (southeast) onto the Glen Boulder Trail, which circles around the rim of the Gulf of Slides, a popular destination for backcountry skiers in winter and spring. Much of the Glen Boulder Trail is above tree line, with long views to the south and good views east toward Wildcat Mountain and the Carter Range. At 1.5 miles from the Davis Path, you'll pass the Glen Boulder, an enormous glacial erratic set precariously on the mountainside. A bit more than a mile past the boulder, back down in the woods, turn left onto the Direttissima, the trail heading back to the visitors center parking lot.

User Groups

Hikers only. No wheelchair facilities. This trail should not be attempted in winter except by hikers experienced in mountaineering and prepared for severe winter weather, and is not for bikes, dogs, horses, or skis. Hunting is prohibited.

Access and Fees

No backcountry permit is needed, but a permit is required for day use or overnight parking at any White Mountain National Forest trailhead, as indicated by signs posted at most trailheads. Permits are available at several area stores and from the national forest at a cost of $5 for seven consecutive days or $20 per year. A $3 one-day permit can be purchased at self-service stations at national forest trailheads, but the pass is good only for the trailhead at which it's purchased.

Maps

For a map of hiking trails, obtain the *Presidential Range* map for $7.95 in waterproof Tyvek, available in many stores and from the Appalachian

Mountain Club, 800/262-4455, website: www.outdoors.org; or the *Trail Map and Guide to the White Mountain National Forest* for $7.95 from the DeLorme Publishing Company, 800/642-0970. For a topographic area map, request Mount Washington from USGS Map Sales, Federal Center, Box 25286, Denver, CO 80225, 888/ASK-USGS (888/275-8747), website: http://mapping.usgs.gov.

Directions
The hike begins from the Appalachian Mountain Club Visitor Center on Route 16 in Pinkham Notch, at the base of Mount Washington, 12 miles south of the junction of Route 16 and U.S. 2 in Gorham and about eight miles north of Jackson. The trailhead is behind the visitors center.

Contact
White Mountain National Forest Supervisor, 719 North Main Street, Laconia, NH 03246, 603/528-8721, TDD for the hearing impaired 603/528-8722, website: www.fs.fed.us/r9/white. The Appalachian Mountain Club's Pinkham Notch Visitor Center has up-to-date reports on weather in the Presidential Range; call 603/466-2721.

25 SQUARE LEDGE
in the White Mountain National Forest in Pinkham Notch

Total distance: 1.2 miles round-trip   **Hiking time:** 0.75 hour

Difficulty: 2   **Rating:** 9

Square Ledge is the aptly named cliff that's obvious when you're standing in the parking lot at the Appalachian Mountain Club Visitor Center on Route 16 and looking due east across the road. The view from atop this cliff is one of the best you can get of Pinkham Notch, and it takes in the deep ravines on the east side of New England's highest peak, 6,288-foot Mount Washington. The hiking trail is 1.2 miles, but you can make a longer loop by getting onto the cross-country skiing trail. A fairly wide skiing trail of only moderate difficulty starts just north of the hiking trail on Route 16, directly across from the Appalachian Mountain Club Visitor Center; it is marked by diamond-shaped plastic markers. This hike is a great trip on snowshoes because the trees are bare, the forest more open, and you get almost continuous views of the east side of Mount Washington (see this chapter's six hikes up Mount Washington). I snowshoed up here on a gorgeous late March afternoon, as the sun was dropping behind Washington. In winter, there may be ice just below the cliffs of Square

Ledge, or you may have to remove your snowshoes if there's no snow or ice and the rocks at the cliff's base are exposed. There is a bit of easy scrambling up six or eight feet of rock to get onto Square Ledge.

From the Appalachian Mountain Club Visitor Center, cross Route 16 and walk south about 100 feet to where the Lost Pond Trail, a part of the white-blazed Appalachian Trail, crosses a bog on a boardwalk and enters the woods. About 50 feet into the woods, turn left on the blue-blazed Square Ledge Trail. The trail almost immediately crosses the ski trail. It ascends gradually—you will only gain about 400 feet in elevation from the road to Square Ledge—through a mixed forest with lots of white birch trees, some of them pretty fat. Watch for the sporadic blazes marking the trail, especially in winter, when the pathway may be less obvious. At 0.1 mile from the road, turn left and follow a side path 100 feet to Ladies Lookout, where you'll get a decent view toward Washington. Back on the Square Ledge Trail, continue through the woods, skirt around Hangover Rock—easy to recognize—then turn right and climb more steeply uphill. As you reach the bottom of the gully on the right (south) side of the Square Ledge cliffs, turn and look to your right; you will see the ski trail about 20 feet through the trees. Remember this spot for your descent. Scramble up the gully to the right of the cliffs. At the top of the gully, scramble up the rocks to the top of the ledge.

After enjoying the view, backtrack down the gully to its base. From here, you can either return the same way you came, making a 1.2-mile round-trip, or turn left, cut through the woods, and extend your hike by less than a mile on the ski trail. Once on the ski trail, turn left and follow it to the Loop Trail, which loops off and returns to the ski trail. At the far end of the Loop Trail, you'll get another view toward Washington. After completing the loop, descend on the ski trail to the point where it crosses the hiking trail. Turn left on the hiking trail, and you'll be back at Route 16 within minutes.

User Groups

Hikers and snowshoers. There is a separate trail for cross-country skiers. No wheelchair access. Dogs must be under control at all times. Hunting is allowed in season.

Access and Fees

No backcountry permit is needed, but a permit is required for day use or overnight parking at any White Mountain National Forest trailhead, as indicated by signs posted at most trailheads. Permits are available at several area stores and from the national forest at a cost of $5 for seven consecutive days or $20 per year. A $3 one-day permit can be purchased at self-service stations at national forest trailheads, but the permit is good only for the trailhead at which it's purchased.

Maps

For a map of hiking trails in this area, obtain the *Presidential Range* map for $7.95 in waterproof Tyvek, available in many stores and from the Appalachian Mountain Club, 800/262-4455, website: www.outdoors.org; or the *Trail Map and Guide to the White Mountain National Forest* for $7.95 from the DeLorme Publishing Company, 800/642-0970. For a topographic area map, request Mount Washington from USGS Map Sales, Federal Center, Box 25286, Denver, CO 80225, 888/ASK-USGS (888/275-8747), website: http://mapping.usgs.gov.

Directions

The hike begins from the Appalachian Mountain Club Visitor Center on Route 16 in Pinkham Notch, at the base of Mount Washington, 12 miles south of the junction of Route 16 and U.S. 2 in Gorham and about eight miles north of Jackson. The trailhead is across the highway from the visitors center.

Contact

White Mountain National Forest Supervisor, 719 North Main Street, Laconia, NH 03246, 603/528-8721, TDD for the hearing impaired 603/528-8722, website: www.fs.fed.us/r9/white. The Appalachian Mountain Club's Pinkham Notch Visitor Center has up-to-date reports on weather in the Presidential Range; call 603/466-2721.

26 MOUNT HIGHT/CARTER DOME/ CARTER NOTCH

in the White Mountain National Forest north of Pinkham Notch

Total distance: 10 miles round-trip   **Hiking time:** 7.5 hours

Difficulty: 9   **Rating:** 10

This very scenic 10-mile loop takes you over the most rugged summit with the most expansive views in the Carter Range—craggy Mount Hight—onto the ninth-highest peak in the Granite State, 4,832-foot Carter Dome, and into a boulder-strewn mountain notch where towering cliffs flank a pair of tiny ponds. The total elevation gained is about 3,500 feet.

From the trailhead, hike the Nineteen-Mile Brook Trail for nearly two miles, and turn left (east) onto the Carter Dome Trail. In about two miles, at Zeta Pass, you might exercise the option of exploring 4,430-foot South Carter (adding 1.5 miles to this hike) by heading north (left) on the Carter-Moriah Trail; then double back to Zeta Pass. This hike heads south (right) on the Carter-Moriah Trail, which follows the Appalachian Trail from Zeta Pass to the junction of the Nineteen-Mile Brook and Wildcat Ridge Trails. The trail climbs steeply, requiring some scrambling over rocks, to the bare summit of 4,675-foot Mount Hight. There you have a 360-degree panorama of the Presidential Range dominating the skyline to the west, the Carters running north, and the lower hills of eastern New Hampshire and western Maine to the south and east. Continue south on the Carter-Moriah Trail, over the viewless summit of Carter Dome, and descend into Carter Notch. There's a great view of the notch from open ledges before you start the knee-pounding drop. At the larger of the two Carter Lakes in the notch, two miles past Mount Hight, turn right (northwest) onto the Nineteen-Mile Brook Trail for the nearly four-mile walk back to the parking area.

User Groups

Hikers and dogs. No wheelchair facilities. This trail would be difficult to snowshoe in severe winter weather, and is not suitable for skis. Bikes, horses, and hunting are prohibited.

Access and Fees

No backcountry permit is needed, but a permit is required for day use or overnight parking at any White Mountain National Forest trailhead, as indicated by signs posted at most trailheads. Permits are available at several area stores and from the national forest at a cost of $5 for seven consecutive days or $20 per year. A $3 one-day permit can be purchased at self-service stations at national forest trailheads, but the pass is good only for the trailhead at which it's purchased.

Maps

For a map of hiking trails, obtain the *Carter Range–Evans Notch/North Country–Mahoosuc* map, $7.95 in waterproof Tyvek, available in many stores and from the Appalachian Mountain Club, 800/262-4455, website: www.outdoors.org; the *Trail Map and Guide to the White Mountain National Forest* for $7.95 from the DeLorme Publishing Company, 800/642-0970; or map 2 in the *Map and Guide to the Appalachian Trail in New Hampshire and Vermont,* an eight-map set and guidebook for $19.95 ($14.95 for the maps alone) from the Appalachian Trail Conference. For a topographic area map, request Carter Dome from USGS Map Sales, Federal Center,

Box 25286, Denver, CO 80225, 888/ASK-USGS (888/275-8747), website: http://mapping.usgs.gov.

Directions
The Nineteen-Mile Brook Trail begins at a turnout on Route 16, a mile north of the Mount Washington Auto Road.

Contact
White Mountain National Forest Supervisor, 719 North Main Street, Laconia, NH 03246, 603/528-8721, TDD for the hearing impaired 603/528-8722, website: www.fs.fed.us/r9/white. Appalachian Trail Conference, 799 Washington Street, P.O. Box 807, Harpers Ferry, WV 25425-0807, 304/535-6331, website: www.appalachiantrail.org.

27 WILDCAT MOUNTAIN
in the White Mountain National Forest in Pinkham Notch

Total distance: 8.5 miles round-trip   **Hiking time:** 5.5 hours

Difficulty: 9   **Rating:** 9

The summit of this 4,000-foot peak is wooded and uninteresting, but the walk along Nineteen-Mile Brook and the view from the top of the cliffs overlooking Carter Notch and the Carter Range—reached via a short spur trail just below Wildcat Mountain's 4,422-foot summit—make this hike very worthwhile. Because this end of Wildcat Mountain does not tend to lure many hikers, you might have that viewpoint to yourself (as a friend and I once did at the tail end of a backpacking trip through the Carter Range). This hike climbs nearly 3,000 feet.

From Route 16, the Nineteen-Mile Brook Trail ascends very gently toward Carter Notch, paralleling the wide, rock-strewn streamed and crossing two tributaries. Just 0.2 mile before the trail drops down into the notch—and 3.5 miles from Route 16—turn right onto the Wildcat Ridge Trail, which is also part of the Appalachian Trail. It climbs the steep east face of Wildcat Mountain and crosses a rockslide path about 25 feet across that is steep and severely eroded, with loose footing in summer and often dangerous, icy conditions in winter. Upon reaching more level ground, shortly before topping the long ridge of Wildcat Mountain, watch for the spur trail branching left that leads about 30 feet to the top of the cliffs overlooking Carter Notch. Return to the parking area the way you came—and on the descent, I highly recommend the 0.5-mile detour down into Carter Notch on the Nineteen-Mile Brook Trail.

User Groups

Hikers, snowshoers, and dogs. No wheelchair facilities. This trail is not suitable for skis. Bikes, horses, and hunting are prohibited.

Access and Fees

No backcountry permit is needed, but a permit is required for day use or overnight parking at any White Mountain National Forest trailhead, as indicated by signs posted at most trailheads. Permits are available at several area stores and from the national forest at a cost of $5 for seven consecutive days or $20 per year. A $3 one-day permit can be purchased at self-service stations at national forest trailheads, but the pass is good only for the trailhead at which it's purchased.

Maps

For a map of hiking trails, obtain the *Presidential Range* map or the *Carter Range-Evans Notch/North Country-Mahoosuc* map, $7.95 each in waterproof Tyvek, available in many stores and from the Appalachian Mountain Club, 800/262-4455, website: www.outdoors.org; the *Trail Map and Guide to the White Mountain National Forest* for $7.95 from the De-Lorme Publishing Company, 800/642-0970; or map 2 in the *Map and Guide to the Appalachian Trail in New Hampshire and Vermont,* an eight-map set for $19.95 ($14.95 for the maps alone) from the Appalachian Trail Conference. For a topographic area map, request Carter Dome from USGS Map Sales, Federal Center, Box 25286, Denver, CO 80225, 888/ASK-USGS (888/275-8747), website: http://mapping.usgs.gov.

Directions

The Nineteen-Mile Brook Trail begins at a turnout on Route 16, a mile north of the Mount Washington Auto Road.

Contact

White Mountain National Forest Supervisor, 719 North Main Street, Laconia, NH 03246, 603/528-8721, TDD for the hearing impaired 603/528-8722, website: www.fs.fed.us/r9/white. Appalachian Trail Conference, 799 Washington Street, P.O. Box 807, Harpers Ferry, WV 25425-0807, 304/535-6331, website: www.appalachiantrail.org.

28 CARTER NOTCH: WILDCAT RIVER TRAIL

in the White Mountain National Forest north of Jackson

Total distance: 8.6 miles round-trip   **Hiking time:** 5 hours

Difficulty: 8   **Rating:** 8

This relatively easy hike accesses spectacular Carter Notch via a trail less traveled than the popular Nineteen-Mile Brook Trail (see the Mount Hight/Carter Dome/Carter Notch listing earlier in this chapter). It's arguably a more scenic outing on snowshoes in winter, when the leaves are down and you get better views of the mountains. For beginner snowshoers, it's also well protected from the severe winter weather that can pound the higher summits, though at 8.6 miles round-trip, you shouldn't underestimate how tiring it can be snowshoeing this entire route. The elevation gain is about 1,500 feet.

From the parking area, follow the Bog Brook Trail for 0.7 mile. Just after crossing the Wildcat River, which can be difficult at times of high water, the Bog Brook Trail bears right, but you will continue straight ahead onto the Wildcat River Trail. Follow it along the gorgeous river, then away from the river into the woods. It ascends steadily but gently except for brief, steep pitches, for 3.6 miles from the Bog Brook Trail junction to the Appalachian Mountain Club hut in Carter Notch. After exploring the notch a bit, return the way you came.

User Groups

Hikers, snowshoers, skiers, and dogs. No wheelchair facilities. Bikes, horses, and hunting are prohibited.

Access and Fees

No backcountry permit is needed, but a permit is required for day use or overnight parking at any White Mountain National Forest trailhead, as indicated by signs posted at most trailheads. Permits are available at several area stores and from the national forest at a cost of $5 for seven consecutive days or $20 per year. A $3 one-day permit can be purchased at self-service stations at national forest trailheads, but the pass is good only for the trailhead at which it's purchased. Carry cash for camping overnight at the Appalachian Mountain Club hut in Carter Notch.

Maps

For a contour map of hiking trails, obtain the *Carter Range–Evans Notch/North Country–Mahoosuc* map, $7.95 in waterproof Tyvek, available in many stores and from the Appalachian Mountain Club, 800/262-4455, website: www.outdoors.org; or the *Trail Map and Guide to the White Mountain National Forest* for $7.95 from the DeLorme Publishing Company, 800/642-0970. For a topographic area map, request Jackson and Carter Dome from USGS Map Sales, Federal Center, Box 25286, Denver, CO 80225, 888/ASK-USGS (888/275-8747), website: http://mapping.usgs.gov.

Directions

From Route 16A in Jackson, Route 16B loops through the north end of town, its two endpoints leaving Route 16A very near each other; take the left, or westernmost, endpoint of Route 16B and follow it uphill. Where Route 16B turns sharply right, continue straight ahead onto Carter Notch Road. Three miles after leaving Route 16B, just after a sharp left turn in the road, park at a turnout for the Bog Brook Trail.

Contact

White Mountain National Forest Supervisor, 719 North Main Street, Laconia, NH 03246, 603/528-8721, TDD for the hearing impaired 603/528-8722, website: www.fs.fed.us/r9/white.

29 LOST POND

in the White Mountain National Forest in Pinkham Notch

Total distance: 2 miles round-trip **Hiking time:** 1 hour

Difficulty: 1 **Rating:** 8

While this pond is no more lost than the popular Lonesome Lake on the other side of the Whites is lonesome, this is a nice short hike that's flat and offers opportunities for wildlife viewing and a unique view of Mount Washington. Cross Route 16 from the Appalachian Mountain Club Visitor Center and follow the Lost Pond Trail, a section of the Appalachian Trail, around the pond. Immediately you will see signs of beaver activity— probably dams and a lodge—and, if you're lucky, a moose will be grazing in the swampy area to the left. About halfway around the pond, look across it to a fine view up at Washington above the still water. The trail ends at the Wildcat Ridge Trail, just minutes from Glen Ellis Falls, which can be reached by turning right (west) toward Route 16; in spring and early summer, crossing the Ellis River between this trail junction and Route 16 can be difficult and dangerous. You can also reach some nice views of this valley and Mount Washington by turning left at this junction and climbing less than a mile up the Wildcat Ridge Trail. This hike returns the way you came.

User Groups

Hikers, dogs, skiers, and snowshoers. No wheelchair facilities. Bikes, horses, and hunting are prohibited.

Access and Fees

No backcountry permit is needed, but a permit is required for day use or overnight parking at any White Mountain National Forest trailhead, as indicated by signs posted at most trailheads. Permits are available at several area stores and from the national forest at a cost of $5 for seven consecutive days or $20 per year. A $3 one-day permit can be purchased at self-service stations at national forest trailheads, but the pass is good only for the trailhead at which it's purchased.

Maps

Contour maps covering this area include the *Presidential Range* map and *Carter Range-Evans Notch/North Country-Mahoosuc* map, both for $7.95 in waterproof Tyvek, available in many stores and from the Appalachian Mountain Club, 800/262-4455, website: www.outdoors.org. For topographic area maps, request Mount Washington, Carter Dome, Jackson, and Stairs Mountain from USGS Map Sales, Federal Center, Box 25286, Denver, CO 80225, 888/ASK-USGS (888/275-8747), website: http://mapping.usgs.gov.

Directions

The hike begins from the Appalachian Mountain Club Visitor Center on Route 16 in Pinkham Notch, at the base of Mount Washington, 12 miles south of the junction of Route 16 and U.S. 2 in Gorham and about eight miles north of Jackson. The trailhead is across the highway from the visitors center.

Contact

White Mountain National Forest Supervisor, 719 North Main Street, Laconia, NH 03246, 603/528-8721, TDD for the hearing impaired 603/528-8722, website: www.fs.fed.us/r9/white. Appalachian Mountain Club Pinkham Notch Visitor Center, P.O. Box 298, Gorham, NH 03581, 603/466-2721, website: www.outdoors.org.

30 GLEN ELLIS FALLS

in the White Mountain National Forest south of
Pinkham Notch

Total distance: 0.3 miles round-trip   **Hiking time:** 0.75 hour

Difficulty: 2   **Rating:** 8

Here's a scenic, short walk that's ideal for young children and enjoyable
for adults—though it could be troublesome for people who have difficulty
climbing steep steps. Follow the wide gravel trail through a tunnel under
Route 16. It descends steeply at times, but there are rock steps and a
handrail. The waterfall is less than a half-mile walk from the parking area
and more than worth the effort: a 70-foot wall of water makes a sheer
drop into a small pool at its base. This is a popular walk with tourists, and
it's especially spectacular in late spring, when water flow is heaviest.

Special note: If you're coming from Lost Pond or Wildcat Mountain
(see listings in this chapter), be aware that the Wildcat River Trail makes a
crossing of the Ellis River near Route 16 that can be treacherous in times
of high water and unsafe for young children.

User Groups

Hikers and dogs. No wheelchair facilities. This trail would be difficult to
snowshoe and is not suitable for bikes, horses, or skis. Hunting is allowed
in season.

Access and Fees

No backcountry permit is needed, but a permit is required for day use or
overnight parking at any White Mountain National Forest trailhead, as indicated by signs posted at most trailheads. Permits are available at several
area stores and from the national forest at a cost of $5 for seven consecu-
tive days or $20 per year. A $3 one-day permit can be purchased at self-
service stations at national forest trailheads, but the pass is good only for
the trailhead at which it's purchased.

Maps

Although no map is needed for this hike, several maps cover it, including
the Presidential Range for $10.95 (paper), and the *Presidential Range* map
and *Carter Range-Evans Notch/North Country-Mahoosuc* map, both for
$7.95 in waterproof Tyvek, available in many stores and from the Ap-
palachian Mountain Club, 800/262-4455, website: www.outdoors.org; and
the *Trail Map and Guide to the White Mountain National Forest* for $7.95
from the DeLorme Publishing Company, 800/642-0970. For topographic

area maps, request Mount Washington, Carter Dome, Jackson, and Stairs Mountain from USGS Map Sales, Federal Center, Box 25286, Denver, CO 80225, 888/ASK-USGS (888/275-8747), website: http://mapping.usgs.gov.

Directions
The trail begins at a parking lot for Glen Ellis Falls off Route 16, less than a mile south of the Appalachian Mountain Club Visitor Center in Pinkham Notch.

Contact
White Mountain National Forest Supervisor, 719 North Main Street, Laconia, NH 03246, 603/528-8721, TDD for the hearing impaired 603/528-8722, website: www.fs.fed.us/r9/white. Appalachian Mountain Club Pinkham Notch Visitor Center, P.O. Box 298, Gorham, NH 03581, 603/466-2721, website: www.outdoors.org.

31 ZEALAND NOTCH/WILLEY RANGE
in the White Mountain National Forest southeast of Twin Mountain

Total distance: 17 miles round-trip **Hiking time:** 2–3 days

Difficulty: 8 **Rating:** 9

This 17-mile loop, best spread over two or three days, passes through spectacular Zealand Notch and traverses the Willey Range, a less-well-known corner of the Whites with a pair of 4,000-foot peaks and rugged terrain, if limited views. Two friends and I made this trip one Thanksgiving weekend, hiking through the notch on a chilly but calm night under a full moon. We enjoyed views from Mount Willey of clouds swirling around the Presidentials before a storm blew in and dampened our spirits with a cold, driving rain. The cumulative elevation gained is less than 3,000 feet.

From the Zealand Road parking lot, follow the Zealand Trail south, paralleling the Zealand River. At 2.3 miles, the A-Z Trail enters from the left; you will return on that trail. The Zealand Trail reaches a junction with the Twinway and the Ethan Pond Trail at 2.5 miles. The Appalachian Mountain Club's Zealand Falls hut lies 0.2 mile uphill on the Twinway; on the way, you pass a short side path to a view of Zealand Falls, and there are views of the notch from the hut. Instead, this hike bears left onto the Ethan Pond Trail, which runs for two miles to the opposite end of the notch, passing numerous overlooks through the trees. Reaching the Thoreau Falls Trail at 4.6 miles, bear right and follow it for 0.1 mile to Thoreau Falls, which tumbles more than 100 feet down through several steps. Backtrack and turn right (east) on the Ethan Pond Trail, which follows level ground for 2.5 miles to the side path leading left less than 0.1 mile to Ethan Pond and the shelter just above the pond.

A mile beyond the junction, turn left (north) onto the Willey Range Trail, which soon begins a steep and sustained climb—employing wooden ladders in spots—of 1.1 miles up 4,285-foot Mount Willey, where there are some views from just below the summit. The trail continues north, dropping into a saddle, then ascending to the 4,340-foot summit of Mount Field—named for Darby Field, the first known person to climb Mount Washington—1.4 miles from Willey's summit. Field is wooded, with no views. Just beyond the summit, the Avalon Trail branches right, but stay left with the Willey Range Trail, descending steadily to the A-Z Trail, 0.9 mile from the summit of Field. Turn left (west), descending easily for 2.7 miles to the Zealand Trail. Turn right (north) and walk 2.5 miles back to the Zealand Road parking lot.

User Groups

Hikers and dogs. No wheelchair facilities. This trail may be difficult to snowshoe because of severe winter weather, and is not suitable for bikes, horses, or skis. Hunting is allowed in season, except along the Appalachian Trail, which coincides with the Twinway and the Ethan Pond Trail.

Access and Fees

No backcountry permit is needed, but a permit is required for day use or overnight parking at any White Mountain National Forest trailhead, as indicated by signs posted at most trailheads. Permits are available at several area stores and from the national forest at a cost of $5 for seven consecutive days or $20 per year. A $3 one-day permit can be purchased at self-service stations at national forest trailheads, but the pass is good only for the trailhead at which it's purchased. Zealand Road is not maintained in winter; the winter parking lot is on U.S. 302, immediately east of Zealand Road. The Appalachian Mountain Club operates the Zealand Falls hut year-round; it is on the Twinway, 0.2 mile from the junction of the Zealand, Twinway, and Ethan Pond Trails and 2.7 miles from the end of Zealand Road. Contact the Appalachian Mountain Club for information on cost and reservations. The Appalachian Mountain Club also operates the first-come, first-served Ethan Pond shelter, located just off the Ethan Pond Trail, 7.3 miles from the Zealand Road parking lot along this hike's route. A caretaker collects the $6 per person nightly fee from late spring to fall.

Maps

Several maps cover this area's hiking trails, including the *Franconia-Pemigewasset Range* map and the *Crawford Notch-Sandwich Range/Moosilauke-Kinsman* map, each $7.95 in waterproof Tyvek, available in many stores and from the Appalachian Mountain Club, 800/262-4455, website: www.outdoors.org; the *Trail Map and Guide to the White Mountain National Forest* for $7.95 from the DeLorme Publishing Company, 800/642-0970 and map 3 in the *Map and Guide to the Appalachian Trail in New Hampshire and Vermont,* an eight-map set and guidebook available for $19.95 ($14.95 for the maps alone) from the Appalachian Trail Conference. For a topographic area map, request Crawford Notch from USGS Map Sales, Federal Center, Box 25286, Denver, CO 80225, 888/ASK-USGS (888/275-8747), website: http://mapping.usgs.gov.

Directions

From the junction of U.S. 3 and U.S. 302 in Twin Mountain, drive east on U.S. 302 for 2.3 miles and turn right onto Zealand Road. Continue 3.5 miles to a parking lot at the end of the road.

Contact

White Mountain National Forest Supervisor, 719 North Main Street, Laconia, NH 03246, 603/528-8721, TDD for the hearing impaired 603/528-8722, website: www.fs.fed.us/r9/white. Appalachian Mountain Club Pinkham Notch Visitor Center, P.O. Box 298, Gorham, NH 03581, 603/466-2721, website: www.outdoors.org. Appalachian Trail Conference, 799 Washington Street, P.O. Box 807, Harpers Ferry, WV 25425-0807, 304/535-6331, website: www.appalachiantrail.org. New Hampshire Division of Parks and Recreation, Bureau of Trails, P.O. Box 1856, Concord, NH 03302-1856, 603/271-3254.

32 MOUNT HALE

in the White Mountain National Forest southeast of Twin Mountain

Total distance: 4.6 miles round-trip **Hiking time:** 2.5 hours

Difficulty: 8 **Rating:** 8

Mount Hale, at 4,054 feet, is one of New Hampshire's 48 4,000-foot peaks—and one of the least-visited in that group because its summit isn't nearly as spectacular as many of the others. But from the tree-ringed clearing atop Hale, you do get views of the Sugarloafs to the north, the

Presidential Range to the northeast, Zealand Notch to the southeast, and North and South Twin to the southwest. The elevation gain is about 2,200 feet, less than other 4,000-footers, but don't assume this is a walk in the park: The Hale Brook Trail presents a rugged, relentlessly steep 2.3-mile climb to the summit, passing cascades along the brook, including rocky sections that grow slick in the wet season. Some friends and I had an enjoyable hike up it one June day when intermittent, heavy rain and low clouds precluded attempting a peak that involved more exposure or time commitment. One curiosity about Hale is that rocks near its summit are magnetized and will interfere with a magnetic compass.

From the parking lot, follow the Hale Brook Trail all the way to the summit. This hike returns by descending the same trail, but another option is to create a loop of eight or nine miles—depending on whether you shuttle two vehicles—by descending on the Lend-a-Hand Trail from Hale's summit for 2.7 miles to the Twinway. Turn left on the Twinway, passing the Appalachian Mountain Club's Zealand Falls hut in 0.1 mile, and reaching the Zealand Trail 0.3 mile farther. Turn left (north) on the Zealand Trail and follow its fairly flat course 2.5 miles back to Zealand Road. Unless you've shuttled a second vehicle to the Zealand Trail parking area, walk just over a mile down the road back to the parking area for the Hale Brook Trail. You can make an enjoyable two-day outing of this loop—a great one for families—with a stay in the Zealand Falls hut.

User Groups

Hikers, snowshoers, and dogs. No wheelchair facilities. Bikes and horses are prohibited, and the trail is not suitable for skis. Hunting is allowed in season.

Access and Fees

No backcountry permit is needed, but a permit is required for day use or overnight parking at any White Mountain National Forest trailhead, as indicated by signs posted at most trailheads. Permits are available at several area stores and from the national forest at a cost of $5 for seven consecutive days or $20 per year. A $3 one-day permit can be purchased at self-service stations at national forest trailheads, but the pass is good only for the trailhead at which it's purchased. Zealand Road is not maintained in winter. The Appalachian Mountain Club operates the Zealand Falls hut year-round; it is on the Twinway, 0.2 mile from the junction of the Zealand, Twinway, and Ethan Pond Trails and 2.7 miles from the end of Zealand Road. Contact the Appalachian Mountain Club for information on cost and reservations.

Maps

For a map of hiking trails in this area, get the *Franconia–Pemigewasset Range* map, $7.95 in waterproof Tyvek, available in many stores and from the Appalachian Mountain Club, 800/262-4455, website: www.outdoors.org; or the *Trail Map and Guide to the White Mountain National Forest* for $7.95 from the DeLorme Publishing Company, 800/642-0970. For a topographic area map, request Crawford Notch from USGS Map Sales, Federal Center, Box 25286, Denver, CO 80225, 888/ASK-USGS (888/275-8747), website: http://mapping.usgs.gov.

Directions

From the junction of U.S. 3 and U.S. 302 in Twin Mountain, drive east on U.S. 302 for 2.3 miles and turn right onto Zealand Road. Continue 2.4 miles to a parking lot on the right. The winter parking lot is on U.S. 302, 0.1 mile east of Zealand Road.

Contact

White Mountain National Forest Supervisor, 719 North Main Street, Laconia, NH 03246, 603/528-8721, TDD for the hearing impaired 603/528-8722, website: www.fs.fed.us/r9/white. Appalachian Mountain Club Pinkham Notch Visitor Center, P.O. Box 298, Gorham, NH 03581, 603/466-2721, website: www.outdoors.org.

33 ZEALAND NOTCH

in the White Mountain National Forest southeast of Twin Mountain

Total distance: 7.6 miles round-trip   **Hiking time:** 5 hours

Difficulty: 6   **Rating:** 9

Partly due to the convenience provided by the Appalachian Mountain Club's Zealand Falls hut, but also simply because of its splendor, Zealand Notch ranks as one of the most-visited spots in the White Mountains year-round. Although the trail tends to be muddy and has a lot of slippery, exposed roots, this is a nice hike in summer and fall—and fairly easy, gaining only about 500 feet in elevation. On snowshoes or cross-country skis in winter, however, it's arguably even more beautiful. The Zealand Road is not maintained in winter—you have to ski or snowshoe up it—making the round-trip distance into the notch 14.6 miles, instead of 7.6 miles. On skis, the trail is easy to moderately difficult, though possible for an experienced cross-country skier to do in one day without metal-edged skis. Two friends and I skied to the hut one bitterly cold December Sunday after a series of storms had dumped at least a few feet of dry powder in the mountains. The forest wore a thick comforter of white that smothered all sound, and the skiing was fabulous.

From the end of Zealand Road, follow the Zealand Trail south, paralleling the Zealand River. At 2.3 miles, the A-Z Trail diverges left. Continuing on the Zealand Trail, you reach the junction with the Twinway and the Ethan Pond Trail at 2.5 miles. The Appalachian Mountain Club's Zealand Falls hut lies 0.2 mile to the right on the Twinway (adding 0.4 mile to this hike's distance). Continue straight ahead onto the Ethan Pond Trail into Zealand Notch. After about a mile, the trail breaks out of the woods and traverses a shelf across the boulder field left behind by an old rockslide on the side of Whitewall Mountain; the views of Zealand Notch are spectacular. Cross this open area to where the Ethan Pond Trail reenters the woods near the junction with the Zeacliff Trail, 1.3 miles from the Twinway/Zealand Trail junction. Return the way you came.

Special note: For the ambitious or those with more time because they are spending a night at the Zealand Falls hut, hiking all the way to Thoreau Falls would add 1.6 miles round-trip to this hike. Continue on the Ethan Pond Trail beyond the Zeacliff Trail junction for 0.7 mile, then bear right onto the Thoreau Falls Trail. In another 0.1 mile, the trail reaches the top of the falls, which drops more than 100 feet through several steps and creates a very impressive cascade of ice in winter.

User Groups

Hikers, dogs, skiers, and snowshoers. No wheelchair facilities. Bikes and horses are prohibited. Hunting is allowed in season, except along the Appalachian Trail, which coincides with the Twinway and the Ethan Pond Trail.

Access and Fees

No backcountry permit is needed, but a permit is required for day use or overnight parking at any White Mountain National Forest trailhead, as indicated by signs posted at most trailheads. Permits are available at several area stores and from the national forest at a cost of $5 for seven consecutive days or $20 per year. A $3 one-day permit can be purchased at self-service stations at national forest trailheads, but the pass is good only for the trailhead at which it's purchased. Zealand Road is not maintained in winter. The Appalachian Mountain Club operates the Zealand Falls hut year-round; it is on the Twinway, 0.2 mile from the junction of the Zealand, Twinway, and Ethan Pond Trails and 2.7 miles from the end of Zealand Road. Contact the Appalachian Mountain Club for information on cost and reservations.

Maps

Several maps cover this area's hiking trails, including the *Franconia-Pemigewasset Range* map, $7.95 in waterproof Tyvek, available in many stores and from the Appalachian Mountain Club, 800/262-4455, website: www.outdoors.org; the *Trail Map and Guide to the White Mountain National Forest* for $7.95 from the DeLorme Publishing Company, 800/642-0970; and map 3 in the *Map and Guide to the Appalachian Trail in New Hampshire and Vermont,* an eight-map set and guidebook available for $19.95 ($14.95 for the maps alone) from the Appalachian Trail Conference. For a topographic area map, request Crawford Notch from USGS Map Sales, Federal Center, Box 25286, Denver, CO 80225, 888/ASK-USGS (888/275-8747), website: http://mapping.usgs.gov.

Directions

From the junction of U.S. 3 and U.S. 302 in Twin Mountain, drive east on U.S. 302 for 2.3 miles and turn right onto Zealand Road. Continue 3.5 miles to a parking lot at the end of the road. The winter parking lot is on U.S. 302, 0.1 mile east of Zealand Road.

Contact

White Mountain National Forest Supervisor, 719 North Main Street, Laconia, NH 03246, 603/528-8721, TDD for the hearing impaired 603/528-8722, website: www.fs.fed.us/r9/white. Appalachian Mountain Club Pinkham Notch Visitor Center, P.O. Box 298, Gorham, NH 03581, 603/466-2721, website: www.outdoors.org. Appalachian Trail Conference, 799 Washington Street, P.O. Box 807, Harpers Ferry, WV 25425-0807, 304/535-6331, website: www.appalachiantrail.org.

34 ZEALAND NOTCH/TWINS LOOP

in the White Mountain National Forest south
of Twin Mountain

Total distance: 16.1 miles one-way   **Hiking time:** 2 days

Difficulty: 8   **Rating:** 9

This moderately difficult 16-mile trek was one of my first overnight trips in the White Mountains. With superb views, lots of relatively easy terrain, and a reasonable distance to cover in two days, it's a fairly popular weekend loop for backpackers. The cumulative elevation gained is about 3,500 feet. From the Zealand Road parking lot, follow the relatively easy Zealand Trail for 2.5 miles to its junction with the Ethan Pond Trail and the Twinway. Turn right onto the Twinway, which coincides with the Appalachian Trail, climbing 0.2 mile to the Appalachian Mountain Club's Zealand Falls hut.

Beyond the hut, the Twinway passes nice cascades and the Lend-a-Hand Trail junction, climbing high above Zealand Notch. Where the trail takes a right turn at 3.9 miles into this trip, a short side path loops out to the Zeacliff overlook, with a spectacular view of Zealand Notch and mountains—from Carrigain to the south to Mount Washington and the Presidential Range to the northeast. Just 0.1 mile farther up the Twinway, the Zeacliff Trail departs to the left, descending steeply into the notch. Continue along the Twinway, which traverses more level terrain on Zealand Mountain, passing a side path 4.4 miles into the hike that leads left 0.1 mile to Zeacliff Pond. After a short climb above the pond, the Twinway passes a side path at 5.6 miles that leads right a flat 0.1 mile to the summit of 4,260-foot Zealand Mountain. The Twinway then dips and climbs again to the flat, open summit of Mount Guyot, with views in every direction.

At 8.1 miles, the Twinway bears right and the Bondcliff Trail diverges left (south); the Guyot campsite, a logical stop for the night, is 0.8 mile away along the Guyot, down a side path marked by a sign. (The 1.6 miles round-trip to the campsite is figured into this hike's total distance.) Following the Twinway, you will traverse easy terrain, then climb more steeply on the final short stretch up South Twin Mountain, 8.9 miles into this trek, at 4,902 feet the highest point on this trip and the eighth-highest mountain in New Hampshire. The views span much of the Pemigewasset Wilderness and stretch to the Presidential Range. Turn north off the Twinway onto the North Twin Spur, descending into a saddle, then climbing to the wooded and viewless summit of North Twin Mountain (4,761 feet), 1.3 miles from South Twin's summit and 10.2 miles into this trek. Turn right onto the North Twin Trail, soon emerging from the trees onto open ledges with one of the best views of the White Mountains on this trip. The trail descends, quite steeply for long stretches, for two miles to the Little River; it then swings left and follows an old railroad bed along the river for more than two miles to the parking area where your second vehicle awaits.

User Groups

Hikers and dogs. No wheelchair facilities. This trail should not be attempted in winter except by hikers experienced in mountaineering and prepared for severe winter weather, and is not suitable for bikes, horses, or skis. Hunting is allowed in season except along the Appalachian Trail, which coincides with the Twinway.

Access and Fees

No backcountry permit is needed, but a permit is required for day use or overnight parking at any White Mountain National Forest trailhead, as indicated by signs posted at most trailheads. Permits are available at several area stores and from the national forest at a cost of $5 for seven consecutive days or $20 per year. A $3 one-day permit can be purchased at self-service stations at national forest trailheads, but the pass is good only for the trailhead at which it's purchased. Zealand Road is not maintained in winter; the winter parking lot is on U.S. 302 immediately east of Zealand Road. The Appalachian Mountain Club operates the Zealand Falls hut year-round; it is on the Twinway, 0.2 mile from the junction of the Zealand, Twinway, and Ethan Pond Trails and 2.7 miles from the end of Zealand Road. Contact the Appalachian Mountain Club for information on cost and reservations. The Appalachian Mountain Club also operates the first-come, first-served Guyot campsite, with a shelter and several tent platforms, located just off the Bondcliff Trail 0.8 mile from the Twinway on Mount Guyot. A caretaker collects the $8 per person nightly fee from late spring to fall.

Maps

Several maps cover this area's hiking trails, including the *Franconia–Pemigewasset Range* map, $7.95 in waterproof Tyvek, available in many stores and from the Appalachian Mountain Club, 800/262-4455, website: www.outdoors.org; and the *Trail Map and Guide to the White Mountain National Forest* for $7.95 from the DeLorme Publishing Company, 800/642-0970. For topographic area maps, request Mount Washington, Bethlehem, South Twin Mountain, and Crawford Notch from USGS Map Sales, Federal Center, Box 25286, Denver, CO 80225, 888/ASK-USGS (888/275-8747), website: http://mapping.usgs.gov.

Directions

You will need to shuttle two vehicles for this trip. To reach this hike's endpoint from the junction of U.S. 302 and U.S. 3 in Twin Mountain, drive south on U.S. 3 for 2.5 miles and turn left onto Haystack Road (Fire Road 304). Or from I-93 north of Franconia Notch State Park, take Exit 35 for U.S. 3 north and continue about 7.5 miles, then turn right onto Fire Road 304. Follow Fire Road 304 to its end and a parking area at the trailhead. Leave one vehicle there. To reach the start of this hike from the junction of U.S. 3 and U.S. 302 in Twin Mountain, drive east on U.S. 302 for 2.3 miles and turn right onto Zealand Road. Continue 3.5 miles to a parking lot at the end of the road.

Contact

White Mountain National Forest Supervisor, 719 North Main Street, Laconia, NH 03246, 603/528-8721, TDD for the hearing impaired 603/528-8722, website: www.fs.fed.us/r9/white. Appalachian Mountain Club Pinkham Notch Visitor Center, P.O. Box 298, Gorham, NH 03581, 603/466-2721, website: www.outdoors.org.

35 NORTH TWIN MOUNTAIN
in the White Mountain National Forest south
of Twin Mountain

Total distance: 8.6 miles round-trip   **Hiking time:** 6 hours

Difficulty: 9   **Rating:** 9

Although it is the 12th-highest mountain in New Hampshire at 4,761 feet, North Twin lies sufficiently out of the way and attracts far fewer hikers than nearby Franconia Ridge and Zealand Notch. Every time I've stood atop this mountain, my only company was my own companions. But from open ledges just below the summit, you get a commanding view south over the Pemigewasset Wilderness, east toward the Presidential Range, and west to Franconia. The vertical ascent is about 2,800 feet.

Take the North Twin Trail for 4.3 miles to the summit. It follows an old railroad bed along the Little River for more than two miles, then turns sharply west, crosses the Little River—a daunting ford when the water is high—and makes a steep and sustained ascent of the mountain's east side. The trail may be heavily eroded in places. It emerges abruptly from the scrub forest onto the ledges more than four miles from the trailhead. Just a few hundred feet farther lies the summit, which is wooded, and the junction with the North Twin Spur Trail. Hike back the same way. For a scenic ridge walk to a summit with arguably better views, follow the North Twin Spur Trail to the 4,902-foot summit of South Twin Mountain, adding 2.6 miles round-trip to this hike's distance.

User Groups
Hikers and dogs. No wheelchair facilities. This trail should not be attempted in winter except by hikers experienced in mountaineering and prepared for severe winter weather, and is not suitable for bikes, horses, or skis. Hunting is allowed in season.

Access and Fees
No backcountry permit is needed, but a permit is required for day use or overnight parking at any White Mountain National Forest trailhead, as indicated by signs posted at most trailheads. Permits are available at several

area stores and from the national forest at a cost of $5 for seven consecutive days or $20 per year. A $3 one-day permit can be purchased at self-service stations at national forest trailheads, but the pass is good only for the trailhead at which it's purchased.

Maps

For a map of hiking trails, get the *Franconia–Pemigewasset Range* map, $7.95 in waterproof Tyvek, available in many stores and from the Appalachian Mountain Club, 800/262-4455, website: www.outdoors.org; or the *Trail Map and Guide to the White Mountain National Forest* for $7.95 from the DeLorme Publishing Company, 800/642-0970. For topographic area maps, request Bethlehem and South Twin Mountain from USGS Map Sales, Federal Center, Box 25286, Denver, CO 80225, 888/ASK-USGS (888/275-8747), website: http://mapping.usgs.gov.

Directions

From the junction of U.S. 302 and U.S. 3 in Twin Mountain, drive south on U.S. 3 for 2.5 miles and turn left onto Haystack Road/Fire Road 304, which may be marked only by a faded post reading "USFS 304." Or from I-93 north of Franconia Notch State Park, take Exit 35 for U.S. 3 north and continue about 7.5 miles; then turn right onto Fire Road 304. Follow Fire Road 304 to its end and a parking area at the trailhead for the North Twin Trail.

Contact

White Mountain National Forest Supervisor, 719 North Main Street, Laconia, NH 03246, 603/528-8721, TDD for the hearing impaired 603/528-8722, website: www.fs.fed.us/r9/white.

36 GALEHEAD MOUNTAIN
in the White Mountain National Forest south of Twin Mountain

Total distance: 10.2 miles round-trip   **Hiking time:** 7 hours

Difficulty: 8   **Rating:** 7

Galehead Mountain, despite being an official 4,000-footer, attracts few hikers because trees cover its 4,024-foot summit, blocking any views. There is a good view of the tight valley of Twin Brook and a ridge of South Twin Mountain, however, from an overlook on the Frost Trail halfway between the Galehead hut and the summit. For visitors to the Galehead hut, the summit demands no more than a fairly easy one-mile hike—one that promises an opportunity for some quiet. This hike's elevation gain is about 2,400 feet.

From the parking area, follow the Gale River Trail, a wide and relatively flat path, until right before it crosses the north branch of the Gale River—over a wooden footbridge—at about 1.5 miles. For more than a mile beyond that bridge, the trail parallels the river, one of this 10-mile hike's most appealing stretches. It then makes a second river crossing on rocks, which could be difficult in high water. Four miles from the trailhead, the Gale River Trail ends at a junction with the Garfield Ridge Trail, which coincides with the Appalachian Trail. Bear left on the Ridge Trail and follow it another 0.6 mile to its junction with the Twinway. Turn right onto the Twinway for the Galehead hut. Behind the hut, pick up the Frost Trail, which leads 0.5 mile to Galehead's summit. A short side path 0.25 mile from the hut leads to the overlook described above. Descend the same way you came. For a longer hike combining Galehead and Mount Garfield, see the special note in the trail notes for Mount Garfield (see next listing).

User Groups

Hikers and dogs. No wheelchair facilities. This trail may be difficult to snowshoe because of severe winter weather, and is not suitable for skis. Bikes, horses, and hunting are prohibited.

Access and Fees

No backcountry permit is needed, but a permit is required for day use or overnight parking at any White Mountain National Forest trailhead, as indicated by signs posted at most trailheads. Permits are available at several area stores and from the national forest at a cost of $5 for seven consecutive days or $20 per year. A $3 one-day permit can be purchased at self-service stations at national forest trailheads, but the pass is good only for the trailhead at which it's purchased. The Appalachian Mountain Club operates the Galehead hut, where a crew prepares meals and guests share bunkrooms and bathrooms. The hut lies at the western end of the trail called the Twinway, about 100 feet from the junction of the Twinway and the Garfield Ridge Trail; contact the Appalachian Mountain Club for reservation and rate information.

Maps

For a contour map of hiking trails, get the *Franconia-Pemigewasset Range* map, $7.95 in waterproof Tyvek, available in many stores and from the Appalachian Mountain Club, 800/262-4455, website: www.outdoors.org; or the *Trail Map and Guide to the White Mountain National Forest* for $7.95

from the DeLorme Publishing Company, 800/642-0970. For topographic area maps, request South Twin Mountain and Bethlehem from USGS Map Sales, Federal Center, Box 25286, Denver, CO 80225, 888/ASK-USGS (888/275-8747), website: http://mapping.usgs.gov.

Directions
From I-93 north of Franconia Notch State Park, take Exit 35 for U.S. 3 north. Drive about 4.8 miles and then turn right onto the dirt Fire Road 25 at a sign for the Gale River Trail. Or from the junction of U.S. 3 and U.S. 302 in Twin Mountain, drive south on U.S. 3 for 5.3 miles and turn left on Fire Road 25. Follow Fire Road 25 for 1.3 miles and turn right onto Fire Road 92. Continue 0.3 mile to a parking area on the left for the Gale River Trail.

Contact
White Mountain National Forest Supervisor, 719 North Main Street, Laconia, NH 03246, 603/528-8721, TDD for the hearing impaired 603/528-8722, website: www.fs.fed.us/r9/white. Appalachian Mountain Club Pinkham Notch Visitor Center, P.O. Box 298, Gorham, NH 03581, 603/466-2721, website: www.outdoors.org.

37 MOUNT GARFIELD
in the White Mountain National Forest south of Twin Mountain

Total distance: 10 miles round-trip

Hiking time: 7 hours

Difficulty: 9

Rating: 9

Holding down the northwest corner of the Pemigewasset Wilderness in the White Mountains, the craggy, 4,500-foot summit of Garfield offers views in all directions, taking in Franconia Ridge to the southwest, the wooded mound of Owl's Head directly south, the Bonds and Mount Carrigain to the southeast, the valley of the Ammonoosuc River to the north, and Galehead Mountain, as well as the long ridge comprising North and South Twin Mountains, due east. When weather permits, you will see the peaks of the Presidential Range poking above the Twins. I had been hiking for years in the Whites before finally hoofing it up Garfield—and discovered views as nice as those offered by many of my favorite summits in these mountains. The hike up the Garfield Trail, while fairly long and gaining nearly 3,000 feet in elevation, never gets very steep or exposed.

From the parking area, follow the Garfield Trail, which for a short time parallels Spruce Brook on its steady ascent through the woods. The path is

a hiker on Mount Garfield

wide and obvious. At 4.8 miles, the trail terminates at the Garfield Ridge Trail, which is part of the white-blazed Appalachian Trail. To the left (east) on the Garfield Ridge Trail, it's 0.2 mile to the spur trail to the Garfield Ridge campsite. The summit lies 0.2 mile to the right (west), where you'll find the foundation of an old fire tower. Descend the same way you came.

Special note: Mount Garfield and Galehead Mountain (see previous listing) can be combined on a loop of 13.5 miles, in which they are linked by hiking 2.7 miles along the Garfield Ridge Trail between the Garfield Trail and the Gale River Trail. The best way to do the loop is to begin on the Gale River Trail and descend the Garfield Trail; that way you will ascend, rather than descend, the often slick, steep, and rocky stretch of the Garfield Ridge Trail east of Mount Garfield. The Gale River Trail and Garfield Trail both begin on Fire Road 92, 1.6 miles apart (a distance not figured into the 13.5-mile loop).

User Groups
Hikers and dogs. No wheelchair facilities. This trail should not be attempted in winter except by hikers experienced in mountaineering and prepared for severe winter weather, and is not suitable for skis. Bikes, horses, and hunting are prohibited.

Access and Fees
No backcountry permit is needed, but a permit is required for day use or overnight parking at any White Mountain National Forest trailhead, as

indicated by signs posted at most trailheads. Permits are available at several area stores and from the national forest at a cost of $5 for seven consecutive days or $20 per year. A $3 one-day permit can be purchased at self-service stations at national forest trailheads, but the pass is good only for the trailhead at which it's purchased. The Appalachian Mountain Club operates the Garfield Ridge campsite (a shelter and seven tent platforms), reached via a 200-yard spur trail off the Garfield Ridge Trail, 0.2 mile east of its junction with the Garfield Trail. A caretaker collects the $8 per person nightly fee from late springfall.

Maps

For a map of hiking trails, get the *Franconia–Pemigewasset Range* map, $7.95 in waterproof Tyvek, available in many stores and from the Appalachian Mountain Club, 800/262-4455, website: www.outdoors.org. Or the *Trail Map and Guide to the White Mountain National Forest* for $7.95 from the DeLorme Publishing Company, 800/642-0970. For topographic area maps, request South Twin Mountain and Bethlehem from USGS Map Sales, Federal Center, Box 25286, Denver, CO 80225, 888/ASK-USGS (888/275-8747), website: http://mapping.usgs.gov.

Directions

From I-93 north of Franconia Notch State Park, take Exit 35 for U.S. 3 north, continue about 4.5 miles, and then turn right on the dirt Fire Road 92. Or from the junction of U.S. 3 and U.S. 302 in Twin Mountain, drive south on U.S. 3 for 5.6 miles and turn left on Fire Road 92. Follow Fire Road 92 for 1.3 miles to a parking area on the right for the Garfield Trail.

Contact

White Mountain National Forest Supervisor, 719 North Main Street, Laconia, NH 03246, 603/528-8721, TDD for the hearing impaired 603/528-8722, website: www.fs.fed.us/r9/white. Appalachian Mountain Club Pinkham Notch Visitor Center, P.O. Box 298, Gorham, NH 03581, 603/466-2721, website: www.outdoors.org.

38 ETHAN POND/THOREAU FALLS

in the White Mountain National Forest between Zealand
Notch and Crawford Notch

Total distance: 10.4 miles round-trip **Hiking time:** 7 hours

Difficulty: 8 **Rating:** 9

This moderate day hike—much of it following a flat section of the Appalachian Trail—begins at one of New Hampshire's most spectacular notches and takes in a popular backcountry pond and towering waterfall. With a short, easy detour off this route, you can also take in a second notch. I like doing this hike on snowshoes in winter, when Thoreau Falls transforms into a giant staircase of ice; the trail may even be sufficiently packed down by other hikers that you won't need snowshoes, but carry them just in case. The total elevation gained on this hike is about 1,200 feet.

From the parking area in Crawford Notch State Park, follow the white blazes of the Appalachian Trail, which coincides here with the Ethan Pond Trail. After crossing railroad tracks, the trail climbs steadily. At 0.2 mile, in a stand of tall birch trees, the trail to Ripley Falls (a worthwhile side trip of 0.2 mile; see the Ripley Falls listing in this chapter) branches left. But veer right toward Ethan Pond. At 1.6 miles, the Willey Range Trail continues north; turn left (west) with the Ethan Pond Trail/Appalachian Trail, which soon flattens out. A mile farther, turn right onto the side path leading about 0.1 mile to scenic Ethan Pond and the Appalachian Mountain Club's Ethan Pond shelter. Back on the Ethan Pond Trail, continue west on flat ground another 2.5 miles, then turn left onto the Thoreau Falls Trail for the 0.1-mile walk to the waterfall. On the way back, you might want to add about a half mile to this hike by following the Ethan Pond Trail into the southern end of spectacular Zealand Notch. Hike back along the same route.

User Groups

Hikers, dogs, skiers, and snowshoers. No wheelchair facilities. Bikes, horses, and hunting are prohibited.

Access and Fees

No backcountry permit is needed, but a permit is required for day use or overnight parking at any White Mountain National Forest trailhead, as indicated by signs posted at most trailheads. Permits are available at several area stores and from the national forest at a cost of $5 for seven consecutive days or $20 per year. A $3 one-day permit can be purchased at self-service stations at national forest trailheads, but the pass is good only for the trailhead at which it's purchased. The Appalachian Mountain Club operates the Ethan Pond shelter, located just off the Ethan Pond Trail, 2.6 miles from U.S. 302 in Crawford Notch. A caretaker collects the $6 per person nightly fee from late springfall.

Maps

Several maps cover this area's hiking trails, including the *Franconia-Pemigewasset Range* map and the *Crawford Notch-Sandwich Range/Moosilauke-Kinsman* map, $7.95 each in waterproof Tyvek, available in many stores and from the Appalachian Mountain Club, 800/262-4455, website: www.outdoors.org; the *Trail Map and Guide to the White Mountain National Forest* for $7.95 from the DeLorme Publishing Company, 800/642-0970; and map 3 in the *Map and Guide to the Appalachian Trail in New Hampshire and Vermont,* an eight-map set and guidebook available for $19.95 ($14.95 for the maps alone) from the Appalachian Trail Conference. For a topographic area map, request Crawford Notch from USGS Map Sales, Federal Center, Box 25286, Denver, CO 80225, 888/ASK-USGS (888/275-8747), website: http://mapping.usgs.gov.

Directions

From U.S. 302, 3.9 miles south of the Crawford Notch hostel, turn south onto a paved road at a sign for Ripley Falls. Drive 0.3 mile and park at the end of the road.

Contact

White Mountain National Forest Supervisor, 719 North Main Street, Laconia, NH 03246, 603/528-8721, TDD for the hearing impaired 603/528-8722, website: www.fs.fed.us/r9/white. Appalachian Mountain Club Pinkham Notch Visitor Center, P.O. Box 298, Gorham, NH 03581, 603/466-2721, website: www.outdoors.org. Appalachian Trail Conference, 799 Washington Street, P.O. Box 807, Harpers Ferry, WV 25425-0807, 304/535-6331, website: www.appalachiantrail.org. New Hampshire Division of Parks and Recreation, P.O. Box 1856, 172 Pembroke Road, Concord, NH 03302, 603/271-3556, camping reservations 603/271-3628, website: www.nhstateparks.org.

39 MOUNT AVALON

in the White Mountain National Forest and Crawford Notch
State Park north of Bartlett and south of Twin Mountain

Total distance: 3.6 miles round-trip   **Hiking time:** 2.5 hours

Difficulty: 4   **Rating:** 9

From various spots on Mount Avalon's 3,442-foot-high summit, you'll get views of the Whites in virtually every direction that are more than worth the 1,400-foot ascent. From the parking area, cross the railroad tracks behind the visitors center and pick up the Avalon Trail. At about 0.2 mile, turn left onto the Cascade Loop Trail, which passes scenic Beecher and Pearl cascades and rejoins the Avalon Trail about a half mile from the parking lot. (In fact, the cascades are a worthy destination for an easy hike of a mile; Beecher, an impressive flumelike cascade above a gorge, lies just 0.3 mile from the trailhead, and Pearl a short distance farther.) Turning left on the Avalon Trail, follow it another 0.8 mile to a junction with the A-Z Trail; bear left, staying on the Avalon, which grows very steep and rocky for the next half mile. Then turn left onto a spur trail that climbs 100 yards to Avalon's craggy summit. Follow the same route back.

User Groups

Hikers and dogs. Dogs must be leashed. No wheelchair facilities. This trail is not suitable for bikes, horses, or skis, and may be difficult to snowshoe due to its steepness. Hunting is allowed in season.

Access and Fees

Parking and access are free.

Maps

Several maps cover this area's hiking trails, including the *Franconia-Pemigewasset Range* map and the *Crawford Notch-Sandwich Range/Moosilauke-Kinsman* map, each $7.95 in waterproof Tyvek, available in many stores and from the Appalachian Mountain Club, 800/262-4455, website: www.outdoors.org; the *Trail Map and Guide to the White Mountain National Forest* for $7.95 from the DeLorme Publishing Company, 800/642-0970; and map 3 in the *Map and Guide to the Appalachian Trail in New Hampshire and Vermont,* an eight-map set and guidebook available for $19.95 ($14.95 for the maps alone) from the Appalachian Trail Conference. For a topographic area map, request Crawford Notch from USGS Map Sales, Federal Center, Box 25286, Denver, CO 80225, 888/ASK-USGS (888/275-8747), website: http://mapping.usgs.gov.

Directions

Park at the visitors center on U.S. 302 in Crawford Notch.

Contact

White Mountain National Forest Supervisor, 719 North Main Street, Laconia, NH 03246, 603/528-8721, TDD for the hearing impaired 603/528-8722, website: www.fs.fed.us/r9/white. Appalachian Trail Conference, 799 Washington Street, P.O. Box 807, Harpers Ferry, WV 25425-0807, 304/535-6331, website: www.appalachiantrail.org. New Hampshire Division of Parks and Recreation, Bureau of Trails, P.O. Box 1856, Concord, NH 03302-1856, 603/271-3254.

40 MOUNT WILLARD

in Crawford Notch State Park north of Bartlett and south of
Twin Mountain

Total distance: 2.8 miles round-trip   **Hiking time:** 2 hours

Difficulty: 2   **Rating:** 9

The view from the cliffs of Mount Willard is widely considered one of the best in the White Mountains for the relatively minor effort—a gradual ascent of less than 900 feet—required to reach it. From the parking area, cross the railroad tracks behind the visitors center and pick up the Avalon Trail. Within 100 yards, turn left onto the Mount Willard Trail, which ascends at a moderate grade. At 1.2 miles, a side path on the left leads 0.2 mile downhill to the Hitchcock Flume, a dramatic gorge worn into the mountainside by erosion. From that trail junction, it's just another 0.2 mile of flat walking on the Mount Willard Trail to Willard's summit. Its open ledges afford an excellent view from high above the notch, with the Webster Cliffs to the east (left) and the Willey Slide directly south (straight ahead). Hike back the same way.

User Groups

Hikers, snowshoers, and dogs. Dogs must be leashed. No wheelchair facilities. This trail is not suitable for bikes, horses, or skis. Hunting is allowed in season.

Access and Fees

Parking and access are free.

Maps

Several maps cover this area's hiking trails, including the *Franconia-Pemigewasset Range* map, the *Presidential Range* map, and the *Crawford Notch-Sandwich Range/Moosilauke-Kinsman* map, each $7.95 in waterproof Tyvek, available in many stores and from the Appalachian Mountain Club, 800/262-4455, website: www.outdoors.org; the *Trail Map and Guide to the White Mountain National Forest* for $7.95 from the DeLorme Publishing Company, 800/642-0970; and map 3 in the *Map and Guide to the Appalachian Trail in New Hampshire and Vermont,* an eight-map set and guidebook available for $19.95 ($14.95 for the maps alone) from the Appalachian Trail Conference. For a topographic area map, request Crawford Notch from USGS Map Sales, Federal Center, Box 25286, Denver, CO 80225, 888/ASK-USGS (888/275-8747), website: http://mapping.usgs.gov.

Directions
Park at the visitors center on U.S. 302 in Crawford Notch.

Contact
White Mountain National Forest Supervisor, 719 North Main Street, Laconia, NH 03246, 603/528-8721, TDD for the hearing impaired 603/528-8722, website: www.fs.fed.us/r9/white. Appalachian Trail Conference, 799 Washington Street, P.O. Box 807, Harpers Ferry, WV 25425-0807, 304/535-6331, website: www.appalachiantrail.org. New Hampshire Division of Parks and Recreation, Bureau of Trails, P.O. Box 1856, Concord, NH 03302-1856, 603/271-3254.

41 MOUNTS PIERCE AND EISENHOWER
in the White Mountain National Forest and
Crawford Notch State Park

Total distance: 10.8 miles round-trip   **Hiking time:** 6.5 hours

Difficulty: 9   **Rating:** 10

The Crawford Path is reputedly the oldest continuously maintained footpath in the country, dating back to 1819, when Abel Crawford and his son Ethan Allen Crawford cut the first section. It's also the easiest route onto the high ridge of the Presidential Range—the road sits at 2,000 feet, and the trail breaks out above the trees in less than three miles. Once on the ridge, you'll have sweeping views of the Whites; the 4,761-foot Mount Eisenhower itself is one of the more distinctive summits in the southern Presidentials. This can, however, be a difficult trail to follow down in foul weather, particularly when it comes to finding your way into the woods on Mount Pierce. The vertical ascent is more than 2,700 feet.

From the parking lot, the Crawford Connector spur leads 0.2 mile to the Crawford Path. (From there, a 45-minute, 0.8-mile round-trip detour on the

Crawford Cliff Trail leads to a good view of the notch.) Less than 0.5 mile up the Crawford Path, watch for a short side trail to Gibbs Falls. After emerging from the woods nearly three miles from the trailhead, the Crawford Path meets the Webster Cliffs Trail, which leads south 0.1 mile to the summit of 4,312-foot Mount Pierce. (The Webster Cliffs Trail and the Crawford Path from this junction north are part of the Appalachian Trail.) Turning back down the Crawford Path from Pierce makes a six-mile round-trip. This hike follows the Crawford Path—which from here coincides with the Appalachian Trail—north another two miles to the Eisenhower Loop Trail, then 0.4 mile up the loop trail to the Eisenhower summit, which has excellent views in every direction. To the north rises the Northeast's tallest peak, 6,288-foot Mount Washington. Stretching northwest from Washington are the northern Presidentials. The distinct hump in the ridge between Eisenhower and Washington is Mount Monroe. To the east you can see the Montalban Ridge running south from Washington—which includes Mount Isolation (see listing in this chapter), a rocky high point about midway along the ridge—and beyond the ridge into western Maine. To the southwest are the peaks and valleys of the Pemigewasset Wilderness, with Mount Carrigain (see listing in this chapter) the tallest among them. And in the distance, more west than south, rises Franconia Ridge, including Mounts Lincoln and Lafayette (see listing in this chapter) as well as Flume and Liberty (see listing in this chapter). Hike back along the same route.

User Groups

Hikers and dogs. No wheelchair facilities. This trail should not be attempted in winter except by hikers experienced in mountaineering and prepared for severe winter weather, and is not suitable for skis. Bikes, horses, and hunting are prohibited.

Access and Fees

No backcountry permit is needed, but a permit is required for day use or overnight parking at any White Mountain National Forest trailhead, as indicated by signs posted at most trailheads. Permits are available at several area stores and from the national forest at a cost of $5 for seven consecutive days or $20 per year. A $3 one-day permit can be purchased at self-service stations at national forest trailheads, but the pass is good only for the trailhead at which it's purchased.

Maps

For a map of hiking trails, obtain the *Presidential Range* map for $7.95 in waterproof Tyvek, available in many stores and from the Appalachian Mountain Club, 800/262-4455, website: www.outdoors.org; the *Trail Map and Guide to the White Mountain National Forest* for $7.95 from the De-Lorme Publishing Company, 800/642-0970; or map 2 in the *Map and Guide to the Appalachian Trail in New Hampshire and Vermont,* an eight-map set and guidebook available for $19.95 ($14.95 for the maps alone) from the Appalachian Trail Conference. For topographic area maps, request Crawford Notch and Stairs Mountain from USGS Map Sales, Federal Center, Box 25286, Denver, CO 80225, 888/ASK-USGS (888/275-8747), website: http://mapping.usgs.gov.

Directions
From U.S. 302 in Crawford Notch, turn onto Mount Clinton Road opposite the Crawford House site just north of Saco Lake. The trail begins at a parking area within 0.1 mile from U.S. 302.

Contact
White Mountain National Forest Supervisor, 719 North Main Street, Laconia, NH 03246, 603/528-8721, TDD for the hearing impaired 603/528-8722, website: www.fs.fed.us/r9/white. Appalachian Trail Conference, 799 Washington Street, P.O. Box 807, Harpers Ferry, WV 25425-0807, 304/535-6331, website: www.appalachiantrail.org. The Appalachian Mountain Club Pinkham Notch Visitor Center has up-to-date weather and trail information about the Whites; call 603/466-2725. New Hampshire Division of Parks and Recreation, Bureau of Trails, P.O. Box 1856, Concord, NH 03302-1856, 603/271-3254.

42 ELEPHANT HEAD
in Crawford Notch State Park

Total distance: 0.6 miles round-trip   **Hiking time:** 0.5 hour

Difficulty: 2   **Rating:** 8

From the north end of Saco Lake in Crawford Notch, gaze south toward the short but prominent cliff at the far end of the pond; it resembles the head and trunk of an elephant. To hike an easy trail to the top of that cliff and a good view of the notch, cross U.S. 302 from the parking area to the Webster-Jackson Trail. After just 0.1 mile, turn right onto the Elephant Head Trail, and continue 0.2 mile to the top of the cliff. Return the way you came.

User Groups
Hikers and snowshoers. Dogs must be leashed. No wheelchair facilities. This trail is not suitable for bikes, horses, or skis. Hunting is allowed in season.

Access and Fees
Parking and access are free.

Maps
Several maps cover this area's hiking trails, including the *Presidential Range* map and the *Franconia–Pemigewasset Range* map, each $7.95 in waterproof Tyvek, available in many stores and from the Appalachian Mountain Club, 800/262-4455, website: www.outdoors.org; and the *Trail Map and Guide to the White Mountain National Forest,* which is $7.95 from the DeLorme Publishing Company, 800/642-0970. For a topographic area map, request Crawford Notch from USGS Map Sales, Federal Center, Box 25286, Denver, CO 80225, 888/ASK-USGS (888/275-8747), website: http://mapping.usgs.gov.

Directions
Park in the turnout on the west side of U.S. 302, 0.3 mile south of the Crawford Notch hostel.

Contact
White Mountain National Forest Supervisor, 719 North Main Street, Laconia, NH 03246, 603/528-8721, TDD for the hearing impaired 603/528-8722, website: www.fs.fed.us/r9/white. New Hampshire Division of Parks and Recreation, Bureau of Trails, P.O. Box 1856, Concord, NH 03302-1856, 603/271-3254.

43 WEBSTER CLIFFS
in the White Mountain National Forest and Crawford Notch State Park north of Bartlett and south of Twin Mountain

Total distance: 9.4 miles round-trip   **Hiking time:** 6.5 hours

Difficulty: 9   **Rating:** 10

This rugged, 9.4-mile hike along a spectacular stretch of the Appalachian Trail follows the brink of the Webster Cliffs high above Crawford Notch and goes to 4,052-foot Mount Jackson, an open summit with views in every direction. In my opinion, only one other summit offers a better view of the southern Presidentials and Mount Washington, and that's Mount Isolation (see next listing). The elevation gain is about 2,700 feet.

From the parking area, cross U.S. 302 to a sign for the Webster Cliffs Trail/Appalachian Trail. The white-blazed trail ascends steadily with good footing at first, then grows steeper and rockier. The first good view comes within two miles, from a wide, flat ledge overlooking the notch and White

looking down on Crawford Notch from Webster Cliffs

Mountains to the south and west. (Just before that ledge is a smaller ledge with a less-expansive view.)

For a round-trip hike of just four miles, this ledge makes a worthwhile destination. But from there, you can see the next open ledge just 0.2 mile farther and a little higher along the ridge, beckoning you onward. The trail continues past several outlooks along the cliffs with sweeping views of the Whites, including the Willey Range across Crawford Notch and Mount Chocorua, the prominent horned peak to the southeast. At 3.3 miles, the Appalachian Trail passes over Mount Webster's 3,910-foot, partly wooded but craggy summit, with excellent views of the notch and mountains from Chocorua to Mount Carrigain and the Saco River Valley. Descending slightly off Webster, the trail crosses relatively flat and boggy terrain, then slabs up to the open summit of Jackson, 4.7 miles from the trailhead. Head back the same way.

User Groups

Hikers and dogs. No wheelchair facilities. This trail should not be attempted in winter except by hikers experienced in mountaineering and prepared for severe winter weather, and is not suitable for skis. Bikes, horses, and hunting are prohibited.

Access and Fees

Parking and access are free.

Maps

Several maps cover this area's hiking trails, including the *Franconia–Pemigewasset Range* map, the *Presidential Range* map, and the *Crawford Notch–Sandwich Range/Moosilauke–Kinsman* map, each $7.95 in waterproof Tyvek, available in many stores and from the Appalachian Mountain Club, 800/262-4455, website: www.outdoors.org; the *Trail Map and Guide to the White Mountain National Forest* for $7.95 from the DeLorme Publishing Company, 800/642-0970; and map 2 in the *Map and Guide to the Appalachian Trail in New Hampshire and Vermont,* an eight-map set and guidebook available for $19.95 ($14.95 for the maps alone) from the Appalachian Trail Conference. For a topographic area map, request Crawford Notch from USGS Map Sales, Federal Center, Box 25286, Denver, CO 80225, 888/ASK-USGS (888/275-8747), website: http://mapping.usgs.gov.

Directions

Park in the turnout on the west side of U.S. 302 3.9 miles south of the Crawford Notch hostel, at the access road to the Ripley Falls Trail and 1.3 miles north of the access road for Arethusa Falls.

Contact

White Mountain National Forest Supervisor, 719 North Main Street, Laconia, NH 03246, 603/528-8721, TDD for the hearing impaired 603/528-8722, website: www.fs.fed.us/r9/white. Appalachian Trail Conference, 799 Washington Street, P.O. Box 807, Harpers Ferry, WV 25425-0807, 304/535-6331, website: www.appalachiantrail.org. New Hampshire Division of Parks and Recreation, Bureau of Trails, P.O. Box 1856, Concord, NH 03302-1856, 603/271-3254.

44 MOUNT ISOLATION

in the White Mountain National Forest north of Jackson and east of Crawford Notch State Park

Total distance: 20 miles one-way   **Hiking time:** 2 days

Difficulty: 9   **Rating:** 9

In the heart of the Dry River Wilderness, south of Mount Washington, Mount Isolation's bald pate lies too far from any road for most day hikers—which translates into a true sense of isolation. A friend and I made this two-day traverse once in late spring and saw only four other backpackers in two days. The total elevation gain to Isolation's summit is about 3,000 feet.

Follow the Rocky Branch Trail west for 3.7 miles to the Rocky Branch, an aptly named tributary of the Saco River. Cross the stream and turn right (north) on the Isolation Trail (to the left is a lean-to, Rocky Branch shelter 2), which eventually swings west in its 2.5-mile climb onto the Montalban Ridge, where it meets the Davis Path. Find a place to camp well off the trail and leave your backpack behind for the one-mile hike south on the Davis Path to the short but steep spur trail to Mount Isolation's barren summit (4,005 feet). You'll have terrific views west and north to the southern Presidentials and Mount Washington, and to the southwest and south of the sprawling Whites. Return to your campsite.

On day two, hike north 0.3 mile on the Davis Path to where the Isolation Trail turns west (left) toward the valley of the Dry River; be careful, because this trail junction is easily overlooked—especially, I can tell you, when it lies under four feet of snow. In about 2.5 miles, turn left (south) on the Dry River Trail, paralleling the broad, boulder-choked river and crossing countless mountain brooks feeding into it. When the trees are bare, you get some fine views of Mount Washington directly upriver. It's nearly five miles from the Isolation Trail junction to U.S. 302.

User Groups

Hikers and dogs. No wheelchair facilities. This trail should not be attempted in winter except by hikers prepared for severe winter weather, and is not suitable for bikes, horses, or skis. Hunting is allowed in season.

Access and Fees

No backcountry permit is needed, but a permit is required for day use or overnight parking at any White Mountain National Forest trailhead, as indicated by signs posted at most trailheads. Permits are available at several area stores and from the national forest at a cost of $5 for seven consecutive days or $20 per year. A $3 one-day permit can be purchased at self-service stations at national forest trailheads, but the pass is good only for the trailhead at which it's purchased. There is a lean-to shelter (Rocky Branch shelter 2) at the junction of the Rocky Branch Trail and Isolation Trail that is slated to be dismantled as soon as it needs major maintenance.

Maps

For a map of hiking trails, obtain the *Presidential Range* map for $7.95 in waterproof Tyvek, available in many stores and from the Appalachian Mountain Club, 800/262-4455, website: www.outdoors.org; or the *Trail Map and Guide to the White Mountain National Forest* for $7.95 from the DeLorme Publishing Company, 800/642-0970. For topographic area maps, request Jackson and Stairs Mountain from USGS Map Sales,

Federal Center, Box 25286, Denver, CO 80225, 888/ASK-USGS (888/
275-8747), website: http://mapping.usgs.gov.

Directions

You will need to shuttle two vehicles. Leave one at the roadside turnout at
the Dry River Trailhead on U.S. 302, 0.3 mile north of the Dry River
Campground and 4.5 miles south of the Crawford Notch hostel. Then
drive south on U.S. 302 to Glen, turn left onto Route 16 north, and drive
8.1 miles to a large parking lot on the left for the Rocky Branch Trail.

Contact

White Mountain National Forest Supervisor, 719 North Main Street, Laconia, NH 03246, 603/528-8721, TDD for the hearing impaired 603/528-
8722, website: www.fs.fed.us/r9/white. The Appalachian Mountain Club
Pinkham Notch Visitor Center has up-to-date weather and trail information about the Whites; call 603/466-2725.

45 THE BALDIES LOOP
in the White Mountain National Forest near North Chatham

Total distance: 9.7 miles round-trip   **Hiking time:** 7 hours

Difficulty: 10   **Rating:** 10

As their names suggest, the pair of 3,500-foot peaks called the Baldies
mimic higher mountains with their craggy summits, four miles of open
ridge, and some of the best views this side of Mount Washington. This
rugged hike is not to be underestimated. Besides its length of almost 10
miles and some 3,300 feet of vertical ascent, it climbs steep, exposed ledges
on the way up South Baldface that may make some hikers uncomfortable.
The Baldies can also attract harsh conditions—I've encountered winds up
here strong enough to knock me around. Although it's probably the most
popular hike in the Evans Notch area, I've done this loop without passing
more than 10 other hikers—Evans Notch lies far enough from population
centers that it attracts far fewer people than other areas of the Whites.

From the parking area, walk 50 yards north on Route 113 and cross the
road to the start of the Baldface Circle Trail. It's a wide, easy trail for 0.7
mile to Circle Junction, where a side trail leads right 0.1 mile to Emerald
Pool, a highly worthwhile detour (adding 0.2 mile to this hike) to a deep
pool below a narrow gorge and a short falls along Charles Brook. From
Circle Junction, bear left at a sign for South Baldface, following the loop
clockwise because it's easier to ascend than descend the ledges on South

Baldface. At 1.2 miles from the road, a side path marked by a sign leads 0.5 mile to Chandler Gorge (adding a mile to this hike's distance).

Climbing steadily, the trail reaches the South Baldface shelter 2.5 miles from the road. Beyond the lean-to, the trail hits all the prominent ledges visible from the road, and for nearly a half mile winds up them, requiring steep, exposed scrambling. A bit more than three miles from the road, the trail reaches the level shoulder of South Baldface, where the Baldface Knob Trail leads left (south) to Baldface Knob and Eastman Mountain. From here, you'll get your first view into the broad glacial cirque, or ravine, bounded by North and South Baldface and the Bicknell Ridge. The Circle Trail continues 0.5 mile west—and 500 feet up—to the 3,569-foot summit of South Baldface. The summit views extend to much of the White Mountains to the west and south, including Mounts Washington, Carrigain, and Chocorua, the triplet peaks of the Tripyramid above Waterville Valley, the distant Franconia Ridge, and the cliffs of Cathedral Ledge and Whitehorse Ledge near North Conway. To the north rise the Mahoosuc Range and a long chain of mountains reaching far into Maine. East lies a landscape of lakes and low hills, most prominently the long, low ridge of Pleasant Mountain.

Continue northwest on the Circle Trail another 1.2 miles, dropping into the woods and then ascending to the 3,591-foot summit of North Baldface, where the views are equally awesome. Descend north off North Baldy via the Circle Trail, and continue nearly a mile to the signed junction with the Bicknell Ridge Trail. Turn right (east) on Bicknell, a scenic alternative to completing the Circle Trail loop. The Bicknell descends an open ridge for about a mile before entering the forest and reaching its lower junction with the Circle Trail in 2.5 miles, at a stream crossing. Follow the Circle Trail another 0.7 mile to Circle Junction, from which it's 0.7 mile farther to the road.

User Groups

Hikers and dogs. No wheelchair facilities. This trail is not suitable for bikes, horses, skis, or snowshoes. Hunting is allowed in season.

Access and Fees

No backcountry permit is needed, but a permit is required for day use or overnight parking at any White Mountain National Forest trailhead, as indicated by signs posted at most trailheads. Permits are available at several area stores and from the national forest at a cost of $5 for seven consecutive days or $20 per year. A $3 one-day permit can be purchased at self-service stations at national forest trailheads, but the pass is good only for the trailhead at which it's purchased.

Maps

For a map of trails, get the *Map of Cold River Valley and Evans Notch* for $6 from the Chatham Trails Association; the *Carter Range-Evans Notch/North Country-Mahoosuc* map, $7.95 in waterproof Tyvek, available in many stores and from the Appalachian Mountain Club, 800/262-4455, website: www.outdoors.org; or the *Trail Map and Guide to the White Mountain National Forest* for $7.95 from the DeLorme Publishing Company, 800/642-0970. For a topographic area map, request Chatham from USGS Map Sales, Federal Center, Box 25286, Denver, CO 80225, 888/ASK-USGS (888/275-8747), website: http://mapping.usgs.gov.

Directions

The trail begins near a large parking lot on the east side of Route 113, 2.7 miles north of the northern junction of Routes 113 and 113B, and 13 miles south of the junction of U.S. 2 and Route 113.

Contact

White Mountain National Forest Supervisor, 719 North Main Street, Laconia, NH 03246, 603/528-8721, TDD for the hearing impaired 603/528-8722, website: www.fs.fed.us/r9/white. Chatham Trails Association, P.O. Box 605, Center Conway, NH 03813, website: http://chathamtrails.org/.

46 EMERALD POOL

in the White Mountain National Forest near
North Chatham

Total distance: 1.6 miles round-trip   **Hiking time:** 1 hour

Difficulty: 1   **Rating:** 9

The aptly named and gorgeous Emerald Pool is a deep hole below a narrow flume and gorge and a short falls along Charles Brook. It's a flat, easy walk to the pool, making this a good hike for young children. From the parking area, walk 50 yards north on Route 113 and cross the road to the start of the Baldface Circle Trail. Follow the wide, easy trail for 0.7 mile to Circle Junction, where a side trail leads right 0.1 mile to Emerald Pool. Return the same way you came in.

User Groups

Hikers, dogs, snowshoers, and skiers. No wheelchair facilities. This trail is not suitable for bikes or horses. Hunting is allowed in season.

Access and Fees

No backcountry permit is needed, but a permit is required for day use or overnight parking at any White Mountain National Forest trailhead, as indicated by signs posted at most trailheads. Permits are available at several area stores and from the national forest at a cost of $5 for seven consecutive days or $20 per year. A $3 one-day permit can be purchased at self-service stations at national forest trailheads, but the permit is good only for the trailhead at which it's purchased.

Maps

For a contour map of trails, get the *Map of Cold River Valley and Evans Notch* for $6 from the Chatham Trails Association; the *Carter Range-Evans Notch/North Country-Mahoosuc* map, $7.95 in waterproof Tyvek, available in many stores and from the Appalachian Mountain Club, 800/262-4455, website: www.outdoors.org; or the *Trail Map and Guide to the White Mountain National Forest* for $7.95 from the DeLorme Publishing Company, 800/642-0970. For a topographic area map, request Chatham from USGS Map Sales, Federal Center, Box 25286, Denver, CO 80225, 888/ASK-USGS (888/275-8747), website: http://mapping.usgs.gov.

Directions

The trail begins near a large parking lot on the east side of Route 113, 2.7 miles north of the northern junction of Routes 113 and 113B, and 13 miles south of the junction of U.S. 2 and Route 113.

Contact

White Mountain National Forest Supervisor, 719 North Main Street, Laconia, NH 03246, 603/528-8721, TDD for the hearing impaired 603/528-8722, website: www.fs.fed.us/r9/white. Chatham Trails Association, P.O. Box 605, Center Conway, NH 03813, website: http://chathamtrails.org/.

47 MOUNT LAFAYETTE: SKOOKUMCHUCK TRAIL

in the White Mountain National Forest north of Franconia Notch State Park

Total distance: 10 miles round-trip

Hiking time: 8 hours

Difficulty: 9

Rating: 10

Compared to other routes up popular Mount Lafayette, the Skookumchuck is less traveled, a bit longer than some, and ascends more gradually. Still, it's 10 miles round-trip, and you will gain more than 3,500 feet in elevation, so it's a taxing hike. Some friends and I recently hiked this on a very chilly winter day, under a cobalt sky and through a forest blanketed thickly with clean snow. Once above tree line, though, it was a bitterly cold walk to the summit; this trail offers a nice winter outing on snowshoes, but turn around before reaching the Garfield Ridge Trail if you're not prepared for severe cold and wind. This is also a great hike for seeing woodland wildflowers in May. For more description about the views from atop Lafayette, see the Mounts Lincoln and Lafayette listing in this chapter.

From the parking lot, pick up the Skookumchuck Trail, which is sporadically marked with blue blazes (the trail corridor is fairly obvious). It contours southward around the west slope of a hill called Big Bickford Mountain, crossing an overgrown logging road a few times. Upon reaching Skookumchuck Brook at a little over a mile, the trail turns east to climb steadily along the brook for more than a half mile. It then leaves the brook and ascends a steep mountainside, passing through beautiful birch forest. Ascending into subalpine forest, you get your first views through the trees of the upper slopes of Lafayette. Shortly after breaking out of the forest, the Skookumchuck terminates at the Garfield Ridge Trail at 4.3 miles. Turn right (south) and follow the Garfield Ridge Trail another 0.7 mile along the exposed ridge to the summit of Lafayette. Return the way you came.

User Groups

Hikers and dogs. Dogs must be leashed. No wheelchair facilities. This trail should not be attempted in winter except by hikers experienced in mountaineering and prepared for severe winter weather, and is not suitable for skis. Bikes, horses, and hunting are prohibited.

Access and Fees

No backcountry permit is needed, but a permit is required for day use or overnight parking at any White Mountain National Forest trailhead, as indicated by signs posted at most trailheads. Permits are available at several area stores and from the national forest at a cost of $5 for seven consecutive days or $20 per year. A $3 one-day permit can be purchased at self-service stations at national forest trailheads, but the pass is good only for the trailhead at which it's purchased.

Maps

For a map of hiking trails, get the *Franconia-Pemigewasset Range* map or the *Crawford Notch-Sandwich Range/Moosilauke-Kinsman* map, each $7.95 in waterproof Tyvek, available in many stores and from the Appalachian Mountain Club, 800/262-4455, website: www.outdoors.org; or the *Trail Map and Guide to the White Mountain National Forest* for $7.95 from the DeLorme Publishing Company, 800/642-0970. For a topographic area map, request Franconia from USGS Map Sales, Federal Center, Box 25286, Denver, CO 80225, 888/ASK-USGS (888/275-8747), website: http://mapping.usgs.gov.

Directions

The Skookumchuck Trail begins at a parking lot on Route 3, about 0.6 mile north of Exit 35 off I-93 in Franconia.

Contact

White Mountain National Forest Supervisor, 719 North Main Street, Laconia, NH 03246, 603/528-8721, TDD for the hearing impaired 603/528-8722, website: www.fs.fed.us/r9/white.

48 CANNON MOUNTAIN: KINSMAN RIDGE TRAIL

in Franconia Notch State Park north of Lincoln and south of Franconia

Total distance: 4.4 miles round-trip   **Hiking time:** 3 hours

Difficulty: 8   **Rating:** 7

Cannon Mountain (4,077 feet) stands out at the north end of spectacular Franconia Notch because of the 1,000-foot cliff on its east face. That cliff is famous for the Old Man of the Mountain, a stone profile that for decades was visible from the notch's north end, but in early May 2003 finally succumbed to gravity and crumbled off the cliff. (Today, at the roadside parking area off I-93 where for many years tourists ogled the Old Man, there stands an information kiosk explaining why and how the stone profile fell.)

This moderate hike of 4.4 miles round-trip, climbing 2,100 feet in elevation, leads to the excellent views from Cannon's summit. Although popular, the Kinsman Ridge Trail has become severely eroded. A more pleasant trail up Cannon Mountain is the Hi-Cannon route (see next listing).

From the parking lot, follow the Kinsman Ridge Trail through a picnic area and briefly along a ski area trail before entering the woods. The trail ascends at a moderate grade, passing a short side path at 1.5 miles that leads to open ledges and a nice view across the notch to Franconia Ridge. The Kinsman Ridge Trail swings right, soon climbing more steeply to the summit, where there is an observation platform and the summit tramway station. To the east, the views extend to Mounts Lafayette and Lincoln. To the west, you can see Vermont's Green Mountains and New York's Adirondacks on a clear day. Head back along the same route.

User Groups

Hikers and dogs. Dogs must be leashed. No wheelchair facilities. This trail should not be attempted in winter except by hikers prepared for severe winter weather, and is not suitable for bikes, horses, or skis. Hunting is allowed in season, but not near trails.

Access and Fees

Parking and access are free.

Maps

For a map of hiking trails, get the *Franconia-Pemigewasset Range* map or the *Crawford Notch-Sandwich Range/Moosilauke-Kinsman* map, each $7.95 in waterproof Tyvek, available in many stores and from the Appalachian Mountain Club, 800/262-4455, website: www.outdoors.org; or the *Trail Map and Guide to the White Mountain National Forest* for $7.95 from the DeLorme Publishing Company, 800/642-0970. For a topographic area map, request Franconia from USGS Map Sales, Federal Center, Box 25286, Denver, CO 80225, 888/ASK-USGS (888/275-8747), website: http://mapping.usgs.gov.

Directions

The hike begins from the tramway parking lot at Exit 2 off I-93, at the north end of Franconia Notch. Look for a sign for the Kinsman Ridge Trail.

Contact

White Mountain National Forest Supervisor, 719 North Main Street, Laconia, NH 03246, 603/528-8721, TDD for the hearing impaired 603/528-8722, website: www.fs.fed.us/r9/white. Franconia Notch State Park,

Franconia, NH 03580, 603/745-8391, website: www.franconianotch-statepark.com. New Hampshire Division of Parks and Recreation, P.O. Box 1856, 172 Pembroke Road, Concord, NH 03302, 603/271-3556, camping reservations 603/271-3628, website: www.nhstateparks.org.

49 CANNON MOUNTAIN: HI-CANNON TRAIL
in Franconia Notch State Park north of Lincoln
and south of Franconia

Total distance: 5.6 miles round-trip   **Hiking time:** 3.5 hours

Difficulty: 8   **Rating:** 9

See the preceding hike's trail notes for more description of Cannon Mountain. This hike up Cannon is actually a far more pleasant route than the previous hike, on a more scenic trail that's in far better condition. I've done this hike in winter with friends, carrying telemark skis up the mountain on our packs, skiing down the Cannon Mountain Ski Area trails, then kicking and gliding down the Franconia Notch Bike Path (see listing in this chapter; watch out for snowmobiles) back to the parking lot. Snow was caked to the trees and lots of blowdowns blocked the way—we had to climb around or over them and sometimes crawl on our hands and knees under them. But the trail is actually well protected from wind until you near the summit. This hike climbs about 2,300 feet.

From the parking lot, follow the Lonesome Lake Trail through the campground and ascend steadily toward Lonesome Lake (see next listing). At 0.4 mile, turn right onto the Hi-Cannon Trail. It climbs relentlessly through forest, gaining elevation quickly until you're traversing at the crest of towering cliffs high above Franconia Notch, with a great view across the notch toward Franconia Ridge. The trail features a wooden ladder to climb about 20 feet up a rock slab. After about 1.5 miles, the trail levels out, ascending at a more gentle angle through subalpine forest toward the summit. Two miles from the Lonesome Lake Trail, turn right on the Kinsman Ridge Trail and follow it 0.4 mile to Cannon's summit, with good views in every direction, most spectacularly toward Franconia Ridge. Return the way you came. To do the combined hike/ski outing I described above, from the Hi-Cannon Trail, walk directly across the Kinsman Ridge Trail, following an obvious trail a few hundred yards to the top of the Cannon Mountain Ski Area. Take your choice of ski trails to the bottom, then pick up the bike path in the parking lot and follow it south back to

Lafayette Place. The entire outing might take five hours—with a stop for a hot chocolate at the ski area's summit restaurant.

User Groups

Hikers and dogs. Dogs must be leashed. No wheelchair facilities. This trail should not be attempted in winter and is not suitable for bikes, horses, or skis. Hunting is allowed in season, but not near trails.

Access and Fees

Parking and access are free.

Maps

For a map of hiking trails, get the *Franconia-Pemigewasset Range* map, or the *Crawford Notch-Sandwich Range/Moosilauke-Kinsman* map, each $7.95 in waterproof Tyvek, available in many stores and from the Appalachian Mountain Club, 800/262-4455, website: www.outdoors.org; or the *Trail Map and Guide to the White Mountain National Forest* for $7.95 from the DeLorme Publishing Company, 800/642-0970. For a topographic area map, request Franconia from USGS Map Sales, Federal Center, Box 25286, Denver, CO 80225, 888/ASK-USGS (888/275-8747), website: http://mapping.usgs.gov.

Directions

Drive to one of the large parking lots on the east and west side of I-93 at the Lafayette Place Campground in Franconia Notch State Park. From the east side parking lot, hikers can cross under the highway to the Lafayette Place Campground on the west side, where the trail begins.

Contact

Franconia Notch State Park, Franconia, NH 03580, 603/745-8391, website: www.franconianotchstatepark.com. New Hampshire Division of Parks and Recreation, P.O. Box 1856, 172 Pembroke Road, Concord, NH 03302, 603/271-3556, camping reservations 603/271-3628, website: www.nhstateparks.org. White Mountain National Forest Supervisor, 719 North Main Street, Laconia, NH 03246, 603/528-8721, TDD for the hearing impaired 603/528-8722, website: www.fs.fed.us/r9/white.

50 LONESOME LAKE

in Franconia Notch State Park north of Lincoln
and south of Franconia

Total distance: 3.2 miles round-trip   **Hiking time:** 2 hours

Difficulty: 4   **Rating:** 10

Lonesome Lake's name gives a newcomer to Franconia Notch no forewarning of the crowds that flock to this scenic mountain tarn; nonetheless, if you accept the likelihood of sharing this beautiful spot with dozens of other visitors, the view from the lake's southwest corner across its crystal waters to Mounts Lafayette and Lincoln on Franconia Ridge has no comparison. This trail passes through extensive boggy areas, which, combined with the heavy foot traffic it sees, can make for a muddy hike. It ascends about 1,000 feet in elevation.

From the parking lot, pick up the Lonesome Lake Trail, which crosses Lafayette Place Campground and ascends at a moderate grade for 1.2 miles to the northeast corner of the lake. Turn left (south) on the Cascade Brook Trail, following it nearly 0.3 mile to the south end of the lake. Turn right on the Fishin' Jimmy Trail, crossing the lake's outlet and reaching a small beach area where people often swim in the lake. The Appalachian Mountain Club hut lies a short distance off the lake, in the woods. Bear right off the Fishin' Jimmy Trail onto the Around-Lonesome-Lake Trail, which heads north along the lake's west shore, crossing boggy areas on boardwalks. In 0.3 mile, turn right (east) on the Lonesome Lake Trail and follow it 1.4 miles back to the campground.

User Groups

Hikers and snowshoers. Dogs must be leashed. No wheelchair facilities. This trail is not suitable for bikes, horses, or skis. Hunting is allowed in season, but not near trails.

Access and Fees

Parking and access are free. The Appalachian Mountain Club operates the Lonesome Lake hut on the Fishin' Jimmy Trail near Lonesome Lake; contact the Appalachian Mountain Club for reservation and rate information.

Maps

For a map of hiking trails, get the *Franconia-Pemigewasset Range* map or the *Crawford Notch-Sandwich Range/Moosilauke-Kinsman* map, each $7.95 in waterproof Tyvek, available in many stores and from the Appalachian Mountain Club, 800/262-4455, website: www.outdoors.org;

the *Trail Map and Guide to the White Mountain National Forest* for $7.95 from the DeLorme Publishing Company, 800/642-0970; or map 3 in the *Map and Guide to the Appalachian Trail in New Hampshire and Vermont,* an eight-map set and guidebook available for $19.95 ($14.95 for the maps alone) from the Appalachian Trail Conference. For a topographic area map, request Franconia from USGS Map Sales, Federal Center, Box 25286, Denver, CO 80225, 888/ASK-USGS (888/275-8747), website: http://mapping.usgs.gov.

Directions
Drive to one of the large parking lots on the east and west side of I-93 at the Lafayette Place Campground in Franconia Notch State Park. From the east side parking lot, hikers can cross under the highway to the Lafayette Place Campground on the west side, where the trail begins.

Contact
White Mountain National Forest Supervisor, 719 North Main Street, Laconia, NH 03246, 603/528-8721, TDD for the hearing impaired 603/528-8722, website: www.fs.fed.us/r9/white. Franconia Notch State Park, Franconia, NH 03580, 603/745-8391, website: www.franconianotchstatepark.com. New Hampshire Division of Parks and Recreation, P.O. Box 1856, 172 Pembroke Road, Concord, NH 03302, 603/271-3556, camping reservations 603/271-3628, website: www.nhstateparks.org. Appalachian Mountain Club Pinkham Notch Visitor Center, P.O. Box 298, Gorham, NH 03581, 603/466-2721, website: www.outdoors.org. Appalachian Trail Conference, 799 Washington Street, P.O. Box 807, Harpers Ferry, WV 25425-0807, 304/535-6331, website: www.appalachiantrail.org.

51 NORTH AND SOUTH KINSMAN
in the White Mountain National Forest and Franconia Notch State Park north of Lincoln and south of Franconia

Total distance: 11.1 miles round-trip   **Hiking time:** 8 hours

Difficulty: 9   **Rating:** 9

Rising high above Franconia Notch, opposite the 5,000-foot peaks of Lafayette and Lincoln, Kinsman Mountain's two distinct peaks offer good views of the notch. But the more popular attractions on this 11.1-mile hike are the 1.5 miles of falls and cascades along Cascade Brook and the views across Lonesome Lake to Franconia Ridge. Many hikers, especially families with young children, explore only as far as the brook—a refreshing place on

Kinsman Pond

a hot summer day (steer clear of the drops). Most of the stream crossings on this hike utilize rocks or downed trees, and can be difficult at times of high water. Also, the heavily used trails described here are often wet and muddy, making rocks and exposed roots slick and footing difficult. This hike ascends about 2,500 feet in elevation.

You can begin this hike on either side of I-93. From the parking lot on the northbound side of I-93, follow the signs to the Basin, passing beneath I-93 and crossing a footbridge over the Pemigewasset River. Beyond the bridge, the trail bends right; within 100 feet, bear left at a sign for the Basin-Cascades Trail. From the parking lot on the southbound side, follow the walkway south to the Basin. Turn right on the bridge over the Pemigewasset and watch for the Basin-Cascades Trail branching left. Hikers from either parking lot will converge at this trailhead at the Basin, a natural stone bowl carved out by the Pemigewasset River and a popular spot for tourists. Follow the Basin-Cascades Trail, where open ledges provide views to Franconia Ridge across the notch. Kinsman Falls lies 0.5 mile up the trail and Rocky Glen Falls is 0.9 mile up, just 0.1 mile before the Basin-Cascades Trail meets the Cascade Brook Trail.

From this junction to the summit of 4,356-foot South Kinsman, the hike follows the white-blazed Appalachian Trail. Turn right (northwest) on the Cascade Brook Trail, immediately crossing the brook on stones or a downed tree. A half mile farther, the Kinsman Pond Trail bears left and crosses Cascade Brook; however, you should bear right and continue roughly north on the Cascade Brook Trail another mile to a junction with the Fishin' Jimmy Trail at the south end of Lonesome Lake. Turn left (west) on the Fishin' Jimmy, crossing a log bridge over the lake's outlet to a beachlike area popular for swimming. There's an outstanding view across Lonesome Lake to Franconia Ridge and Mounts Lafayette and Lincoln and Little Haystack (from left to right). Stay on the Fishin' Jimmy, passing the Appalachian Mountain Club's Lonesome Lake hut, which sits back in the woods just above the beach area. The trail rises and falls, passing over the hump separating Lonesome Lake from the upper flanks of Kinsman Mountain. After crossing a feeder stream to Cascade Brook, the trail ascends steeply, often up rock slabs into which wooden steps have been drilled in places. Two miles from Lonesome Lake, the Fishin' Jimmy Trail terminates at Kinsman Junction, a confluence of three trails—and a point you will return to on the descent.

Walk straight (west) onto the Kinsman Ridge Trail, climbing steep rock. Within 0.2 mile from Kinsman Junction, you begin to see views back toward Franconia Ridge; you reach the wooded summit of 4,293-foot North Kinsman at 0.4 mile. A side path leads 20 feet from the summit cairn to an open ledge with a sweeping view eastward that takes in Cannon Mountain, Lonesome Lake, Franconia Ridge, and the mountains above Waterville Valley. Continue south on the Kinsman Ridge Trail, descending past two open areas with good views. The trail drops into the saddle between the two peaks, then ascends steadily to the broad, flat summit of South Kinsman, nearly a mile from North Kinsman's summit. From various spots on South Kinsman's summit, you have views toward Franconia Ridge, North Kinsman, and Moosilauke to the south.

Backtrack to North Kinsman and descend to Kinsman Junction. Turn right (south) on the Kinsman Pond Trail, reaching the Appalachian Mountain Club shelter at Kinsman Pond in 0.1 mile. The trail follows the eastern shore of this scenic mountain tarn, below the summit cone of North Kinsman. It then hooks southeast into the forest, leading steadily downhill and making four stream crossings; this stretch of trail may be poorly marked, wet, and difficult to follow. It reaches the Cascade Brook Trail 2.5 miles from Kinsman Junction, right after crossing Cascade Brook. Bear right (southeast) onto the Cascade Brook Trail, following it 0.5 mile. Immediately after crossing Cascade Brook again, turn left onto the Basin-Cascades Trail, which leads a mile back to the Basin.

Special note: Some hikers go just to the summit of North Kinsman, skipping the 1.8-mile round-trip hike from North to South Kinsman. That would make for a 9.3-mile hike along the route described here, reducing this hike's time by about 1.5 hours.

User Groups

Hikers and dogs. No wheelchair facilities. This trail should not be attempted in winter except by hikers experienced in mountaineering and prepared for severe winter weather, and is not suitable for skis. Bikes, horses, and hunting are prohibited.

Access and Fees

Parking and access are free. This hike begins in Franconia Notch State Park, but much of it lies within the White Mountain National Forest. The Appalachian Mountain Club operates the Kinsman Pond campsite, with a shelter and three tent platforms, located along the Kinsman Pond Trail, 0.1 mile from Kinsman Junction and 4.5 miles from the Basin. A caretaker collects the $8 per person nightly fee during the warmer months. The Appalachian Mountain Club also operates the Lonesome Lake hut, where a crew prepares meals, and guests share bunkrooms and bathrooms; contact the Appalachian Mountain Club for reservation and rate information.

Maps

For a map of hiking trails, get the *Franconia-Pemigewasset Range* map or the *Crawford Notch-Sandwich Range/Moosilauke-Kinsman* map, each $7.95 in waterproof Tyvek, available in many stores and from the Appalachian Mountain Club, 800/262-4455, website: www.outdoors.org; the *Trail Map and Guide to the White Mountain National Forest* for $7.95 from the DeLorme Publishing Company, 800/642-0970; or map 3 in the *Map and Guide to the Appalachian Trail in New Hampshire and Vermont,* an eight-map set and guidebook available for $19.95 ($14.95 for the maps alone) from the Appalachian Trail Conference. For topographic area maps, request Franconia and Lincoln from USGS Map Sales, Federal Center, Box 25286, Denver, CO 80225, 888/ASK-USGS (888/275-8747), website: http://mapping.usgs.gov.

Directions

From I-93 in Franconia Notch, take the exit for the Basin. There are separate parking lots on the northbound and southbound sides of the highway; see trail notes above for details on locating the trailhead from each lot.

Contact

White Mountain National Forest Supervisor, 719 North Main Street, Laconia, NH 03246, 603/528-8721, TDD for the hearing impaired 603/528-8722, website: www.fs.fed.us/r9/white. Franconia Notch State Park, Franconia, NH 03580, 603/745-8391, website: www.franconianotch-statepark.com. New Hampshire Division of Parks and Recreation, P.O. Box 1856, 172 Pembroke Road, Concord, NH 03302, 603/271-3556, camping reservations 603/271-3628, website: www.nhstateparks.org. Appalachian Mountain Club Pinkham Notch Visitor Center, P.O. Box 298, Gorham, NH 03581, 603/466-2721, website: www.outdoors.org. Appalachian Trail Conference, 799 Washington Street, P.O. Box 807, Harpers Ferry, WV 25425-0807, 304/535-6331, website: www.appalachiantrail.org.

52 FRANCONIA NOTCH: PEMI TRAIL

in Franconia Notch State Park north of Lincoln
and south of Franconia

Total distance: 5.5 miles one-way　　　　**Hiking time:** 2.5 hours

Difficulty: 4　　　　　　　　　　　　　　　　**Rating:** 8

The Pemi Trail offers an easy and scenic 5.5-mile, one-way walk (a shuttling of cars is suggested) through Franconia Notch, with periodic views of
the cliffs and peaks flanking the notch. The trail follows the west shore of
Profile Lake, with excellent views across the water to Eagle Cliff on
Mount Lafayette. When the light is right, you can distinguish a free-stand-
ing rock pinnacle in a gully separating two major cliffs on this shoulder of
Lafayette; known as the Eaglet, this pinnacle is a destination for rock
climbers and has been a nesting site in spring for peregrine falcons, which
you might see flying around in spring. After crossing the paved bike path
through the notch just south of Profile Lake and a second time just north
of Lafayette Place Campground, the Pemi Trail follows a campground
road along the west bank of the Pemigewasset River, then leaves the campground and parallels the river all the way to the water-sculpted rock at the
Basin. It crosses the Basin-Cascades Trail, then meets the Cascade Brook
Trail before crossing east beneath I-93 and finishing at the parking lot immediately north of the flume.

User Groups

Hikers and snowshoers. Dogs must be leashed. No wheelchair facilities.
This trail is not suitable for bikes, horses, or skis. Hunting is allowed in
season, but not near trails.

Access and Fees

Parking and access are free.

Maps

Obtain the free map of Franconia Notch State Park, available from the
state park or the New Hampshire Division of Parks and Recreation; the
Franconia-Pemigewasset Range map or the *Crawford Notch-Sandwich
Range/Moosilauke-Kinsman* map, each $7.95 in waterproof Tyvek, avail-
able in many stores and from the Appalachian Mountain Club, 800/262-
4455, website: www.outdoors.org. For topographic area maps, request
Franconia and Lincoln from USGS Map Sales, Federal Center, Box
25286, Denver, CO 80225, 888/ASK-USGS (888/275-8747), website:
http://mapping.usgs.gov.

Directions

This one-way trail requires a shuttling of cars. The trail's endpoints are at the parking area off I-93 at the exit immediately north of the Flume near the south end of Franconia Notch State Park; and the parking area for the Kinsman Ridge Trail, reached via Exit 2 at the north end of the notch.

Contact

Franconia Notch State Park, Franconia, NH 03580, 603/745-8391, website: www.franconianotchstatepark.com. New Hampshire Division of Parks and Recreation, P.O. Box 1856, 172 Pembroke Road, Concord, NH 03302, 603/271-3556, camping reservations 603/271-3628, website: www.nhstateparks.org.

53 MOUNT LAFAYETTE: OLD BRIDLE PATH

in the White Mountain National Forest and Franconia Notch State Park north of Lincoln and south of Franconia

Total distance: 8 miles round-trip　　　　**Hiking time:** 6.5 hours

Difficulty: 9　　　　　　　　　　　　　　　　**Rating:** 10

This eight-mile hike provides the most direct and popular route to the 5,260-foot summit of Mount Lafayette, the sixth-highest peak in the White Mountains. The elevation gain is about 3,500 feet, ranking this hike among the most difficult in New England, though it does not present the exposure of hikes like Mount Washington's Huntington Ravine. It is also a fairly well-traveled route in winter, often with a packed trough through the snow, but the route is completely exposed to weather once you venture beyond the Greenleaf hut. I've hiked it many times, including winter outings on days so cold we wore every stitch of clothing we'd brought—even while hiking uphill—and turned back before the summit because of strong, brutally cold winds pounding the upper mountain. The Appalachian Mountain Club's Greenleaf hut offers a scenic location for making this hike a two-day trip and a way to catch the sunset high up the mountain. See next listing for more description of the views from the Old Bridle Path, Greenleaf Trail, and Lafayette's summit.

From the parking lot on the east side of I-93, follow the Falling Waters Trail and Old Bridle Path for 0.2 mile. Where the Falling Waters Trail turns sharply right, continue straight ahead on the Old Bridle Path. It climbs fairly easily at first through mostly deciduous forest, then grows steeper as it ascends the prominent west ridge hooking down from the summit of Lafayette. Once on the crest of that ridge, you'll get great views from a few open ledges of the summits of Lafayette to the left, and Mount

Lincoln (5,089 feet) to the right of Lafayette. At 2.9 miles from the trail-head, the Old Bridle Path terminates at the Greenleaf Trail and Greenleaf hut. From there, follow the Greenleaf Trail as it dips down into a shallow basin, passes through subalpine forest, and soon emerges onto the rocky, open west slope of Lafayette, climbing another 1.1 miles and more than 1,000 feet in elevation to Lafayette's summit, where the views take in most of the White Mountains and New Hampshire's north country, and west to Vermont's Green Mountains. Return the way you came.

User Groups
Hikers and dogs. Dogs must be leashed. No wheelchair facilities. This trail should not be attempted in winter except by hikers experienced in moun-taineering and prepared for severe winter weather, and is not suitable for skis. Bikes, horses, and hunting are prohibited.

Access and Fees
Parking and access are free. The Appalachian Mountain Club operates the Greenleaf hut at the junction of the Greenleaf Trail and Old Bridle Path; con-tact the Appalachian Mountain Club for reservation and rate information.

Maps
For a map of hiking trails, get the *Franconia–Pemigewasset Range* map or the *Crawford Notch–Sandwich Range/Moosilauke–Kinsman* map, each $7.95 in waterproof Tyvek, available in many stores and from the Appalachian Mountain Club, 800/262-4455, website: www.outdoors.org; the *Trail Map and Guide to the White Mountain National Forest* for $7.95 from the De-Lorme Publishing Company, 800/642-0970; or map 3 in the *Map and Guide to the Appalachian Trail in New Hampshire and Vermont,* an eight-map set and guidebook available for $19.95 ($14.95 for the maps alone) from the Appalachian Trail Conference. For a topographic area map, request Franco-nia from USGS Map Sales, Federal Center, Box 25286, Denver, CO 80225, 888/ASK-USGS (888/275-8747), website: http://mapping.usgs.gov.

Directions
Drive to one of the large parking lots on the east and west side of I-93 at the Lafayette Place Campground in Franconia Notch State Park. From the west side parking lot, hikers can walk under the highway to the east side, where the trails begin.

Contact
White Mountain National Forest Supervisor, 719 North Main Street, Laco-nia, NH 03246, 603/528-8721, TDD for the hearing impaired 603/528-8722,

website: www.fs.fed.us/r9/white. Franconia Notch State Park, Franconia, NH 03580, 603/745-8391, website: www.franconianotchstatepark.com. New Hampshire Division of Parks and Recreation, P.O. Box 1856, 172 Pembroke Road, Concord, NH 03302, 603/271-3556, camping reservations 603/271-3628, website: www.nhstateparks.org. Appalachian Mountain Club Pinkham Notch Visitor Center, P.O. Box 298, Gorham, NH 03581, 603/466-2721, website: www.outdoors.org. Appalachian Trail Conference, 799 Washington Street, P.O. Box 807, Harpers Ferry, WV 25425-0807, 304/535-6331, website: www.appalachiantrail.org.

54 MOUNTS LINCOLN AND LAFAYETTE

in the White Mountain National Forest and Franconia Notch State Park north of Lincoln and south of Franconia

Total distance: 8.8 miles round-trip **Hiking time:** 6.5 hours

Difficulty: 10 **Rating:** 10

For many New England hikers—myself included—this 8.8-mile loop over the sixth- and seventh-highest peaks in New Hampshire represented a dramatic introduction to the White Mountains and has become a favorite hike revisited many times over the years. With nearly two miles of continuous, exposed ridgeline high above the forest connecting Mounts Lincoln (5,089

a hiker on Mount Lincoln, Franconia Ridge

feet) and Lafayette (5,260 feet), this hike lures hundreds of people on warm weekends in summer and fall. The views from Franconia Ridge encompass most of the White Mountains, spanning the peaks and valleys of the Pemigewasset Wilderness all the way to the Presidential Range, Vermont's Green Mountains, and, on a very clear day, New York's Adirondacks. The Falling Waters Trail passes several waterfalls and cascades, and the Old Bridle Path follows a long shoulder of Mount Lafayette over some open ledges that offer excellent views of Lincoln and Lafayette.

It's also a rugged hike, with some 3,600 feet of cumulative elevation gain and a considerable amount of steep, rocky trail. Because of the heavy foot traffic on Franconia Ridge and the fragility of the alpine flora, you should take care to walk only on the clearly marked trail or on bare rock.

From the parking lot on the east side of I-93, follow the Falling Waters Trail, which coincides for 0.2 mile with the Old Bridle Path, then turns sharply right and crosses Walker Brook on a bridge. The trail climbs steadily and steeply, crossing Dry Brook at 0.7 mile, which could be difficult in high water. Over the ensuing mile, it passes several cascades and waterfalls, including Cloudland Falls, with a sheer drop of 80 feet, and makes two more crossings of the brook.

At 2.8 miles, a side path leads to the right a short distance to Shining Rock, a huge slab on the mountainside that appears to shimmer when viewed from the road far below. The views of the notch are excellent, but bear in mind that the shining is caused by running water, making the slab slippery and dangerous to scramble around on. Continue up the Falling Waters Trail, emerging above the trees about 0.1 mile before reaching the Franconia Ridge Trail (which is part of the Appalachian Trail) at the summit of Little Haystack Mountain, 3.2 miles from the trailhead. Turn left (north), following the cairns and white blazes of the Franconia Ridge Trail/Appalachian Trail along the open ridge.

Among the peaks in view as you head over Lincoln and Lafayette are the bald cap of Mount Garfield immediately northeast of Lafayette; North and South Twin Mountains, east of Garfield; Mount Washington and the high peaks of the Presidential Range in the more distant northeast; the wooded mound of Owl's Head, standing alone across the valley immediately east of Franconia Ridge; the Bonds and Bondcliff on the other side of Owl's Head; the towering mass of Mount Carrigain southeast of Owl's Head and the Bonds; the jumble of peaks above Waterville Valley farther south and east, including the three pointed summits of Mount Tripyramid; the distinct horn of Mount Chocorua in the distance between Carrigain and Waterville Valley; Cannon Cliff and Mountain to the west across Franconia Notch; the north and south peaks of Kinsman Mountain, south of and behind Cannon; and to the southwest, sprawling Mount Moosilauke. (This book describes hikes up all of the peaks listed here, except for the Owl's Head.)

From Haystack, the trail drops slightly but follows easy ground until climbing steeply to the summit of Lincoln, 0.7 mile from Haystack. It passes over a subsidiary summit of Lincoln immediately to the north, then drops into a saddle with the tallest scrub vegetation on the ridge before making the long ascent of Mount Lafayette, 0.9 mile from Lincoln's summit. This highest point on the ridge, predictably, tends to be the windiest and coldest spot as well, although there are sheltered places in the rocks on the summit's north side. Turn left (west) and descend the Greenleaf Trail, much of it over open terrain, for 1.1 miles to the Appalachian Mountain Club's Greenleaf hut. Just beyond the hut, bear left onto the Old Bridle Path, descending southwest over the crest of a long ridge, with occasional views of Franconia Ridge and the steep, green western slopes of Lafayette and Lincoln, before reentering the woods and eventually reaching the parking lot, 2.9 miles from the hut.

Special note: Under most conditions, it's desirable to hike this loop in the direction described here because the steep sections of the Falling Waters Trail are easier to ascend than descend, especially when, as often occurs, the trail is wet. But if you're doing the hike on a day with cold wind, consider reversing the direction; the wind generally comes from the northwest, and reversing this hike's direction would put it at your back while atop Franconia Ridge, rather than in your face.

User Groups

Hikers and dogs. Dogs must be leashed. No wheelchair facilities. This trail should not be attempted in winter except by hikers experienced in mountaineering and prepared for severe winter weather, and is not suitable for skis. Bikes, horses, and hunting are prohibited.

Access and Fees

Parking and access are free. The Appalachian Mountain Club operates the Greenleaf hut at the junction of the Greenleaf Trail and Old Bridle Path; contact the Appalachian Mountain Club for reservation and rate information.

Maps

For a map of hiking trails, get the *Franconia-Pemigewasset Range* map or the *Crawford Notch-Sandwich Range/Moosilauke-Kinsman* map, each $7.95 in waterproof Tyvek, available in many stores and from the Appalachian Mountain Club, 800/262-4455, website: www.outdoors.org; the *Trail Map and Guide to the White Mountain National Forest* for $7.95 from the DeLorme Publishing Company, 800/642-0970; or map 3 in the *Map and Guide to the Appalachian Trail in New Hampshire and Vermont,* an eight-map set and guidebook available for $19.95 ($14.95 for the maps alone) from the Appalachian Trail Conference. For a topographic area map, request Franconia from USGS Map Sales, Federal Center, Box 25286, Denver, CO 80225, 888/ASK-USGS (888/275-8747), website: http://mapping.usgs.gov.

Directions

Drive to one of the large parking lots on the east and west sides of I-93 at the Lafayette Place Campground in Franconia Notch State Park. From the west side parking lot, hikers can walk under the highway to the east side, where the trails begin.

Contact

White Mountain National Forest Supervisor, 719 North Main Street, Laconia, NH 03246, 603/528-8721, TDD for the hearing impaired 603/528-8722, website: www.fs.fed.us/r9/white. Franconia Notch State Park, Franconia, NH 03580, 603/745-8391, website: www.franconianotchstatepark.com. New Hampshire Division of Parks and Recreation, P.O. Box 1856, 172 Pembroke Road, Concord, NH 03302, 603/271-3556, camping reservations 603/271-3628, website: www.nhstateparks.org. Appalachian Mountain Club Pinkham Notch Visitor Center, P.O. Box 298, Gorham, NH 03581, 603/466-2721, website: www.outdoors.org. Appalachian Trail Conference, 799 Washington Street, P.O. Box 807, Harpers Ferry, WV 25425-0807, 304/535-6331, website: www.appalachiantrail.org.

55 FRANCONIA NOTCH LOOP

in the White Mountain National Forest and Franconia Notch State Park north of Lincoln and south of Franconia

Total distance: 14 miles round-trip   **Hiking time:** 9 hours or 1–2 days

Difficulty: 9   **Rating:** 10

While this loop of about 14 miles can be done in a day by fit hikers, I like to make an overnight trip of it, staying either in the Greenleaf hut or at the Liberty Springs campsite. Either place gives you a great high-elevation base from which to catch the sunset. I once spent a September evening sitting alone atop Mount Liberty, watching shadows grow long over the White Mountains and Franconia Notch while the setting sun fired long rays of light through the thin clouds, creating spectacular prisms of light that glowed luminously above Mount Moosilauke and the Kinsmans to the

a backpacker on Franconia Ridge

west. See the trail notes for the preceding hike, Mounts Lincoln and Lafayette, for more description of the views from Franconia Ridge. The cumulative elevation gained on this hike is about 4,700 feet.

From the parking lot on the east side of I-93, follow the Falling Waters Trail and the Old Bridle Path for 0.2 mile to where the trails split; then continue straight ahead on the Old Bridle Path. It climbs easily at first, then steeply, for 2.9 miles from the trailhead to a junction with the Greenleaf Trail at the Greenleaf hut. From the hut, continue east on the Greenleaf Trail as it dips down into a shallow basin, passes through subalpine forest, and soon emerges onto the rocky, open west slope of Lafayette, climbing another 1.1 miles and more than 1,000 feet in elevation to Lafayette's summit. Turn right (south) on the Franconia Ridge Trail, which coincides with the Appalachian Trail, and hike the rugged, open, and in places narrow Franconia Ridge—enjoying constant 360-degree views—for a mile to the 5,089-foot summit of Mount Lincoln, then another 0.7 mile to the summit of Little Haystack (4,780 feet), where the Falling Waters Trail turns right (west).

This hike continues south on the Franconia Ridge Trail, soon dropping into subalpine forest—although the forest cover is thin and the ridge narrow enough that you can see through the trees and know how abruptly the earth drops off to either side. At 1.8 miles past Little Haystack, the Liberty Spring Trail and Appalachian Trail turn right (west); you will eventually descend that way. But continue south on the Franconia Ridge Trail another 0.3 mile, climbing less than 300 feet to the rocky summit of Mount Liberty for excellent, 360-degree views of the Whites (see the trail notes for the preceding hike, Mounts Lincoln and Lafayette, for more description of these views).

From Liberty's summit, backtrack to the Liberty Spring Trail and descend it. Within 0.3 mile you'll reach the Liberty Spring campsite, where you can spend the night if backpacking. From the campsite, descend the Liberty Spring Trail another 2.6 miles to the Whitehouse Trail and the Franconia Notch Bike Path. Cross the Pemigewasset River on a bridge, and just beyond the bridge turn right onto the Pemi Trail. Walk under the highway, then stay to the right (north) on the Pemi Trail and follow it nearly a mile to the Basin, where the Pemigewasset River has carved impressive natural bowls and cascades into the granite bedrock. From the Basin, you can stay on the Pemi Trail, or follow the paved bike path, about two miles farther to the parking lot on the west side of the highway at Lafayette Place Campground. If you parked on the east side of the highway, you can walk under the highway to that parking lot.

User Groups

Hikers and dogs. Dogs must be leashed. No wheelchair facilities. This trail should not be attempted in winter except by hikers experienced in mountaineering and prepared for severe winter weather, and is not suitable for skis. Bikes, horses, and hunting are prohibited.

Access and Fees

Parking and access are free. The Appalachian Mountain Club operates the Greenleaf hut at the junction of the Greenleaf Trail and Old Bridle Path; contact the Appalachian Mountain Club for reservation and rate information. The Appalachian Mountain Club also manages the Liberty Spring campsite, with 12 tent platforms, located along the Liberty Spring Trail, 2.6 miles from the Whitehouse Trail and 0.3 mile from the Franconia Ridge Trail. A caretaker collects the $8 nightly fee during the warmer months.

Maps

For a map of hiking trails, get the *Franconia-Pemigewasset Range* map or the *Crawford Notch–Sandwich Range/Moosilauke–Kinsman* map, each $7.95 in waterproof Tyvek, available in many stores and from the Appalachian Mountain Club, 800/262-4455, website: www.outdoors.org; the *Trail Map and Guide to the White Mountain National Forest* for $7.95 from the DeLorme Publishing Company, 800/642-0970; or map 3 in the *Map and Guide to the Appalachian Trail in New Hampshire and Vermont,* an eight-map set and guidebook available for $19.95 ($14.95 for the maps alone) from the Appalachian Trail Conference. For a topographic area map, request Franconia from USGS Map Sales, Federal Center, Box 25286, Denver, CO 80225, 888/ASK-USGS (888/275-8747), website: http://mapping.usgs.gov.

Directions

Drive to one of the large parking lots on the east and west side of I-93 at the Lafayette Place Campground in Franconia Notch State Park. From the west side parking lot, hikers can walk under the highway to the east side, where the trails begin.

Contact

White Mountain National Forest Supervisor, 719 North Main Street, Laconia, NH 03246, 603/528-8721, TDD for the hearing impaired 603/528-8722, website: www.fs.fed.us/r9/white. Franconia Notch State Park, Franconia, NH 03580, 603/745-8391, website: www.franconianotchstatepark.com. New Hampshire Division of Parks and Recreation, P.O. Box 1856, 172 Pembroke Road, Concord, NH 03302, 603/271-3556, camping reservations 603/271-3628, website: www.nhstateparks.org. Appalachian Mountain Club Pinkham Notch Visitor Center, P.O. Box 298, Gorham, NH 03581, 603/466-2721, website: www.outdoors.org. Appalachian Trail Conference, 799 Washington Street, P.O. Box 807, Harpers Ferry, WV 25425-0807, 304/535-6331, website: www.appalachiantrail.org.

56 FRANCONIA NOTCH BIKE PATH

in the White Mountain National Forest and Franconia Notch State Park north of Lincoln and south of Franconia

Total distance: 8.5 miles round-trip   **Hiking time:** 3.5 hours

Difficulty: 6   **Rating:** 8

The Franconia Notch Bike Path runs like a stream, north/south for about 8.5 miles through Franconia Notch, providing a paved route for exploring one of the most spectacular notches in New England. Popular with families, it's great for cycling, walking, running, snowshoeing, and cross-country skiing. With several access points, you can do as much of the path as you like. Much of it is in the forest, but there are numerous views of the surrounding peaks from the path. There are some pretty steep, though short, hills along the path. The path may be accessible by wheelchairs provided the user can manage the short but steep climbs.

Its elevation begins at about 1,700 feet at the Skookumchuck trailhead, rises to around 2,000 feet at the base of Cannon Mountain and Profile Lake, then drops to about 1,100 feet at the Flume; going north to south is easier, especially from anywhere south of Profile Lake. Scenic points along it include the Flume, a natural cleavage in the mountainside; the Basin, where the still-small Pemigewasset River pours through natural bowls in the bedrock; a view of Cannon Cliff from a spot immediately north of Profile Lake; and the truck-sized boulder, estimated to weigh between 20 and 30 tons, lying right beside the paved path north of Lafayette Place campground, deposited there by a rockslide off Cannon Cliff on June 19, 1997.

User Groups

Hikers, bikers, snowshoers, skiers, horses, wheelchairs. Dogs must be leashed. Hunting and in-line skating are prohibited.

Access and Fees

Parking and access are free within Franconia Notch State Park, but the Skookumchuck Trail parking lot lies within the White Mountain National Forest, and a permit is required for day use or overnight parking. Permits are available at several area stores and from the national forest at a cost of $5 for seven consecutive days or $20 per year. A $3 one-day permit can be purchased at self-service stations at national forest trailheads, but the pass is good only for the trailhead at which it's purchased.

Maps

For a map that shows the bike path, get the *Franconia–Pemigewasset Range* map, $7.95 in waterproof Tyvek, available in many stores and from the Appalachian Mountain Club, 800/262-4455, website: www.outdoors.org. For topographic area maps, request Franconia and Lincoln from USGS Map Sales, Federal Center, Box 25286, Denver, CO 80225, 888/ASK-USGS (888/275-8747), website: http://mapping.usgs.gov.

Directions

The bike path can be accessed from several points. Its northern end is at the parking lot for the Skookumchuck Trail, on Route 3 about 0.6 mile north of Exit 35 off I-93 in Franconia. Its southern end is at the Flume, reached via the exit for the Flume off I-93 in Franconia Notch. Other access points in Franconia Notch include the Cannon Mountain parking lot at Exit 2, the former Old Man of the Mountains viewpoint parking area (see the description of the Cannon Mountain: Kinsman Ridge Trail hike for details on the Old Man's demise), the Profile Lake parking lot, the Lafayette Place Campground, and the Basin parking lot.

Contact

Franconia Notch State Park, Franconia, NH 03580, 603/745-8391, website: www.franconianotchstatepark.com. New Hampshire Division of Parks and Recreation, P.O. Box 1856, 172 Pembroke Road, Concord, NH 03302, 603/271-3556, camping reservations 603/271-3628, website: www.nhstateparks.org. White Mountain National Forest Supervisor, 719 North Main Street, Laconia, NH 03246, 603/528-8721, TDD for the hearing impaired 603/528-8722, website: www.fs.fed.us/r9/white.

57 MOUNTS FLUME AND LIBERTY

in the White Mountain National Forest and Franconia Notch State Park north of Lincoln and south of Franconia

Total distance: 9.8 miles round-trip   **Hiking time:** 7 hours

Difficulty: 9   **Rating:** 9

If these two summits were located virtually anywhere else, this loop hike would enjoy enormous popularity. But the 5,000-footers to the north, Lafayette and Lincoln, are what capture the attention of most hikers venturing onto spectacular Franconia Ridge. Many people who call the Lafayette-Lincoln Loop (see the Mounts Lincoln and Lafayette listing in this chapter) their favorite hike in the Whites have never enjoyed the uninterrupted views from the rocky summits of 4,325-foot Flume or 4,459-foot Liberty: Franconia Notch, west to Mount Moosilauke and the Green Mountains, and a grand sweep of peaks to the east all the way to the Presidential Range. I hiked this loop on a March day when the sun felt like July—although the notion of summer approaching was

a backpacker on Mount Flume, Franconia Ridge

dispelled by the cool wind, snow, and ice. This hike's cumulative elevation gain is nearly 2,500 feet.

From the parking lot, take the blue-blazed Whitehouse Trail north for nearly a mile (it coincides briefly with the Franconia Notch Bike Path). Pick up the white-blazed Liberty Spring Trail—a part of the Appalachian Trail—heading east. Within 0.5 mile, signs mark where the Flume Slide Trail branches right. From that junction to the slide, the trail is somewhat overgrown, marked very sporadically with light-blue blazes and can be hard to follow. It grows steep on the upper part of the slide, and you will scramble over rocks that can be very slick when wet. (For a less exposed route to the summit of Mount Liberty, go up and down the Liberty Spring Trail.)

Where the Flume Slide Trail hits the ridge crest 3.3 miles from the Liberty Spring Trail, turn left onto the Osseo Trail, which leads a short distance to Mount Flume's summit. Continue over the summit on the Franconia Ridge Trail, dipping into the saddle between the peaks, then climbing to Liberty's summit a mile past the top of Flume. Another 0.3 mile beyond the summit, turn left onto the Liberty Spring Trail and descend for 2.9 miles to the Whitehouse Trail, following it back to the parking lot.

User Groups

Hikers and dogs. Dogs must be leashed. No wheelchair facilities. This trail should not be attempted in winter except by hikers experienced in mountaineering and prepared for severe winter weather, and is not suitable for skis. Bikes, horses, and hunting are prohibited.

Access and Fees

Parking and access are free. This hike begins in Franconia Notch State Park, but much of it lies within the White Mountain National Forest. The Appalachian Mountain Club operates the Liberty Spring campsite, with 12 tent platforms, located along the Liberty Spring Trail, 2.6 miles from the Whitehouse Trail and 0.3 mile from the Franconia Ridge Trail. A caretaker collects the $8 nightly fee during the warmer months.

Maps

For a map of hiking trails, get the *Franconia-Pemigewasset Range* map or the *Crawford Notch-Sandwich Range/Moosilauke-Kinsman* map, each $7.95 in waterproof Tyvek, available in many stores and from the Appalachian Mountain Club, 800/262-4455, website: www.outdoors.org; the *Trail Map and Guide to the White Mountain National Forest* for $7.95 from the DeLorme Publishing Company, 800/642-0970; or map 3 in the *Map and Guide to the Appalachian Trail in New Hampshire and Vermont,* an eight-map set and guidebook available for $19.95 ($14.95 for the maps alone) from the Appalachian Trail Conference. For topographic area maps, request Franconia and Lincoln from USGS Map Sales, Federal Center, Box 25286, Denver, CO 80225, 888/ASK-USGS (888/275-8747), website: http://mapping.usgs.gov.

Directions

From I-93 in Franconia Notch, take the exit for the Flume. Follow the sign to trailhead parking for the Whitehouse Trail and the Appalachian Trail, which coincides with the Liberty Spring Trail and is reached via the Whitehouse.

Contact

Franconia Notch State Park, Franconia, NH 03580, 603/745-8391, website: www.franconianotchstatepark.com. New Hampshire Division of Parks and Recreation, P.O. Box 1856, 172 Pembroke Road, Concord, NH 03302, 603/271-3556, camping reservations 603/271-3628, website: www.nhstateparks.org. White Mountain National Forest Supervisor, 719 North Main Street, Laconia, NH 03246, 603/528-8721, TDD for the hearing impaired 603/528-8722, website: www.fs.fed.us/r9/white. Appalachian Mountain Club Pinkham Notch Visitor Center, P.O. Box 298, Gorham, NH 03581, 603/466-2721, website: www.outdoors.org. Appalachian Trail Conference, 799 Washington Street, P.O. Box 807, Harpers Ferry, WV 25425-0807, 304/535-6331, website: www.appalachiantrail.org.

58 TWINS–BONDS TRAVERSE

in the White Mountain National Forest between Twin Mountain and the Kancamagus Highway

Total distance: 20 miles one-way　　　**Hiking time:** 2.5–3 days

Difficulty: 9　　　　　　　　　　　　　　**Rating:** 10

Of the many good routes to backpack across the Pemigewasset Wilderness—the vast roadless area in the heart of the White Mountains—this ranks as my favorite because it traverses the spectacular Bondcliff Ridge, which splits the Pemi down the middle. The views are great from the summits of all five official 4,000-footers along this trek: North Twin (4,761 feet) and South Twin (4,902 feet), Bond (4,698 feet), Bondcliff (4,265 feet), and West Bond (4,540 feet), the last a wonderful knob of rock jutting above the dense scrub forest with terrific views of Franconia Ridge, Bondcliff, and the southern White Mountains. Two companions and I once caught a fabulous, burning-red sunrise from the shelter at the Guyot campsite.

a backpacker on Bondcliff, White Mountains

Hiking north to south, follow the North Twin Trail 4.3 miles to the summit of North Twin, and the North Twin Spur 1.3 miles to South Twin.
Turn left (southeast) on the Twinway and follow it for two miles. Turn
right (south) onto the Bondcliff Trail. Within 0.5 mile—a short distance beyond the spur trail leading left to Guyot campsite—turn right onto a spur
trail for the one-mile round-trip to the summit of West Bond. Return to
the Bondcliff Trail, and turn right (south) and continue about a half mile
to the summit of Mount Bond, with excellent views in all directions, including Mount Washington to the east and the spectacular Bondcliff
Ridge immediately south. Continuing south, you'll reach the ridge within a
mile and walk its open crest above tall cliffs. From Bondcliff's summit, it's
4.4 miles down through the woods to the Wilderness Trail. Turn right
(west) and follow the Wilderness Trail 3.8 miles to the parking area at Lincoln Woods. If you're planning to camp at the Franconia Brook campsite,
you will turn east (left) from the Bondcliff Trail onto the Wilderness Trail,
and ultimately reach the Lincoln Woods trailhead via the trail known as
the East Branch Road.

User Groups

Hikers and dogs. No wheelchair facilities. The Wilderness Trail (see listing
in this chapter) stretch of this hike is flat and is a popular day trip with
skiers and snowshoers, but the rest of this route should not be attempted
in winter except by hikers experienced in mountaineering and prepared for

severe winter weather, and is not suitable for skis. Bikes and horses are prohibited. Hunting is allowed in season.

Access and Fees

No backcountry permit is needed, but a permit is required for day use or overnight parking at any White Mountain National Forest trailhead, as indicated by signs posted at most trailheads. Permits are available at several area stores and from the national forest at a cost of $5 for seven consecutive days or $20 per year. A $3 one-day permit can be purchased at self-service stations at national forest trailheads, but the pass is good only for the trailhead at which it's purchased. The Guyot campsite, operated by the Appalachian Mountain Club, 800/262-4455, has a shelter and six tent platforms and is reached via a short spur trail (marked by a sign) off the Bondcliff Trail about a quarter mile south of the Twinway junction. A caretaker collects the $8 per person nightly fee at Guyot from late spring to fall. The Franconia Brook campsite (16 tent platforms), operated by the White Mountain National Forest, costs $8 per person; it has been moved to the east side of the Pemigewasset River's East Branch, almost directly across the river from its former location at the river's confluence with Franconia Brook. The campsite is reached by hiking the trail known as East Branch Road for three miles from the Lincoln Woods trailhead. Hikers on this hike would reach this campsite by turning east (left) from the Bondcliff Trail onto the Wilderness Trail and following it for 0.7 mile to a bridge over the East Branch, crossing the bridge, following the Cedar Brook Trail west for a bit more than a half mile, then turning right onto the East Branch Road, which is overgrown and may be easily overlooked. The Guyot and Franconia Brook campsites are popular and often full on weekends. Camping in the forest is legal, provided you remain at least 200 feet from a trail and 0.25 mile from established camping areas such as Guyot campsite.

Maps

For a map of hiking trails, get the *Franconia-Pemigewasset Range* map, $7.95 in waterproof Tyvek, available in many stores and from the Appalachian Mountain Club, 800/262-4455, website: www.outdoors.org. Or the *Trail Map and Guide to the White Mountain National Forest* for $7.95 from the DeLorme Publishing Company, 800/642-0970. For topographic area maps, request Bethlehem, South Twin Mountain, and Mount Osceola from USGS Map Sales, Federal Center, Box 25286, Denver, CO 80225, 888/ASK-USGS (888/275-8747), website: http://mapping.usgs.gov.

Directions

You will need to shuttle two vehicles for this trek. Leave one in the large parking lot at Lincoln Woods, where there is a White Mountain National

Forest ranger station. It is along the Kancamagus Highway (Route 112) five miles east of McDonald's in Lincoln and just east of the bridge where the Kancamagus crosses the East Branch of the Pemigewasset River. The Wilderness Trail—also known for its initial three miles as the Lincoln Woods Trail—begins here.

The other trailhead—where this hike begins—is off U.S. 3. From the junction of U.S. 302 and U.S. 3 in Twin Mountain, drive south on U.S. 3 for 2.5 miles and turn left onto Haystack Road/Fire Road 304. Or from I-93 north of Franconia Notch State Park, take Exit 35 for U.S. 3 north and continue approximately 7.5 miles, then turn right onto Fire Road 304. Follow this road to its end and a parking area at the North Twin Trail.

Contact

White Mountain National Forest Supervisor, 719 North Main Street, Laconia, NH 03246, 603/528-8721, TDD for the hearing impaired 603/528-8722, website: www.fs.fed.us/r9/white.

59 PEMIGEWASSET WILDERNESS TRAVERSE

in the White Mountain National Forest between U.S. 302
near Twin Mountain and Route 112 east of Lincoln

Total distance: 19.5 miles one-way   **Hiking time:** 10–12 hours/1–2 days

Difficulty: 8   **Rating:** 10

The Pemigewasset Wilderness is the sprawling roadless area of mountains and wide valleys in the heart of the White Mountains. A federally designated wilderness area, the Pemi harbors spectacular big-mountain hikes such as the Twins-Bonds Traverse (see previous listing) and Mount Carrigain (see listing later in this chapter). This traverse, however, follows the valleys of the Pemi, much of it relatively easy hiking along routes once followed by the railroads of 19th-century logging companies. It could be done in a two-day backpacking trip. But I've included this mainly because it's considered a classic ski tour, feasible to accomplish in a day for experienced cross-country skiers also skilled in winter mountain travel. For that reason, I've included in this hike's distance the 3.5 miles you have to ski up Zealand Road, which is not plowed in winter. This hike is thus 3.5 miles shorter in the warmer months. The route may follow lower elevations and climb only about 1,000 feet in elevation over its course, but weather can change quickly in here, and 20 miles on skis is a long day. You may have to break trail through varied snow conditions much of the way, and not finish until after dark (which is what happened to three friends and me when we skied this route). Zealand Notch is even more wild in winter than in the warmer months, and there's some nice skiing along these other trails. The Thoreau Falls Trail presents significant amounts of steeper terrain; you will have to carry skis and hike intermittently for a mile or more. Depending upon the amount of snowfall and how much freezing has occurred, numerous brooks crossing the Thoreau trail may not be frozen, necessitating repeated removal of skis to cross the brooks. Do not underestimate how long or difficult a winter trip like this can be.

From the winter parking lot, follow the Zealand Road, climbing gradually for 3.5 miles to its end (where this hike begins in warmer months). Then pick up the blue-blazed Zealand Trail, winding through the forest on fairly flat ground, with some short, steep steps, for 2.5 miles to a trail junction. To the right, the Twinway leads 0.2 mile uphill to the Appalachian Mountain Club's Zealand Falls hut. This hike continues straight ahead onto the Ethan Pond Trail, which coincides with the Appalachian Trail. The Ethan Pond Trail contours along the west slope of Whitewall Mountain.

About 1.3 miles past the Zealand Trail, the Ethan Pond Trail emerges from the forest onto the open scar of an old rockslide on Whitewall, in the middle of Zealand Notch. Above loom the towering cliffs of the mountain; below, the rockslide's fallout, a broad boulder field. Across the notch rises Zealand Mountain, and straight ahead, to the south, stands Carrigain. The trail crosses the rockslide for about 0.2 mile, then reenters the woods. At 2.1 miles past the Zealand Trail, bear right onto the Thoreau Falls Trail, following easy terrain for 0.1 mile to Thoreau Falls, which tumbles more than 100 feet and forms an impressive cascade of ice in winter. The trail crosses the stream immediately above the brink of the falls. Be careful here in any season, but especially in winter do not assume that any snow or ice bridge is safe; two days before my friends and I skied through here in January 1997, someone had fallen through the ice.

Once across the stream, the trail climbs steeply, angling across a wooded hillside, then dropping just as steeply down the other side. The trail may be difficult or impossible to ski for a mile or more, but it eventually reaches more level ground. At 4.7 miles from the Ethan Pond Trail, the trail crosses a bridge over the east branch of the Pemigewasset River. Just 0.4 mile past the bridge, turn right (west) onto the Wilderness Trail, which is the easiest trail on this route (making it the preferred way to finish if there's a chance of finishing after dark). The Wilderness Trail crosses the river again in 0.9 mile, on a 180-foot suspension bridge, then parallels the river for the remaining 5.4 flat miles to the Lincoln Woods parking lot on the Kancamagus Highway.

Special note: Skiers who do not want to wrestle their skis up and down the steep sections of the Thoreau Falls Trail might consider another option, two miles longer but easier. After passing through Zealand Notch, instead of turning right onto the Thoreau Falls Trail, continue left with the Ethan Pond Trail for 0.5 mile, and then turn right (south) onto the Shoal Pond Trail. Follow it for four miles to a spot called Stillwater Junction, then turn right (west) onto the Wilderness Trail and follow it 8.9 miles to Lincoln Woods.

User Groups
Hikers, dogs, skiers, and snowshoers. No wheelchair facilities. Bikes and horses are prohibited. This trail should only be attempted in winter by people prepared for severe winter weather. Hunting is allowed in season, except along the Appalachian Trail, which coincides with the Twinway and the Ethan Pond Trail.

Access and Fees
No backcountry permit is needed, but a permit is required for day use or overnight parking at any White Mountain National Forest trailhead, as indicated by signs posted at most trailheads. Permits are available at several area stores and from the national forest at a cost of $5 for seven consecutive days or $20 per year. A $3 one-day permit can be purchased at self-service stations at national forest trailheads, but the pass is good only for the trailhead at which it's purchased. Zealand Road is not maintained in winter. The Appalachian Mountain Club operates the Zealand Falls hut year-round; it is on the Twinway, 0.2 mile from the junction of the Zealand, Twinway, and Ethan Pond Trails and 2.7 miles from the end of Zealand Road. Contact the Appalachian Mountain Club for information on cost and reservations. The Franconia Brook campsite (16 tent platforms), operated by the White Mountain National Forest, costs $8 per person and is open only during summer and fall; it has been moved to the east side of the Pemigewasset River's east branch, almost directly across the river from its former location at the river's confluence with Franconia Brook. The campsite is reached by hiking the trail known as East Branch Road for three miles from the Lincoln Woods trailhead. On this hike, you would reach this campsite by turning left (south) from the Wilderness Trail onto the Cedar Brook Trail right before the second bridge crossing of the east branch of the Pemigewasset River, and following the Cedar Brook Trail west for a little more than a half mile, then turning right onto the East Branch Road, which is overgrown and may be easily overlooked. Camping in the forest is legal, provided you remain at least 200 feet from a trail and 0.25 mile from established camping areas such as Guyot campsite.

Maps

For a map of hiking trails, get the *Franconia-Pemigewasset Range* map, $7.95 in waterproof Tyvek, available in many stores and from the Appalachian Mountain Club, 800/262-4455, website: www.outdoors.org; the *Trail Map and Guide to the White Mountain National Forest* for $7.95 from the DeLorme Publishing Company, 800/642-0970; or map 3 in the *Map and Guide to the Appalachian Trail in New Hampshire and Vermont,* an eight-map set and guidebook available for $19.95 ($14.95 for the maps alone) from the Appalachian Trail Conference. For topographic area maps, request Bethlehem, Mount Washington, South Twin Mountain, Crawford Notch, Mount Osceola, and Mount Carrigain from USGS Map Sales, Federal Center, Box 25286, Denver, CO 80225, 888/ASK-USGS (888/275-8747), website: http://mapping.usgs.gov.

Directions

You need to shuttle two vehicles for this one-way traverse. To go north to south, as described here, leave one vehicle in the Lincoln Woods parking lot, where there is a White Mountain National Forest ranger station. It is along the Kancamagus Highway (Route 112), five miles east of the McDonald's in Lincoln and just east of the bridge where the Kancamagus crosses the east branch of the Pemigewasset River. The Wilderness Trail—also known for its initial three miles as the Lincoln Woods Trail—begins here. To reach the start of this hike, from the junction of U.S. 3 and U.S. 302 in Twin Mountain, drive east on U.S. 302 for 2.3 miles and turn right onto Zealand Road, then continue 3.5 miles to a parking lot at the end of the road. In winter, park in the lot on the north side of U.S. 302, 0.1 mile east of Zealand Road, and ski or walk up Zealand Road.

Contact

White Mountain National Forest Supervisor, 719 North Main Street, Laconia, NH 03246, 603/528-8721, TDD for the hearing impaired 603/528-8722, website: www.fs.fed.us/r9/white. Appalachian Mountain Club Pinkham Notch Visitor Center, P.O. Box 298, Gorham, NH 03581, 603/466-2721, website: www.outdoors.org. Appalachian Trail Conference, 799 Washington Street, P.O. Box 807, Harpers Ferry, WV 25425-0807, 304/535-6331, website: www.appalachiantrail.org.

60 ARETHUSA FALLS AND FRANKENSTEIN CLIFF

in Crawford Notch State Park north of Bartlett and south
of Twin Mountain

Total distance: 4.7 miles round-trip   **Hiking time:** 3 hours

Difficulty: 5   **Rating:** 10

This fairly easy loop of 4.7 miles takes in both New Hampshire's highest
waterfall and the nice view from the top of Frankenstein Cliff, and ascends a total of about 1,200 feet in elevation. From the far end of the
lower parking lot, you can pick up a connector trail to the upper lot.
There, follow the Arethusa Falls Trail for 0.1 mile and then turn left
onto the Bemis Brook Trail, which parallels the Arethusa Trail for 0.5
mile and eventually rejoins it, but is more interesting for the short cascades it passes—Bemis Falls and Coliseum Falls—as well as Fawn Pool.
After reaching the Arethusa Trail again, turn left and continue uphill
another 0.8 mile to the base of the magnificent falls, which are more
than 200 feet tall.

Many hikers return the same way, making a 2.8-mile round-trip.
But this hike crosses the stream below the falls on rocks, following the
Arethusa–Ripley Falls Trail, which crosses another stream on rocks within 0.3 mile (which could be difficult in high water). At 1.3 miles from
Arethusa Falls, bear right onto the Frankenstein Cliff Trail and continue
0.8 mile to a ledge atop the cliffs with a view south to the lower end of
Crawford Notch and the Saco Valley. Descend steeply another 1.3 miles
on the Frankenstein Cliff Trail to the parking area. See the special note
in the description of Ripley Falls (see next listing) for a loop hike incorporating both waterfalls.

User Groups

Hikers, snowshoers, and dogs. Dogs must be leashed. No wheelchair facilities. This trail is not suitable for bikes, horses, or skis. Hunting is allowed
in season.

Access and Fees

Parking and access are free.

Maps

Several maps cover this area's hiking trails, including the *Franconia-
Pemigewasset Range* map and the *Crawford Notch-Sandwich Range/
Moosilauke-Kinsman* map, each $7.95 in waterproof Tyvek, available in

many stores and from the Appalachian Mountain Club, 800/262-4455, website: www.outdoors.org; and the *Trail Map and Guide to the White Mountain National Forest* for $7.95 from the DeLorme Publishing Company, 800/642-0970. For topographic area maps, request Crawford Notch and Stairs Mountain from USGS Map Sales, Federal Center, Box 25286, Denver, CO 80225, 888/ASK-USGS (888/275-8747), website: http://mapping.usgs.gov.

Directions
From U.S. 302, 5.2 miles south of the Crawford Notch hostel, turn west onto a paved road at a sign for Arethusa Falls. You can park in the lower lot immediately on the right, or drive 0.2 mile and park at the end of the road.

Contact
White Mountain National Forest Supervisor, 719 North Main Street, Laconia, NH 03246, 603/528-8721, TDD for the hearing impaired 603/528-8722, website: www.fs.fed.us/r9/white. New Hampshire Division of Parks and Recreation, Bureau of Trails, P.O. Box 1856, Concord, NH 03302-1856, 603/271-3254.

61 RIPLEY FALLS
in Crawford Notch State Park north of Bartlett and south of Twin Mountain

Total distance: 1 mile round-trip   **Hiking time:** 0.75 hour

Difficulty: 2   **Rating:** 10

This hike in Crawford Notch State Park begins on the Ethan Pond Trail, which coincides with the Appalachian Trail. Within 100 feet of the parking lot, cross railroad tracks and climb steadily uphill on an easy, wide trail. It passes through an area of tall birch trees at 0.2 mile, and then forks; the Ethan Pond Trail/Appalachian Trail bears right, but go left onto the Ripley Falls Trail. Continue 0.3 mile to the beautiful, cascading falls, which tumble from a height of more than 100 feet and are most impressive in late spring and early summer. Return the way you came.

Special note: You can combine this hike with the hike of Arethusa Falls (see previous listing) on a loop of 4.3 miles (about three hours); shuttling vehicles is necessary. Start by hiking to Arethusa. After passing that waterfall, bear left onto the Arethusa–Ripley Falls Trail (instead of right onto the Frankenstein Cliff Trail, as that hike describes) and follow it to Ripley Falls; then descend the Ripley Falls Trail.

User Groups

Hikers, snowshoers, and dogs. No wheelchair facilities. This trail is not suitable for skis. Bikes, horses, and hunting are prohibited.

Access and Fees

Parking and access are free.

Maps

Several maps cover this area's hiking trails, including the *Franconia-Pemigewasset Range* map and the *Crawford Notch-Sandwich Range/Moosilauke-Kinsman* map, each $7.95 in waterproof Tyvek, available in many stores and from the Appalachian Mountain Club, 800/262-4455; website: www.outdoors.org; the *Trail Map and Guide to the White Mountain National Forest* for $7.95 from the DeLorme Publishing Company, 800/642-0970; and map 3 in the *Map and Guide to the Appalachian Trail in New Hampshire and Vermont,* an eight-map set and guidebook available for $19.95 ($14.95 for the maps alone) from the Appalachian Trail Conference. For a topographic area map, request Crawford Notch from USGS Map Sales, Federal Center, Box 25286, Denver, CO 80225, 888/ASK-USGS (888/275-8747), website: http://mapping.usgs.gov.

Directions

From U.S. 302, 3.9 miles south of the Crawford Notch hostel, turn south onto a paved road at a sign for Ripley Falls. Drive 0.3 mile and park at the end of the road.

Contact

White Mountain National Forest Supervisor, 719 North Main Street, Laconia, NH 03246, 603/528-8721, TDD for the hearing impaired 603/528-8722, website: www.fs.fed.us/r9/white. Appalachian Trail Conference, 799 Washington Street, P.O. Box 807, Harpers Ferry, WV 25425-0807, 304/535-6331, website: www.appalachiantrail.org. New Hampshire Division of Parks and Recreation, Bureau of Trails, P.O. Box 1856, Concord, NH 03302-1856, 603/271-3254.

62 STAIRS MOUNTAIN
in the White Mountain National Forest north of Bartlett

Total distance: 9.2 miles round-trip   **Hiking time:** 6 hours

Difficulty: 8   **Rating:** 8

This hike can be done in a day or can be split up over a couple of days with a stay at the shelter. Stairs Mountain is so named because of the Giant Stairs, a pair of steplike ledges on the 3,463-foot mountain's south end. From the cliffs atop the Giant Stairs, you get wide views of the mountains to the south. Although the Rocky Branch Trail attracts backpackers to the shelters along it, many of those people are headed for the 4,000-foot peaks farther north; you might find a little piece of solitude on Stairs Mountain. I snowshoed up Stairs once with a group of friends right after back-to-back blizzards in March—we were walking on several feet of snow, and it was an adventure just staying with the unbroken trail. This hike climbs about 2,100 feet.

From the end of Jericho Road, follow the Rocky Branch Trail north a flat two miles to the Rocky Branch shelter 1, where there is a lean-to and a tent site. Just beyond it, the Stairs Col Trail turns left (west) and ascends steadily for nearly two miles, passing below the Giant Stairs and through Stairs Col to the Davis Path. Turn right (north) on the Davis Path and follow it for a bit less than a half mile to a side path leading right for about 0.2 mile to the cliffs above the Giant Stairs. Return the way you came.

User Groups
Hikers, snowshoers, and dogs. No wheelchair facilities. The Rocky Branch Trail is fairly easy to ski as far as the Stairs Col Trail junction. Bikes and horses are prohibited. Hunting is allowed in season.

Access and Fees
No backcountry permit is needed, but a permit is required for day use or overnight parking at any White Mountain National Forest trailhead; signs indicating so are posted at most of them. Permits are available at several area stores and from the national forest at a cost of $5 for seven consecutive days or $20 per year. A $3 one-day permit can be purchased at self-service stations at national forest trailheads, but the pass is good only for the trailhead at which it's purchased. Rocky Branch Shelter 1 consists of an open lean-to and tent site, reached via a short spur trail just south of the junction of the Rocky Branch Trail and the Stairs Col Trail (just outside the boundary of the Dry River Wilderness).

Maps

For a map of hiking trails, get the *Crawford Notch-Sandwich Range/Moosilauke-Kinsman* map, $7.95 in waterproof Tyvek, available in many stores and from the Appalachian Mountain Club, 800/262-4455, website: www.outdoors.org; or the *Trail Map and Guide to the White Mountain National Forest* for $7.95 from the DeLorme Publishing Company, 800/642-0970. For topographic area maps, request North Conway West, Bartlett, and Stairs Mountain from USGS Map Sales, Federal Center, Box 25286, Denver, CO 80225, 888/ASK-USGS (888/275-8747), website: http://mapping.usgs.gov.

Directions

From the junction of Route 16 and U.S. 302 in Glen, drive west on U.S. 302 for one mile and turn right onto Jericho Road/Rocky Branch Road. Follow that road, which is paved for about a mile and then becomes gravel (passable by car), for five miles to its end, where there is parking and the Rocky Branch Trail begins.

Contact

White Mountain National Forest Supervisor, 719 North Main Street, Laconia, NH 03246, 603/528-8721, TDD for the hearing impaired 603/528-8722, website: www.fs.fed.us/r9/white. The Appalachian Mountain Club Pinkham Notch Visitor Center has up-to-date weather and trail information about the Whites; call 603/466-2725.

63 THE WILDERNESS TRAIL

in the White Mountain National Forest, east of Lincoln

Total distance: 10.8 miles round-trip   **Hiking time:** 5 hours

Difficulty: 6   **Rating:** 8

While this is a scenic hike or overnight backpacking trip along the east branch of the Pemigewasset River in any season, I've included it mainly for its popularity among cross-country skiers and snowshoers as a winter day trip. The season generally runs from December to March, and you can usually find ski tracks already laid down and a beaten path from previous snowshoers shortly after every fresh snowfall. Some visitors only go the nearly three miles out to the first bridge, over Franconia Brook, and return. This description covers the 5.4 miles out to the suspension bridge over the east branch of the Pemi at the junction with the Thoreau Falls Trail. The route is virtually flat the entire distance.

From the parking lot, take the bridge over the east branch of the

Pemigewasset River, then turn right onto the Lincoln Woods Trail—the name given in recent years to the first three miles of what was formerly known entirely as the Wilderness Trail. The trail follows an old railroad grade from logging days, paralleling the river. At 2.6 miles, the Black Pond Trail branches left, leading 0.8 mile to this quiet little pond—a worthwhile detour where you will see far fewer people than on this popular trail. At 2.8 miles you reach the Franconia Brook campsite on the left. Just beyond it, the trail crosses a footbridge over Franconia Brook, and at 2.9 miles the Franconia Brook Trail branches left. Here the Lincoln Woods Trail enters the Pemigewasset Wilderness and becomes the Wilderness Trail. Continuing straight ahead on it, you reach a junction with the Bondcliff Trail, which branches left, at 4.7 miles. Continue on the Wilderness Trail, crossing Black Brook on a bridge near an old logging railroad bridge. From there, it's just another 0.7 mile to the suspension bridge over the Pemi's east branch at the junction with the Thoreau Falls Trail. Return the way you came.

Special note: You can make a loop of about the same distance from the Lincoln Woods trailhead by going out the trail known as the East Branch Road, which begins just beyond the ranger station and follows the Pemigewasset River's east branch on its east side. This trail can become obscure and is generally not nearly as well traveled as the Lincoln Woods/Wilderness Trail. Within four miles, you'll turn left (east) onto the Cedar Brook Trail; follow it about a half mile, cross the bridge over the east branch of the Pemi River, then turn left (west) and follow the Wilderness Trail back to the trailhead. If you're looking for a bigger adventure in this part of the Pemigewasset Wilderness, see either the Twins-Bonds Traverse or the Pemigewasset Wilderness Traverse (both in this chapter).

User Groups

Hikers, dogs, skiers, and snowshoers. No wheelchair facilities. Bikes and horses are prohibited. Hunting is allowed in season.

Access and Fees

No backcountry permit is needed, but a permit is required for day use or overnight parking at any White Mountain National Forest trailhead, as indicated by signs posted at most trailheads. Permits are available at several area stores and from the national forest at a cost of $5 for seven consecutive days or $20 per year. A $3 one-day permit can be purchased at self-service stations at national forest trailheads, but the pass is good only for the trailhead at which it's purchased. The Franconia Brook campsite (16 tent platforms), operated by the White Mountain National Forest, costs $8 per person and is open only during summer and fall; it has been moved to the east side of the Pemigewasset River's east branch, almost directly across the river from its former location at the river's confluence with Franconia Brook. The campsite is reached by hiking the trail known as East Branch Road for three miles from the Lincoln Woods trailhead. On this hike, you would reach this campsite from the Wilderness Trail by crossing the bridge over the east branch of the Pemigewasset River and turning right (west) onto the Cedar Brook Trail right before the second bridge crossing of the east branch of the Pemigewasset River, then following the Cedar Brook Trail west for a little more than a half mile before turning right onto the East Branch Road, which is overgrown and may be easily overlooked. Camping in the forest is legal, provided you remain at least 200 feet from a trail and 0.25 mile from established camping areas such as Franconia Brook campsite.

Maps

For a map of hiking trails, get the *Franconia-Pemigewasset Range* map or the *Crawford Notch-Sandwich Range/Moosilauke-Kinsman* map, $7.95 each in waterproof Tyvek, available in many stores and from the Appalachian Mountain Club, 800/262-4455, website: www.outdoors.org; or the *Trail Map and Guide to the White Mountain National Forest* for $7.95 from the DeLorme Publishing Company, 800/642-0970. For a topographic area map, request the Mount Osceola map from USGS Map Sales, Federal Center, Box 25286, Denver, CO 80225, 888/ASK-USGS (888/275-8747), website: http://mapping.usgs.gov.

Directions

Drive to the large parking lot at Lincoln Woods, along the Kancamagus Highway/Route 112, five miles east of the McDonald's in Lincoln, and just east of the bridge where the Kancamagus crosses the east branch of the Pemigewasset River. The Wilderness Trail—also known for its initial three miles as the Lincoln Woods Trail—begins here.

Contact

White Mountain National Forest Supervisor, 719 North Main Street, Laconia, NH 03246, 603/528-8721, TDD for the hearing impaired 603/528-8722, website: www.fs.fed.us/r9/white.

64 MOUNT CARRIGAIN

in the White Mountain National Forest southwest of
Crawford Notch State Park

Total distance: 10 miles round-trip   **Hiking time:** 7 hours

Difficulty: 9   **Rating:** 10

The tallest peak in this corner of the Whites, 4,700-foot Carrigain offers one of the finest—and unquestionably unique—views in these mountains from the observation tower on its summit. On a clear day, the panorama takes in Mount Washington and the Presidential Range, the vast sweep of peaks across the Pemigewasset Wilderness to Franconia Ridge, Moosilauke to the west, and the peaks above Waterville Valley and the distinctive horn of Chocorua to the south. Although 10 miles round-trip, with a vertical ascent of about 3,300 feet, this hike grows steep only for the ascent to the crest of Signal Ridge, which itself has spectacular views, including one toward the cliffs of Mount Lowell to the east.

Follow the Signal Ridge Trail, which follows Whiteface Brook at first, passing picturesque cascades. At 1.7 miles from the road, the Carrigain Notch Trail branches right; continue up the Signal Ridge Trail. Reaching the open terrain of Signal Ridge at about 4.5 miles, you enjoy excellent views, particularly east across Carrigain Notch to Mount Lowell's cliffs. The ridge ascends easily to the summit observation tower. Return the same way you came.

User Groups

Hikers and dogs. No wheelchair facilities. This trail should not be attempted in winter except by hikers experienced in mountaineering and prepared for severe winter weather, and is not suitable for bikes, horses, or skis. Hunting is allowed in season.

Access and Fees

No backcountry permit is needed, but a permit is required for day use or overnight parking at any White Mountain National Forest trailhead, as indicated by signs posted at most trailheads. Permits are available at several area stores and from the national forest at a cost of $5 for seven consecutive days or $20 per year. A $3 one-day permit can be purchased at self-service stations at national forest trailheads, but the pass is good only for the trailhead at which it's purchased. Sawyer River Road (Fire Road 34) is usually closed to vehicles once the snow arrives.

Maps

For a map of hiking trails, get the *Franconia–Pemigewasset Range* map or the *Crawford Notch–Sandwich Range/Moosilauke–Kinsman* map, $7.95 each in waterproof Tyvek, available in many stores and from the Appalachian Mountain Club, 800/262-4455, website: www.outdoors.org. Or get the *Trail Map and Guide to the White Mountain National Forest* for $7.95 from the DeLorme Publishing Company, 800/642-0970. For topographic area maps, request Mount Carrigain and Bartlett from USGS Map Sales, Federal Center, Box 25286, Denver, CO 80225, 888/ASK-USGS (888/275-8747), website: http://mapping.usgs.gov.

Directions

From U.S. 302, 10.7 miles south of the visitor information center in Crawford Notch and 10.3 miles north of the junction of U.S. 302 and Route 16 in Glen, turn south onto Sawyer River Road/Fire Road 34. Follow it for two miles to the Signal Ridge Trail on the right, just before a bridge over Whiteface Brook. There is parking on the left, just past the brook.

Contact

White Mountain National Forest Supervisor, 719 North Main Street, Laconia, NH 03246, 603/528-8721, TDD for the hearing impaired 603/528-8722, website: www.fs.fed.us/r9/white.

65 MOUNT STANTON

in the White Mountain National Forest between Bartlett and Glen

Total distance: 3 miles round-trip   **Hiking time:** 2 hours

Difficulty: 4   **Rating:** 8

At just 1,716 feet above sea level, Mount Stanton offers spectacular views and the feel of a big mountain for relatively little work—just three miles and 1,000 feet of climbing. These factors make it a good hike for children or for a day when clouds descend upon the big mountains. The trail does have a few moderately steep stretches, but they are neither sustained nor very difficult; fit people could easily run up the path for a quick workout. Near Mount Stanton's summit, you will see open ledges to the left (south) worth exploring. Out on the ledges, you will find yourself on the brink of a 500-foot sheer drop, atop a cliff called White's Ledge (a wonderful technical rock climb for those with experience). You might see rock climbers reaching the top; be careful not to kick stones over the edge. The ledges offer broad views of the Saco River Valley. Follow the same route back.

User Groups

Hikers, snowshoers, and dogs. No wheelchair facilities. This trail is not suitable for bikes, horses, or skis. Hunting is allowed in season.

Access and Fees

Parking and access are free.

Maps

For a map of hiking trails, get the *Crawford Notch–Sandwich Range/Moosilauke–Kinsman* map, $7.95 in waterproof Tyvek, available in many stores and from the Appalachian Mountain Club, 800/262-4455, website: www.outdoors.org; or the *Trail Map and Guide to the White Mountain National Forest* for $7.95 from the DeLorme Publishing Company, 800/642-0970. For a topographic area map, request North Conway West from USGS Map Sales, Federal Center, Box 25286, Denver, CO 80225, 888/ASK-USGS (888/275-8747), website: http://mapping.usgs.gov.

Directions

From junction of U.S. 302 and Highway 16 in Glen, drive on U.S. 302 west toward Bartlett for about two miles. Just before the covered bridge, turn right onto Covered Bridge Lane (there is a small sign high on a tree). Follow the paved road 0.2 mile and bear right onto Oak Ridge Drive. Almost immediately, make a sharp right turn onto Hemlock Drive, which is dirt for a short distance before becoming paved, and continue for 0.3 mile. Park at a trail sign on the road. The trail begins just uphill on the left side of the driveway near the trail sign.

Contact

White Mountain National Forest Supervisor, 719 North Main Street, Laconia, NH 03246, 603/528-8721, TDD for the hearing impaired 603/528-8722, website: www.fs.fed.us/r9/white.

66 MOUNT MOOSILAUKE: BEAVER BROOK TRAIL

west of North Woodstock

Total distance: 7.8 miles round-trip **Hiking time:** 5.5 hours

Difficulty: 9 **Rating:** 10

A number of years ago, a friend invited me to hike Mount Moosilauke with a group of people—my first of many trips up this 4,802-foot massif in the southwest corner of the White Mountains. We went up the Beaver Brook Trail, past its numerous cascades and on to a summit with an extensive alpine area and views that span much of the White Mountains and extend west to the Green Mountains in Vermont and New York's Adirondacks. Moosilauke is one of the most popular peaks in the Whites, and the Beaver Brook Trail is a popular route up the mountain. But it is steep and rugged. This hike climbs about 3,000 feet.

The Beaver Brook Trail, which coincides with the Appalachian Trail, leaves Route 112 and soon begins the steep, sustained climb up the narrow drainage of Beaver Brook. At 0.3 mile, you may notice a side path that formerly led a short distance to the Dartmouth Outing Club's Beaver Brook lean-to. (The lean-to has been torn down and a new DOC shelter built farther up the trail, about 1.5 miles from the trailhead and less than a half mile from the Asquam-Ridge Trail junction.) Beyond there, the Beaver Brook Trail levels somewhat, and at 1.9 miles the Asquam-Ridge Trail branches left. The Beaver Brook Trail/Appalachian Trail then ascends over the wooded shoulder known as Mount Blue and finally emerges above the trees for the nearly flat final 0.2 mile to the summit. Visible to the northeast are Franconia Ridge and, much farther to the northeast, the Presidential Range. Hike back the way you came.

Special note: By shuttling two vehicles to the trailheads, this hike can be combined with the Glencliff Trail (see next listing) for a traverse of Moosilauke via the Appalachian Trail. Hike up the Beaver Brook Trail and descend the Glencliff.

User Groups

Hikers and dogs. No wheelchair facilities. This trail should not be attempted in winter except by hikers experienced in mountaineering and prepared for severe winter weather, and is not suitable for skis. Bikes, horses, and hunting are prohibited.

Access and Fees

No backcountry permit is needed, but a permit is required for day use or overnight parking at any White Mountain National Forest trailhead, as indicated by signs posted at most trailheads. Permits are available at several area stores and from the national forest at a cost of $5 for seven consecutive days or $20 per year. A $3 one-day permit can be purchased at self-service stations at national forest trailheads, but the pass is good only for the trailhead at which it's purchased.

Maps

Several maps cover this area's hiking trails, including the *Crawford Notch-Sandwich Range/Moosilauke-Kinsman* map, $7.95 in waterproof Tyvek, available in many stores and from the Appalachian Mountain Club, 800/262-4455, website: www.outdoors.org; the *Trail Map and Guide to the White Mountain National Forest* for $7.95 from the DeLorme Publishing Company, 800/642-0970; and map 3 in the *Map and Guide to the Appalachian Trail in New Hampshire and Vermont,* an eight-map set and guidebook available for $19.95 ($14.95 for the maps alone) from the Appalachian Trail Conference. For a topographic area map, request Mount Moosilauke from USGS Map Sales, Federal Center, Box 25286, Denver, CO 80225, 888/ASK-USGS (888/275-8747), website: http://mapping.usgs.gov.

Directions

The Beaver Brook Trail, which coincides with the Appalachian Trail, begins from a parking lot along Route 112 at the height of land in Kinsman Notch, 6.2 miles west of North Woodstock and 4.8 miles south of the junction of Routes 112 and 116.

Contact

White Mountain National Forest Supervisor, 719 North Main Street, Laconia, NH 03246, 603/528-8721, TDD for the hearing impaired 603/528-8722, website: www.fs.fed.us/r9/white. Appalachian Trail Conference, 799 Washington Street, P.O. Box 807, Harpers Ferry, WV 25425-0807, 304/535-6331, website: www.appalachiantrail.org.

67 MOUNT MOOSILAUKE: GLENCLIFF TRAIL
north of Warren

Total distance: 7.8 miles round-trip   **Hiking time:** 5.5 hours

Difficulty: 9   **Rating:** 10

The Glencliff Trail, a section of the white-blazed Appalachian Trail, offers a difficult and very scenic route to the 4,802-foot summit of Mount

Moosilauke, where an extensive alpine area offers panoramic views stretching across much of the White Mountains and west to Vermont's Green Mountains and New York's Adirondacks. This hike gains about 3,300 feet in elevation.

From the parking lot, follow the white blazes past a gate and along old farm roads through pastures before entering the woods at 0.4 mile, where a side path leads left to a Dartmouth College cabin (not open to the public), and the Hurricane Trail diverges right. The Glencliff Trail ascends steadily but at a moderate grade for the next two miles, then grows steeper as it rises into the mountain's krummholtz, the scrub conifers that grow in the subalpine zone. At three miles the trail hits the old carriage road on Moosilauke. A spur path leads right (south) to Moosilauke's craggy south peak just 0.2 mile distant. This hike turns left (north) and follows the wide carriage road over easy ground along the open ridge—with great views—ascending gently to the summit at 3.9 miles. Return the way you came. For a full traverse of Moosilauke via the Appalachian Trail, see the special note in the description of the previous hike.

User Groups

Hikers and dogs. No wheelchair facilities. This trail should not be attempted in winter except by hikers experienced in mountaineering and prepared for severe winter weather, and is not suitable for skis. Bikes, horses, and hunting are prohibited.

Access and Fees

No backcountry permit is needed, but a permit is required for day use or overnight parking at any White Mountain National Forest trailhead, as indicated by signs posted at most trailheads. Permits are available at several area stores and from the national forest at a cost of $5 for seven consecutive days or $20 per year. A $3 one-day permit can be purchased at self-service stations at national forest trailheads, but the pass is good only for the trailhead at which it's purchased.

Maps

Several maps cover this area's hiking trails, including the *Crawford Notch–Sandwich Range/Moosilauke-Kinsman* map, $7.95 in waterproof Tyvek, available in many stores and from the Appalachian Mountain Club, 800/262-4455, website: www.outdoors.org; the *Trail Map and Guide to the White Mountain National Forest* for $7.95 from the DeLorme Publishing Company, 800/642-0970; and map 3 in the *Map and Guide to the Appalachian Trail in New Hampshire and Vermont,* an eight-map set and guidebook available for $19.95 ($14.95 for the maps alone) from the Appalachian Trail Conference. For a topographic area map, request Mount Moosilauke from USGS Map Sales, Federal Center, Box 25286, Denver, CO 80225, 888/ASK-USGS (888/275-8747), website: http://mapping.usgs.gov.

Directions
From Route 25 in Glencliff Village, turn onto High Street, just past the sign for the Glencliff Home for the Elderly. Drive 1.2 miles to a dirt parking lot on the right.

Contact
White Mountain National Forest Supervisor, 719 North Main Street, Laconia, NH 03246, 603/528-8721, TDD for the hearing impaired 603/528-8722, website: www.fs.fed.us/r9/white. Appalachian Trail Conference, 799 Washington Street, P.O. Box 807, Harpers Ferry, WV 25425-0807, 304/535-6331, website: www.appalachiantrail.org.

68 MOUNT OSCEOLA
in the White Mountain National Forest, north of Waterville Valley and east of Lincoln

Total distance: 6.4 miles round-trip   **Hiking time:** 4 hours

Difficulty: 8   **Rating:** 9

One of the easiest 4,000-footers in New Hampshire to hike—with a vertical ascent of only about 2,000 feet—Osceola's summit ledges, rising 4,340 feet above sea level, give a sweeping view to the south and southeast of Waterville Valley and Mount Tripyramid, and northeast to the Pemigewasset Wilderness and the Presidential Range.

From the parking lot, follow the Mount Osceola Trail as it ascends at a moderate angle through numerous switchbacks and reaches the summit ledges at 3.2 miles. The trail continues one more mile to reach 4,156-foot East Osceola, which will add two miles and approximately 1.5 hours to this hike's distance and time. Hike back along the same route.

User Groups
Hikers and dogs. No wheelchair facilities. This trail should not be attempted in winter except by hikers experienced in mountaineering and prepared for severe winter weather, and is not suitable for bikes, horses, or skis. Hunting is allowed in season.

at the summit of Mount Osceola, overlooking Waterville Valley

Access and Fees

No backcountry permit is needed, but a permit is required for day use or overnight parking at any White Mountain National Forest trailhead; signs indicating so are posted at most of them. Permits are available at several area stores and from the national forest at a cost of $5 for seven consecutive days or $20 per year. A $3 one-day permit can be purchased at self-service stations at national forest trailheads, but the pass is good only for the trailhead at which it's purchased. Tripoli Road is generally not maintained in winter.

Maps

For a contour map of trails, get the *Franconia-Pemigewasset Range* map or the *Crawford Notch-Sandwich Range/Moosilauke-Kinsman* map, $7.95 each in waterproof Tyvek, available in many stores and from the Appalachian Mountain Club, 800/262-4455, website: www.outdoors.org; the *Trail Map and Guide to the White Mountain National Forest* for $7.95 from the DeLorme Publishing Company, 800/642-0970; or the map of the national forest, available by sending a check payable to White Mountain National Forest for $6 to the forest's main office. For topographic area maps, request Mount Osceola and Waterville Valley from USGS Map Sales, Federal Center, Box 25286, Denver, CO 80225, 888/ASK-USGS (888/275-8747), website: http://mapping.usgs.gov.

Directions

From I-93, take Exit 31 for Tripoli Road. Drive east on Tripoli Road for seven miles to a parking lot on the left for the Mount Osceola Trail.

Contact

White Mountain National Forest Supervisor, 719 North Main Street, Laconia, NH 03246, 603/528-8721, TDD for the hearing impaired 603/528-8722, website: www.fs.fed.us/r9/white.

69 GREELEY PONDS NORTH

in the White Mountain National Forest on the Kancamagus Highway/Route 112 between Lincoln and Conway

Total distance: 4.4 miles round-trip   **Hiking time:** 2 hours

Difficulty: 4   **Rating:** 8

This fairly flat 4.4-mile hike offers the shortest and easiest route to the two scenic Greeley Ponds, ascending just a few hundred feet. It's a nice hike in summer, better in the fall, but arguably best on snowshoes or cross-country skis in winter. The ski trail begins at a separate parking area but eventually merges with the hiking trail before reaching the first pond. From the parking area, follow the Greeley Ponds Trail as it winds southward through a mixed deciduous and conifer forest. At 1.3 miles, the Mount Osceola Trail diverges to the right (east), soon to climb steeply up East Osceola and Osceola, a worthwhile side trip. This hike continues south on the Greeley Ponds Trail for nearly another half mile to the upper Greeley Pond, which sits in a scenic basin below the dramatic cliffs of East Osceola. Continuing another half mile on the trail brings you to the lower pond. Return the way you came.

User Groups

Hikers, dogs, skiers, and snowshoers. No wheelchair facilities. This trail is not suitable for bikes or horses. Hunting is allowed in season.

Access and Fees

No backcountry permit is needed, but a permit is required for day use or overnight parking at any White Mountain National Forest trailhead, as indicated by signs posted at most trailheads. Permits are available at several area stores and from the national forest at a cost of $5 for seven consecutive days or $20 per year. A $3 one-day permit can be purchased at self-service stations at national forest trailheads, but the pass is good only for the trailhead at which it's purchased. Camping and fires are prohibited within the Greeley Ponds Scenic Area, the boundary of which is marked by a sign along the trail.

Maps

For a contour map of trails, get the *Franconia-Pemigewasset Range* map or the *Crawford Notch-Sandwich Range/ Moosilauke-Kinsman* map, $7.95 each in waterproof Tyvek, available in many stores and from the Appalachian Mountain Club, 800/262-4455, website: www.outdoors.org; or the *Trail Map and Guide to the White Mountain National For-*

the beach on the northernmost of the Greeley Ponds

est for $7.95 from the DeLorme Publishing Company, 800/642-0970. For a topographic area map, request the Mount Osceola, Mount Carrigain, Mount Tripyramid, and Waterville Valley maps from USGS Map Sales, Federal Center, Box 25286, Denver, CO 80225, 888/ASK-USGS (888/275-8747), website: http://mapping.usgs.gov.

Directions

The hike begins at a small parking area along the Kancamagus Highway/ Route 112, 9.9 miles east of the McDonald's on Route 112 in Lincoln (Exit 32 off I-93), 3.4 miles west of the sign at Kancamagus Pass and 25.6 miles west of the junction of Routes 112 and 16 in Conway. The ski trail begins at a parking lot 0.2 mile farther east.

Contact

White Mountain National Forest Supervisor, 719 North Main Street, Laconia, NH 03246, 603/528-8721, TDD for the hearing impaired 603/528-8722, website: www.fs.fed.us/r9/white.

70 GREELEY PONDS SOUTH

in the White Mountain National Forest in Waterville Valley

Total distance: 7.4 miles round-trip   **Hiking time:** 4 hours

Difficulty: 7   **Rating:** 8

This 7.4-mile hike offers a route from popular Waterville Valley to the two scenic Greeley Ponds that is longer and climbs a little more than the Greeley Ponds North hike. The total vertical ascent on this hike is about 700 feet. I love doing this trail on cross-country skis in winter. The winter and summer parking area is at the start of the Livermore Trail, a former logging road that in winter is groomed and tracked for skating and diagonal skiing by the local ski touring center, although no touring center pass is required because it's a national forest trail.

From the parking lot, follow the wide road for 0.25 mile, then turn left at a sign onto the Greeley Ponds Trail, a fairly wide hiking trail that in winter is not groomed but is often packed and tracked by snowshoers and skiers. Flat at first, the trail begins to rise gradually as it parallels the Mad River, which up here is just a rambunctious stream. The trail grows fairly steep for the last 0.1 mile to the lower Greeley Pond—the one spot where some skiers may want to remove their skis—which can be reached by a short spur path. At one point the ski and hiking trails diverge, with the ski trail following the Mad River's right bank to the lower pond and the hiking trail crossing over the river to its left bank. At the lower pond, both trails cross to the pond's left shoreline, with the ski trail hugging the shore and the hiking trail running parallel a bit farther back into the woods. The trails lead all the way to the upper pond, below the cliffs of East Osceola. Return the way you came.

User Groups

Hikers, dogs, skiers, and snowshoers. No wheelchair facilities. This trail is not suitable for bikes or horses. Hunting is allowed in season.

Access and Fees

No backcountry permit is needed, but a permit is required for day use or overnight parking at any White Mountain National Forest trailhead, as indicated by signs posted at most trailheads. Permits are available at several area stores and from the national forest at a cost of $5 for seven consecutive days or $20 per year. A $3 one-day permit can be purchased at self-service stations at national forest trailheads, but the pass is good only for the trailhead at which it's purchased. Camping and fires are prohibited within the Greeley Ponds Scenic Area, the boundary of which is marked by a sign along the trail.

Maps

For a contour map of trails, get the *Franconia–Pemigewasset Range* map or the *Crawford Notch–Sandwich Range/Moosilauke–Kinsman* map, $7.95 each in waterproof Tyvek, available in many stores and from the Appalachian Mountain Club, 800/262-4455, website: www.outdoors.org; or the *Trail Map and Guide to the White Mountain National Forest* for $7.95 from the DeLorme Publishing Company, 800/642-0970. For a topographic area map, request the Mount Osceola, Mount Carrigain, Mount Tripyramid, and Waterville Valley maps from USGS Map Sales, Federal Center, Box 25286, Denver, CO 80225, 888/ASK-USGS (888/275-8747), website: http://mapping.usgs.gov.

Directions

From I-93 in Campton, take Exit 28 onto Route 49 east. Drive about 11.4 miles into Waterville Valley and turn right onto Valley Road, which is still Route 49. Just 0.4 mile farther, turn left onto West Branch Road, in front of the Osceola Library. Drive another 0.7 mile and turn right (before the bridge) into the parking lot at the start of the Livermore Trail.

Contact

White Mountain National Forest Supervisor, 719 North Main Street, Laconia, NH 03246, 603/528-8721, TDD for the hearing impaired 603/528-8722, website: www.fs.fed.us/r9/white.

71 CATHEDRAL LEDGE

in Echo Lake State Park west of North Conway

Total distance: 0.1 mile round-trip   **Hiking time:** 0.25 hour

Difficulty: 1   **Rating:** 8

This is less a hike than an easy, five-minute walk to the top of Cathedral Ledge, a sheer, 400-foot cliff with a breaktaking view of the Mount Washington Valley. Popular with tourists when the access road is open from late spring to autumn, the lookout is protected by a fence to keep visitors from wandering too close to the brink. Cathedral is one of New Hampshire's most popular rock-climbing areas, so you're likely to see climbers pulling over the top of the cliff right in front of you. Obviously, you should not throw anything off the cliff, given the likelihood of there being people below. From the circle, follow a wide, obvious path to the east, a short distance through the woods to the top of the cliff. Return the same way.

User Groups

Hikers, bikers, dogs, skiers, and snowshoers. No wheelchair facilities. Skiers and snowshoers must begin at the base of the access road, which adds about one mile to the round-trip mileage listed above and is a steep climb. Dogs must be leashed. Hunting is allowed in season.

Access and Fees

Parking and access are free. The access road is not maintained in winter and is blocked by a gate.

Maps

Although no map is necessary for this hike, it is shown on the *Crawford Notch–Sandwich Range/Moosilauke–Kinsman* map, $7.95 in waterproof Tyvek, available in many stores and from the Appalachian Mountain Club, 800/262-4455, website: www.outdoors.org. For a topographic map of the area, request North Conway West from USGS Map Sales, Federal Center, Box 25286, Denver, CO 80225, 888/ASK-USGS (888/275-8747), website: http://mapping.usgs.gov.

Directions

From Route 16 in North Conway in front of the Eastern Slope Inn, turn west at traffic lights onto River Road. Continue 1.5 miles and turn left at a sign for Cathedral Ledge. Follow the road for more than a mile to its end at a circle near the clifftop.

Contact

New Hampshire Division of Parks and Recreation, P.O. Box 1856, 172 Pembroke Road, Concord, NH 03302, 603/271-3556, camping reservations 603/271-3628, website: www.nhstateparks.org.

72 THE MOATS

in the White Mountain National Forest west of North Conway

Total distance: 9.4 miles round-trip   **Hiking time:** 6 hours

Difficulty: 9   **Rating:** 9

The 9.4-mile traverse of the Moats is one of the most scenic hikes that you can make in the White Mountains without going up a big peak. The highest of the three peaks, North Moat Mountain, is just 3,196 feet; the Middle and South peaks are both under 3,000 feet. Yet all three summits, and several open ledges along the ridge connecting them, offer broad views of the Saco Valley. From North Moat on a clear day, you can see Mount Washington almost due north. The full traverse of the Moats entails more than 3,000 feet of climbing. If you do not have two vehicles to shuttle, then park at the northern terminus of the Moat Mountain Trail and hike up North Moat Mountain, which is an 8.4-mile round-trip that gains nearly 2,700 feet in elevation. You could also hike a loop to North Moat on the Moat Mountain Trail and Red Ridge Trail.

To hike the full traverse—which I strongly recommend—from south to north, pick up the Moat Mountain Trail on Dugway Road. As it also does at its northern end, the trail starts out here as an old woods road, eventually narrowing to a footpath. Watch for arrows marking the trail's direction at junctions. After starting out as an easy, flat walk, the trail begins climbing steadily, though never too steeply, up South Moat Mountain, reaching its 2,749-foot summit at 2.3 miles. It dips a bit, reentering the woods, but generally follows the gentle ridge top to the 2,805-foot summit of Middle Moat, just 0.6 mile farther. Behind the Middle, the hiking gets a little more strenuous—though not very difficult—dropping somewhat, passing a junction with the Red Ridge Trail at 3.8 miles from the trailhead, then climbing through dense forest and up rocky ledges to the summit of North Moat, at five miles. The descent is somewhat tiring on the knees— especially if the rock slabs along the trail are slick with water. Stay on the Moat Mountain Trail, passing junctions with the Attitash Trail at 6.8 miles and the other end of the Red Ridge Trail at 8.1 miles, and reaching the northern trailhead at 9.2 miles.

User Groups

Hikers, snowshoers, and dogs. No wheelchair facilities. This trail is not suitable for bikes, skis, or horses. Hunting is allowed in season.

Access and Fees

No backcountry permit is needed, but a permit is required for day use or overnight parking at any White Mountain National Forest trailhead, as indicated by signs posted at most trailheads. Permits are available at several area stores and from the national forest at a cost of $5 for seven consecutive days or $20 per year. A $3 one-day permit can be purchased at self-service stations at national forest trailheads, but the pass is good only for the trailhead at which it's purchased.

Maps

For a map of hiking trails in this area, obtain the *Crawford Notch–Sandwich Range/Moosilauke–Kinsman* map, $7.95 in waterproof Tyvek, available in many stores and from the Appalachian Mountain Club, 800/262-4455, website: www.outdoors.org; or the *Trail Map and Guide to the White Mountain National Forest* for $7.95 from the DeLorme Publishing Company, 800/642-0970. For a topographic area map, request North Conway West from USGS Map Sales, Federal Center, Box 25286, Denver, CO 80225, 888/ASK-USGS (888/275-8747), website: http://mapping.usgs.gov.

Directions

From Route 16 in North Conway, turn west at the traffic lights in front of the Eastern Slope Inn onto River Road. Continue about 2.2 miles to a large parking area on the left for Diana's Baths. The trail begins on the west side of the parking area. To hike the complete traverse south to north, as described here, leave one vehicle here and drive a second vehicle back out, turning right (south) onto West Side Road. Continue for about 0.9 mile, taking Old West Side Road (at the three-way intersection with the road to Cathedral Ledge), which rejoins West Side Road. Turning right (south) onto West Side Road, continue for about 4.5 miles. Turn right onto Passaconaway Road (which becomes Dugway Road), and drive another 2.5 miles to roadside parking and the Moat Mountain Trail's southern end, on the right.

Contact

White Mountain National Forest Supervisor, 719 North Main Street, Laconia, NH 03246, 603/528-8721, TDD for the hearing impaired 603/528-8722, website: www.fs.fed.us/r9/white.

73 SABBADAY FALLS

in the White Mountain National Forest on the Kancamagus Highway/Route 112 between Lincoln and Conway

Total distance: 0.8 mile round-trip   **Hiking time:** 0.75 hour

Difficulty: 1   **Rating:** 10

The early explorers of the Passaconaway Valley reached Sabbaday Falls on a Sunday, and thereafter the spectacular falls became a popular destination on the Sabbath. The falls drop twice through a narrow gorge so perfect in its geometry it seems the work of engineers. The gorge was formed from the gouging action of rocks and sand released by glacial melt-off 10,000 years ago. Below the gorge, Sabbaday Brook settles quietly, if briefly, in a clear pool. This easy hike is a great one for young children.

From the parking area, follow the wide gravel and dirt Sabbaday Brook Trail, which parallels the rocky brook. The trail ascends very little over its first 0.3 mile to where a side path leads left. This path loops past the lower pool and above the gorge and both falls before rejoining the Sabbaday Brook Trail. Turn right to return to the parking area.

User Groups

Hikers, dogs, skiers, and snowshoers. No wheelchair facilities. This trail is not suitable for bikes or horses. Hunting is allowed in season.

Access and Fees

No backcountry permit is needed, but a permit is required for day use or overnight parking at any White Mountain National Forest trailhead, as indicated by signs posted at most trailheads. Permits are available at several area stores and from the national forest at a cost of $5 for seven consecutive days or $20 per year. A $3 one-day permit can be purchased at self-service stations at national forest trailheads, but the pass is good only for the trailhead at which it's purchased.

Maps

For a contour map of trails, get the *Franconia-Pemigewasset Range* map or the *Crawford Notch-Sandwich Range/Moosilauke-Kinsman* map, $7.95 each in waterproof Tyvek, available in many stores and from the Appalachian Mountain Club, 800/262-4455, website: www.outdoors.org; or the *Trail Map and Guide to the White Mountain National Forest* for $7.95 from the DeLorme Publishing Company, 800/642-0970. For a topographic area map, request Mount Tripyramid from USGS Map Sales, Federal Center, Box 25286, Denver, CO 80225, 888/ASK-USGS (888/275-8747), website: http://mapping.usgs.gov.

Directions

The hike begins at the Sabbaday Falls parking area along the Kancamagus Highway/Route 112, 19.9 miles east of the McDonald's on Route 112 in Lincoln, 6.6 miles east of the sign at Kancamagus Pass and 15.6 miles west of the junction of Routes 112 and 16 in Conway.

Contact

White Mountain National Forest Supervisor, 719 North Main Street, Laconia, NH 03246, 603/528-8721, TDD for the hearing impaired 603/528-8722, website: www.fs.fed.us/r9/white.

74 MOUNT TRIPYRAMID

in the White Mountain National Forest east of Waterville Valley

Total distance: 11 miles round-trip   **Hiking time:** 7 hours

Difficulty: 10   **Rating:** 9

Tripyramid's three wooded summits offer little in the way of compelling views. But two friends and I spent a wonderful day mountain biking to the hiking trail loop and scrambling up and down Tripyramid's two rockslides. Although you can hike this entire route, I suggest mountain biking the Livermore Trail, an old logging road, then stashing your bikes in the woods and hiking the Mount Tripyramid Trail. And two of the three summits along this route, the North and Middle Peaks, are both official 4,000-footers. This hike ascends about 3,000 feet over its length and involves some exposed scrambling, especially going up the north slide of Tripyramid; it is not for the faint of heart or anyone not in good shape.

From the parking area, walk around the gate onto Livermore Road (also called the Livermore Trail), a rough road ascending gradually for 2.6 miles to the south end of the Tripyramid Trail, which loops over the mountain. If you have bikes, leave them here at the south end of the loop and walk another mile up the Livermore Trail, then turn right onto the Mount Tripyramid Trail at its north end. The trail ascends the north slide, which is more exposed and steeper than the south slide (making this

a view from near the summit of North Tripyramid

the preferred direction of travel on the loop) and dangerous when wet or icy. At 1.2 miles, the trail reaches the North Peak and true summit at 4,140 feet. There are limited views. Continue on the narrow path, passing a junction with the Sabbaday Brook Trail 0.5 mile past the North Peak, and reaching Middle Peak (4,110 feet) 0.3 mile farther. A pair of outlooks just off the trail offer decent views. The trail continues to the South Peak (4,090 feet), which is wooded. Just beyond that peak, bear right where the Sleeper Trail branches left and descend the steep south slide, which has lots of loose rock. The trail enters the woods again and follows Slide Brook past nice pools to the Livermore Trail, 2.5 miles from South Peak. Turn left and hike (or bike) the 2.6 miles back to the parking area.

User Groups
Hikers and dogs on the Mount Tripyramid Trail; hikers, bikers, dogs, and skiers on the Livermore Trail. No wheelchair facilities. The Mount Tripyramid Trail should not be attempted in winter except by hikers experienced in mountaineering and prepared for severe winter weather. It is not suitable for horses. Hunting is allowed in season.

Access and Fees
No backcountry permit is needed, but a permit is required for day use or overnight parking at any White Mountain National Forest trailhead, as indicated by signs posted at most trailheads. Permits are available at several area stores and from the national forest at a cost of $5 for seven consecutive days or $20 per year. A $3 one-day permit can be purchased at self-service stations at national forest trailheads, but the pass is good only for the trailhead at which it's purchased. In the winter months, you can ski or snowshoe up Livermore Trail, which is groomed and tracked for skating or diagonal skiing, without having to pay the trail fee for the cross-country ski touring center in Waterville Valley because Livermore Trail is within the national forest.

Maps
For a contour map of trails, get the *Franconia–Pemigewasset Range* map or the *Crawford Notch–Sandwich Range/Moosilauke–Kinsman* map, $7.95 each in waterproof Tyvek, available in many stores and from the Appalachian Mountain Club, 800/262-4455, website: www.outdoors.org; or the *Trail Map and Guide to the White Mountain National Forest* for $7.95 from the DeLorme Publishing Company, 800/642-0970. For topographic area maps, request Mount Tripyramid and Waterville Valley from USGS Map Sales, Federal Center, Box 25286, Denver, CO 80225, 888/ASK-USGS (888/275-8747), website: http://mapping.usgs.gov.

Directions

From I-93 in Campton, take Exit 28 onto Route 49 east. Drive about 11.4 miles into Waterville Valley and turn right onto Valley Road, which is still Route 49 east. Just 0.4 mile farther, turn left onto West Branch Road, in front of the Osceola Library. Drive another 0.7 mile and turn right (before the bridge) into the parking lot at the start of the Livermore Trail (also called the Livermore Road).

Contact

White Mountain National Forest Supervisor, 719 North Main Street, Laconia, NH 03246, 603/528-8721, TDD for the hearing impaired 603/528-8722, website: www.fs.fed.us/r9/white.

75 WELCH AND DICKEY

in the White Mountain National Forest southwest of Waterville Valley

Total distance: 4.5 miles round-trip   **Hiking time:** 3.5 hours

Difficulty: 6   **Rating:** 10

My mom, an avid hiker, and I hiked this 4.5-mile loop over Welch (2,605 feet) and Dickey (2,736 feet) at the height of fall foliage color on a day when the higher mountains were swathed in clouds. Yet these lower summits remained clear, giving us colorful views from the many open ledges on this loop hike. Relatively easy, with just a few brief, steep stretches, it's a good hike for children, entailing only about 1,700 feet of uphill over 4.5 miles.

From the parking area, you can do the loop in either direction, but I recommend heading up the Welch Mountain Trail (hiking counterclockwise). Within a mile, the trail emerges onto open ledges just below the summit of Welch Mountain, with a wide view across the Mad River Valley to Sandwich Mountain. The trail turns left and ascends another mile to the summit, with broad views in every direction, including Dickey Mountain to the north. Continuing on the trail, you drop steeply into a shallow saddle, then climb up onto Dickey, 0.5 mile from Welch. Watch for a sign pointing to nearby ledges, where there is a good view toward Franconia Notch. From Dickey's summit, follow an arrow onto an obvious trail north, which soon descends steeply to slab ledges above the cliffs of Dickey Mountain, overlooking a beautiful, narrow valley between Welch and Dickey that blazes with color during the peak of foliage. The Dickey Mountain Trail continues descending the ridge, reentering the woods, then reaching the parking area, two miles from Dickey's summit.

User Groups

Hikers, snowshoers, and dogs. No wheelchair facilities. This trail is not suitable for bikes, horses, or skis. Hunting is allowed in season.

Access and Fees

No backcountry permit is needed, but a permit is required for day use or overnight parking at any White Mountain National Forest trailhead, as indicated by signs posted at most trailheads. Permits are available at several area stores and from the national forest at a cost of $5 for seven consecutive days or $20 per year. A $3 one-day permit can be purchased at self-service stations at national forest trailheads, but the pass is good only for the trailhead at which it's purchased.

Maps

For a contour map of trails, get the *Franconia-Pemigewasset Range* map or the *Crawford Notch-Sandwich Range/Moosilauke-Kinsman* map, $7.95 each in waterproof Tyvek, available in many stores and from the Appalachian Mountain Club, 800/262-4455, website: www.outdoors.org; or the *Trail Map and Guide to the White Mountain National Forest* for $7.95 from the DeLorme Publishing Company, 800/642-0970. For a topographic area map, request Waterville Valley from USGS Map Sales, Federal Center, Box 25286, Denver, CO 80225, 888/ASK-USGS (888/275-8747), website: http://mapping.usgs.gov.

Directions

From I-93 in Campton, take Exit 28 onto Route 49 north, toward Waterville Valley. After passing through the traffic lights in Campton, drive another 4.4 miles on Route 49, then turn left onto Upper Mad River Road, immediately crossing the Mad River on Six Mile Bridge. Continue 0.7 mile from Route 49, then turn right onto Orris Road at a small sign reading Welch Mountain Trail. Drive another 0.7 mile to a parking area on the right, at the trailhead.

Contact

White Mountain National Forest Supervisor, 719 North Main Street, Laconia, NH 03246, 603/528-8721, TDD for the hearing impaired 603/528-8722, website: www.fs.fed.us/r9/white.

76 SANDWICH MOUNTAIN
in the White Mountain National Forest in Waterville Valley

Total distance: 8.3 miles round-trip   **Hiking time:** 5.5 hours
Difficulty: 9   **Rating:** 9

At 3,993 feet, Sandwich Mountain is a tad short to attract the same attention among hikers as many of the 4,000-footers in the White Mountains. But from the small area of rocks jutting just above the forest at its summit, you get a wide view from the northwest to the east of most of the White Mountains—certainly more peaks are visible from here than from many of the smaller 4,000-footers in the Whites. I once caught an amazing sunset up here on a warm and calm autumn day at the peak of fall foliage. The elevation gained on this hike is about 2,500 feet.

The Drake's Brook Trail starts at the north end of the trailhead parking lot, the Sandwich Mountain Trail at the south end. This 8.3-mile loop can be done in either direction—both trails have steep sections that can be difficult to descend, particularly when wet. If the foliage is peaking, I would recommend deciding your direction of travel based on making sure you are on the lower half of the Sandwich Mountain Trail when the sun is high, to enhance the color in the forest seen from open ledges along that trail; by midafternoon, the mountain shadow will fall over those views, dulling the color show. I will describe the hike clockwise.

Follow the old logging road of the Drake's Brook Trail for 0.4 mile to where the ski and bike trail to Fletcher's Cascades branches left (leading nearly a mile to these scenic cascades); bear right with the hiking trail. It soon crosses Drake's Brook, which can be difficult to cross at times of high water. The trail parallels the brook for about 2.5 miles, although it is often separated from the water by dense brush and a steep bank. It then swings right and climbs steeply for more than a half mile to a junction with the Sandwich Mountain Trail (SMT) at 3.2 miles. Turn left for the summit on the SMT. In 0.1 mile a side trail branches right, leading steeply uphill for 0.2 mile to Jennings Peak, a subsidiary summit of Sandwich Mountain with a good view from atop cliffs, taking in the summit of Sandwich Mountain, the valleys of the Mad and Pemigewasset Rivers, and the Lakes Region and Squam Mountains to the south.

Double back to the SMT, turn right, and continue 1.1 miles to the summit of Sandwich Mountain, where you break out of the spruce forest at a rock pile with a spectacular view in a wide sweep north. Jennings Peak lies to the immediate northwest and Waterville Valley in the near foreground, including the peaks surrounding it (left to right): Tecumseh, Osceola, and Tripyramid (the last two are described in this chapter) with its south slide visible. To the east stretches the broad ridge connecting Whiteface, Passaconaway, and Chocorua's bald knob beyond (all three described in this chapter). Massive Mount Moosilauke (described in this chapter) dominates the horizon to the west. The high Franconia Ridge, connecting Mounts Flume, Liberty, Lincoln, and Lafayette (all described in this chapter), rises above everything else in the distant northwest. Due north, the Pemigewasset Wilderness covers the vast roadless area beyond Waterville Valley—and beyond the Kancamagus Highway, which is hidden from view—including the ridge of Mount Bond and Bondcliff, and Mount Carrigain, the prominent high mound at 1 o'clock (all described in this chapter). Finally, to Carrigain's right are the biggest peaks in the Whites, Mount Washington and the Presidential Range (also descriped in this chapter). Behind you, look for a somewhat hidden footpath through scrub trees that leads a few feet to a view south toward the Lakes Region. Descend the Sandwich Mountain Trail for 3.9 miles back to the parking area.

User Groups

Hikers, snowshoers, and dogs. No wheelchair facilities. This trail is not suitable for bikes, horses, or skis. Hunting is allowed in season.

Access and Fees

No backcountry permit is needed, but a permit is required for day use or overnight parking at any White Mountain National Forest trailhead, as indicated by signs posted at most trailheads. Permits are available at several area stores and from the national forest at a cost of $5 for seven consecutive days or $20 per year. A $3 one-day permit can be purchased at self-service stations at national forest trailheads, but the pass is good only for the trailhead at which it's purchased.

Maps

For a contour map of trails, get the *Franconia-Pemigewasset Range* map or the *Crawford Notch-Sandwich Range/Moosilauke-Kinsman* map, $7.95 each in waterproof Tyvek, available in many stores and from the Appalachian Mountain Club, 800/262-4455, website: www.outdoors.org; or the *Trail Map and Guide to the White Mountain National Forest* for $7.95 from the DeLorme Publishing Company, 800/642-0970. For a topographic area map, request the Waterville Valley and Mount Tripyramid maps from USGS Map Sales, Federal Center, Box 25286, Denver, CO 80225, 888/ASK-USGS (888/275-8747), website: http://mapping.usgs.gov.

Directions

From Exit 28 off I-93 in Campton, take Route 49 north for about 10.2 miles and turn right into a parking lot for the Drake's Brook and Sandwich Mountain Trails.

Contact

White Mountain National Forest Supervisor, 719 North Main Street, Laconia, NH 03246, 603/528-8721, TDD for the hearing impaired 603/528-8722, website: www.fs.fed.us/r9/white.

77 MOUNT WHITEFACE
in the southern White Mountain National Forest
north of Wonalancet

Total distance: 8 miles round-trip   **Hiking time:** 5.5 hours

Difficulty: 10   **Rating:** 9

While Whiteface, at 4,010 feet, is not among the best-known 4,000-footers in the Whites, the cliffs just below its summit offer dramatic views of the southern Whites, Mount Washington, and the Lakes Region to the south. The precipices along the upper Blueberry Ledge Trail are a great place to catch the fall foliage; I did one late September morning and also saw my first snowflakes of the season. All trails here are blazed in blue. The vertical ascent is about 3,800 feet. For a longer loop linking Whiteface with Passaconaway, see the special note in the description for the Mount Passaconaway hike.

From the parking lot, walk back to the road and turn right, following the road and signs for the trails for 0.3 mile. Turn left onto the Blueberry Ledge Trail, crossing over Wonalancet Brook on a bridge. Continue hiking on the single-lane dirt road to its end, where the Blueberry Ledge Trail enters the woods. The trail remains fairly easy at first, crossing slab ledges 1.5 miles from the parking lot.

At 3.2 miles, the Wiggin Trail diverges right (east), leading 1.1 miles to the Dicey's Mill Trail—the descent route for this hike. The best views begin at 3.6 miles, where the Blueberry Ledge Trail turns sharply right at a slab and the brink of a cliff that could be hazardous when wet or icy. In winter, you might want the security of roping up and belaying this section; a 60-foot rope would be long enough. To the south and southwest are the lakes of central New Hampshire and Sandwich Mountain. Continue up the Blueberry Ledge Trail for another 0.3 mile; wooden steps on steep slabs along this stretch of the trail have been removed. You will pass ledges with terrific views down into the broad glacial cirque known as the Bowl (which is framed by Whiteface and neighboring Mount Passaconaway), east to Mount Chocorua, and north to Mount Washington. Bear right at a trail junction near open ledges onto the Rollins Trail, following it 0.2 mile to the wooded summit of Whiteface. To descend, return to the Wiggin Trail, turn left, and follow it to the Dicey's Mill Trail; turn right, and descend 1.9 miles to the parking area, the last half mile of hiking following Ferncroft Road.

User Groups
Hikers only. No wheelchair facilities. This trail may be difficult to snow-shoe because of severe winter weather, and is not suitable for bikes, dogs, horses, or skis. Hunting is allowed in season.

Access and Fees
No backcountry permit is needed, but a permit is required for day use or overnight parking at any White Mountain National Forest trailhead, as in-dicated by signs posted at most trailheads. Permits are available at several area stores and from the national forest at a cost of $5 for seven consecu-tive days or $20 per year. A $3 one-day permit can be purchased at self-service stations at national forest trailheads, but the pass is good only for the trailhead at which it's purchased. Trails in this part of the national for-est are accessed through private land; be sure to stay on trails. Camping is permitted on the hardened ground at the former site of the Wonalancet Out Door Club's Camp Heermance (removed in 2002), 3.8 miles from the Ferncroft parking area via the Blueberry Ledge Trail. See the website of the Wonalancet Out Door Club for current information.

Maps
For a map of trails, get the *Crawford Notch–Sandwich Range/Moosilauke-Kinsman* map, $7.95 in waterproof Tyvek, which is available in many stores and from the Appalachian Mountain Club, 800/262-4455, website: www.out-doors.org; the Trail Map and Guide to the Sandwich Range Wilderness, on waterproof Tyvek, for $5 in local stores or from the Wonalancet Out Door Club; or the *Trail Map and Guide to the White Mountain National Forest* for $7.95 from the DeLorme Publishing Company, 800/642-0970. For topo-graphic area maps, request Mount Chocorua and Mount Tripyramid from USGS Map Sales, Federal Center, Box 25286, Denver, CO 80225, 888/ASK-USGS (888/275-8747), website: http://mapping.usgs.gov.

Directions
From Route 113A in Wonalancet, turn north onto Ferncroft Road. Follow it for 0.5 mile and bear right at a sign into the hiker parking lot.

Contact

Wonalancet Out Door Club, HCR 64 Box 248, Wonalancet, NH 03897, website: www.wodc.org. White Mountain National Forest Supervisor, 719 North Main Street, Laconia, NH 03246, 603/528-8721, TDD for the hearing impaired 603/528-8722, website: www.fs.fed.us/r9/white.

78 MOUNT PASSACONAWAY
in the southern White Mountain National Forest north of Wonalancet

Total distance: 9.5 miles round-trip   **Hiking time:** 6.5 hours

Difficulty: 9   **Rating:** 8

Probably one of the least-visited of New Hampshire's 4,000-foot summits, the top of Passaconaway (4,060 feet) is wooded, with no views (unless you're standing on several feet of snow and can see over the low spruce trees). But there are two nice views near the summit. The trails are marked with blue blazes and the vertical ascent is about 3,800 feet.

From the parking lot, walk back to the road and turn right, following the road for 0.8 mile straight onto the Dicey's Mill Trail. Soon after entering the woods, the trail crosses into the national forest. It parallels and eventually crosses Wonalancet Brook at 2.3 miles (0.4 mile beyond the Wiggin Trail junction), then begins ascending more steeply. The trail passes the junction with the Rollins Trail, which comes in from the left (west) at 3.7 miles, then the East Loop Trail departing right (east) at 3.9 miles. At around 4.5 miles, you'll get a view toward the peaks above Waterville Valley to the northwest. The junction with the Walden Trail is reached at 4.6 miles; from there, a spur path leads to the right about 50 yards to Passaconaway's summit. Follow the Walden Trail around the summit cone about 100 yards to the best view on this hike, from a ledge overlooking Mount Chocorua to the east and Mount Washington to the north. Continue descending the Walden Trail, dropping steeply to the East Loop, 0.6 mile from the summit spur path. Turn right (west) on the East Loop, which leads 0.2 mile back to the Dicey's Mill Trail. Turn left (south) and follow that trail 3.9 miles back to the Ferncroft Road parking area.

Special note: You can combine Passaconaway and Mount Whiteface on a rugged loop of nearly 12 miles, with more than 4,600 feet of climbing. Hike the Blueberry Ledge Trail up Whiteface, then the Rollins Trail for 2.3 miles over the high ridge connecting the two peaks; there are some views along the Rollins, though much of it is within the subalpine conifer forest. Turn left (north) on the Dicey's Mill Trail, and then complete the Passaconaway hike described above.

User Groups

Hikers only. No wheelchair facilities. This trail could be difficult to snow-shoe because of severe winter weather and is not suitable for bikes, dogs, horses, or skis. Hunting is allowed in season.

Access and Fees

No backcountry permit is needed, but a permit is required for day use or overnight parking at any White Mountain National Forest trailhead, as indicated by signs posted at most trailheads. Permits are available at several area stores and from the national forest at a cost of $5 for seven consecutive days or $20 per year. A $3 one-day permit can be purchased at self-service stations at national forest trailheads, but the pass is good only for the trailhead at which it's purchased. Trails in this part of the national forest are accessed through private land; be sure to stay on the path. Camping is permitted on the hardened ground at the former site of the Camp Rich shelter, near the junction of the Rollins and Dicey's Mill Trails. See the website of the Wonalancet Out Door Club for current information.

Maps

For a map of trails, get the *Crawford Notch–Sandwich Range/Moosi-lauke-Kinsman* map, $7.95 in waterproof Tyvek, which is available in many stores and from the Appalachian Mountain Club, 800/262-4455, website: www.outdoors.org; the Trail Map and Guide to the Sandwich Range Wilderness, on waterproof Tyvek, for $5 in local stores or from the Wonalancet Out Door Club; or the *Trail Map and Guide to the White Mountain National Forest* for $7.95 from the DeLorme Publishing Company, 800/642-0970. For topographic area maps, request Mount Chocorua and Mount Tripyramid from USGS Map Sales, Federal Center, Box 25286, Denver, CO 80225, 888/ASK-USGS (888/275-8747), website: http://mapping.usgs.gov.

Directions

From Route 113A in Wonalancet, turn north onto Ferncroft Road. Follow it for 0.5 mile and bear right at a sign into the hiker parking lot.

Contact

Wonalancet Out Door Club, HCR 64 Box 248, Wonalancet, NH 03897, website: www.wodc.org. White Mountain National Forest Supervisor, 719 North Main Street, Laconia, NH 03246, 603/528-8721, TDD for the hearing impaired 603/528-8722, website: www.fs.fed.us/r9/white.

79 MOUNT CHOCORUA: BROOK-LIBERTY LOOP

in the White Mountain National Forest north of Tamworth and east of Wonalancet

Total distance: 7.4 miles round-trip   **Hiking time:** 5 hours

Difficulty: 9   **Rating:** 10

Of the two routes described in this guide up the popular, 3,500-foot Mount Chocorua, this one is far less traveled—and, in my opinion, a better hike. Chocorua is a great place to bring children; I hiked this loop with my nephew Nicholas shortly before he turned seven, and he could not contain his excitement as we scrambled up the final slabs and ledges to the open, rocky summit. The summit attracts dozens of hikers on clear weekend days in summer and fall for good reason: The views north to Mount Washington, west across the White Mountains, south to the lakes region, and east over the hills and lakes of western Maine are among the finest attainable in the Whites without climbing a bigger peak. The foliage views are particularly striking. This hike climbs about 2,600 feet in elevation.

On this loop, hike up the Brook Trail, which is steeper, and descend the Liberty Trail—the easiest route on Chocorua. (Hikers looking for a less demanding route could opt to go up and down the Liberty Trail.) From the parking area, walk past the gate and follow the gravel woods road, which the Brook Trail leaves within 0.5 mile. The trail passes a small waterfall along Claybank Brook less than two miles up and after some easy to moderately difficult hiking, emerges from the woods onto the bare rock of Chocorua's summit cone at three miles. The final 0.6 mile ascends steep slabs and ledges; the Liberty Trail coincides with the Brook Trail for the last 0.2 mile. To descend, follow the two trails down for that 0.2 mile, and then bear left onto the Liberty Trail. It traverses somewhat rocky ground high on the mountain, passing the U.S. Forest Service's Jim Liberty cabin within 0.5 mile. The descent grows more moderate, eventually following an old bridle path back to the parking area, 3.8 miles from the summit.

User Groups

Hikers and dogs. No wheelchair facilities. This trail should not be attempted in winter except by hikers experienced in mountaineering and prepared for severe winter weather, and is not suitable for bikes, horses, or skis. Hunting is allowed in season.

Access and Fees

No backcountry permit is needed, but a permit is required for day use or overnight parking at any White Mountain National Forest trailhead, as indicated by signs posted at most trailheads. Permits are available at several area stores and from the national forest at a cost of $5 for seven consecutive days or $20 per year. A $3 one-day permit can be purchased at self-service stations at national forest trailheads, but the pass is good only for the trailhead at which it's purchased. The national forest maintains the Jim Liberty cabin (which has a capacity of nine) on the Liberty Trail, 0.5 mile below Chocorua's summit; a fee is charged and the water source is unreliable in dry seasons. Contact the White Mountain National Forest for rate and reservation information.

Maps
For a map of trails, get the *Crawford Notch–Sandwich Range/Moosilauke–Kinsman* map, $7.95 in waterproof Tyvek, which is available in many stores and from the Appalachian Mountain Club, 800/262-4455, website: www.outdoors.org; or the *Trail Map and Guide to the White Mountain National Forest* for $7.95 from the DeLorme Publishing Company, 800/642-0970. For topographic area maps, request Mount Chocorua and Silver Lake from USGS Map Sales, Federal Center, Box 25286, Denver, CO 80225, 888/ASK-USGS (888/275-8747), website: http://mapping.usgs.gov.

Directions
From the junction of Routes 113 and 113A in Tamworth, drive west on Route 113A for 3.4 miles and turn right onto the dirt Fowler's Mill Road. Continue for 1.2 miles and turn left (at trail signs) onto Paugus Road/Fire Road 68. The parking area and trailhead lie 0.8 mile up the road.

Contact
White Mountain National Forest Supervisor, 719 North Main Street, Laconia, NH 03246, 603/528-8721, TDD for the hearing impaired 603/528-8722, website: www.fs.fed.us/r9/white.

80 MOUNT CHOCORUA: PIPER TRAIL
in the White Mountain National Forest north of Chocorua and west of Conway

Total distance: 9 miles round-trip   **Hiking time:** 6.5 hours

Difficulty: 9   **Rating:** 10

This is the most heavily used route up the popular, 3,500-foot Mount Chocorua, though at nine miles for the round-trip, it is not the shortest. It ascends some 2,700 feet. The trail suffers from erosion due to overuse, which can make the footing difficult in places.

From the parking area, the trail starts out on easy ground, entering the woods. About two miles out, it crosses the Chocorua River and ascends switchbacks up the steepening mountainside. At 3.1 miles, a short side path leads to the Camp Penacook shelter and tent sites. The final half mile of trail passes over open ledges with sweeping views and on to the summit, where the panoramic views take in Mount Washington to the north, New Hampshire's Lakes Region to the south, the hills and lakes of western Maine to the east, and the grand sweep of the White Mountains to the west and northwest. Descend the same trail.

User Groups

Hikers and dogs. No wheelchair facilities. This trail should not be attempted in winter except by hikers experienced in mountaineering and prepared for severe winter weather and is not suitable for bikes, horses, or skis. Hunting is allowed in season.

Access and Fees

No backcountry permit is needed, but a permit is required for day use or overnight parking at any White Mountain National Forest trailhead, as indicated by signs posted at most trailheads. Permits are available at several area stores and from the national forest at a cost of $5 for seven consecutive days or $20 per year. A $3 one-day permit can be purchased at self-service stations at national forest trailheads, but the pass is good only for the trailhead at which it's purchased. The national forest maintains Camp Penacook, which consists of a lean-to shelter and four tent platforms, 3.1 miles up the Piper Trail and 1.4 miles below Chocorua's summit; there is no fee.

Maps

For a map of trails, get the *Crawford Notch–Sandwich Range/Moosilauke–Kinsman* map, $7.95 in waterproof Tyvek, which is available in many stores and from the Appalachian Mountain Club, 800/262-4455, website: www.outdoors.org; or the *Trail Map and Guide to the White Mountain National Forest* for $7.95 from the DeLorme Publishing Company, 800/642-0970. For topographic area maps, request Mount Chocorua and Silver Lake from USGS Map Sales, Federal Center, Box 25286, Denver, CO 80225, 888/ASK-USGS (888/275-8747), website: http://mapping.usgs.gov.

Directions

The Piper Trail begins behind the Piper Trail Restaurant and Cabins on Route 16 between the towns of Chocorua and Conway, six miles south of the junction of Route 16 and Route 112 (the Kancamagus Highway). Follow the dirt road to the right of the store for 0.25 mile to the trailhead parking area.

Contact
White Mountain National Forest Supervisor, 719 North Main Street, Laconia, NH 03246, 603/528-8721, TDD for the hearing impaired 603/528-8722, website: www.fs.fed.us/r9/white.

81 MOUNT ISRAEL
in the southern White Mountain National Forest northwest of Center Sandwich

Total distance: 4.2 miles round-trip   **Hiking time:** 2.5 hours

Difficulty: 6   **Rating:** 8

Just 2,630 feet high, Mount Israel's summit ledges have nice views of the entire Sandwich Range to the north and Mount Moosilauke to the west. This is one of those hikes few people know about, which should be better known considering the relatively easy access to quality views and the ascent of just 1,600 feet. From the parking lot, walk past a sign reading "Israel," left of the main building of Mead Base, to the Wentworth Trail, which is marked by a sign. The trail climbs at a moderate grade for about 1.5 miles to a good overlook south to the Lakes Region. Two miles from the start, you emerge at the summit ledges and a wide view of the Sandwich Range (from left to right): Sandwich Mountain, Tripyramid, Whiteface with a cliff near its summit, Passaconaway immediately behind and to the right of Whiteface, and Chocorua far to the right, barely within sight. From a nearby ledge, you can look west to Moosilauke (see listings for all of these peaks in this chapter). Descend the way you came.

User Groups
Hikers, snowshoers, dogs. No wheelchair facilities. This trail is not suitable for bikes, horses, or skis. Hunting is allowed in season.

Access and Fees
No backcountry permit is needed, but a permit is required for day use or overnight parking at any White Mountain National Forest trailhead, as indicated by signs posted at most trailheads. Permits are available at several area stores and from the national forest at a cost of $5 for seven consecutive days or $20 per year. A $3 one-day permit can be purchased at self-

service stations at national forest trailheads, but the pass is good only for the trailhead at which it's purchased.

Maps

For a map of trails, get the *Crawford Notch–Sandwich Range/Moosilauke–Kinsman* map, $7.95 in waterproof Tyvek, which is available in many stores and from the Appalachian Mountain Club, 800/262-4455, website: www.outdoors.org; or the *Trail Map and Guide to the White Mountain National Forest* for $7.95 from the DeLorme Publishing Company, 800/642-0970. The Squam Lakes Association—which maintains 50 miles of trails in the area—also sells a trail map that covers this hike for $6, and an area guidebook and map for $6, plus $1.25 shipping per item (prices may change). For topographic area maps, request Squam Mountains and Center Sandwich from USGS Map Sales, Federal Center, Box 25286, Denver, CO 80225, 888/ASK-USGS (888/275-8747), website: http://mapping.usgs.gov.

Directions

From Route 113 in Center Sandwich, turn onto Grove Street at a sign for Sandwich Notch. At 0.4 mile, bear left on Diamond Ledge Road (don't be deceived by the name of the road bearing right—Mount Israel Road). At 2.5 miles from Route 113, bear right at a sign for Mead Base Camp. Follow that road another mile to its end at Mead Base Camp and parking on the right.

Contact

White Mountain National Forest Supervisor, 719 North Main Street, Laconia, NH 03246, 603/528-8721, TDD for the hearing impaired 603/528-8722, website: www.fs.fed.us/r9/white. Squam Lakes Association, P.O. Box 204, Holderness, NH 03245, 603/968-7336, fax 603/968-7444, email: Info@squamlakes.org, website: www.squamlakes.org.

82 STINSON MOUNTAIN

in the White Mountain National Forest north of Rumney

Total distance: 3.6 miles round-trip   **Hiking time:** 2.5 hours

Difficulty: 4   **Rating:** 8

Tucked away in the very southwestern corner of the White Mountain National Forest is little Stinson Mountain (2,900 feet), a small mountain with a great summit view of the valley of the Baker River, the state college town of Plymouth, and the surrounding hills. It's a nice spot to catch the sunrise or foliage at its peak. This hike ascends 1,400 feet in a 1.8-mile uphill jaunt.

Follow the Stinson Mountain Trail, which begins quite easily, then grows moderately steep but never very difficult. Within 0.25 mile, the trail crosses an old logging road, and in 0.5 mile it bears right where an old wooden footbridge leads left on a former trail. Although the trail is generally an easy, wide, and obvious path, be careful not to be fooled into these wrong turns. Within a hundred yards of the summit, or 1.8 miles from the trailhead, the trail forks, with both branches leading to the summit ledges. Trees block the view somewhat to the north, but you can see Mount Moosilauke (see the two Moosilauke hike listings in this chapter). Immediately north of the summit ledges, a side path leads 200 feet to a better view of Stinson Lake and Moosilauke. Return the way you came.

User Groups

Hikers, snowshoers, and dogs. No wheelchair facilities. This trail is not suitable for bikes, horses, or skis. Hunting is allowed in season.

Access and Fees

No backcountry permit is needed, but a permit is required for day use or overnight parking at any White Mountain National Forest trailhead, as indicated by signs posted at most trailheads. Permits are available at several area stores and from the national forest at a cost of $5 for seven consecutive days or $20 per year. A $3 one-day permit can be purchased at self-service stations at national forest trailheads, but the pass is good only for the trailhead at which it's purchased.

Maps

For a map of trails, get the *Crawford Notch–Sandwich Range/Moosilauke–Kinsman* map, $7.95 in waterproof Tyvek, which is available in many stores and from the Appalachian Mountain Club, 800/262-4455, website: www.outdoors.org. For a topographic area map, request Rumney from USGS Map Sales, Federal Center, Box 25286, Denver, CO 80225, 888/ASK-USGS (888/275-8747), website: http://mapping.usgs.gov.

Directions

From Route 25 in Rumney Village (3.5 miles north of the traffic circle at Routes 25 and 3A, 2.1 miles north of the Polar Caves Park, 7.7 miles west of I-93 Exit 26, and 4.2 miles south of the junction of Routes 25 and 118), turn at a blinking yellow light onto Main Street. In a mile, the street becomes Stinson Lake Road. At 5.1 miles from Route 25, bear right on Cross Road at a sign for Hawthorne Village. In 0.3 mile, bear right onto a gravel road, then drive another half mile and turn right at a sign for the Stinson Mountain Trail. Drive 0.3 mile farther to parking on the left and a trail sign.

Contact

White Mountain National Forest Supervisor, 719 North Main Street, Laconia, NH 03246, 603/528-8721, TDD for the hearing impaired 603/528-8722, website: www.fs.fed.us/r9/white.

Chapter 2

© MICHAEL LANZA

Central and Southern New Hampshire

Central and Southern New Hampshire

The White Mountains may be the star attraction for hikers in the Granite State, but New Hampshire has several smaller peaks in the lower part of the state that are no less spectacular, and are easier to climb up and closer to where most people live. I've trekked up Mounts Monadnock and Cardigan more times than I know and never grown tired of them. Peaks like Kearsarge, Sunapee, Major, and Smarts are equally enjoyable, for adults and children. State parks scattered across the central and southern portion of the state offer great local hiking on miles of trails and old woods roads. Two long-distance trails in southern New Hampshire—the 21-mile Wapack Trail and the 50-mile Monadnock-Sunapee Greenway—offer scenic hiking over hills that see far fewer boots than popular corners of the Whites.

This chapter covers everything below the White Mountains, from hills along the Appalachian Trail in the Upper Connecticut Valley and the Lakes Region to the Seacoast and Massachusetts border. The prime, snow-free hiking season in these places generally goes from April or May through October or November, with the exception of the Seacoast area, where snow is less frequent and the hiking season longer.

This chapter includes hikes along the Appalachian Trail in western New Hampshire (Moose Mountain, Smarts Mountain, and Holt's Ledge). Along the trail, dogs must be kept under control, and horses, bikes, hunting, and firearms are prohibited. Cross-country skiing and snowshoeing are allowed, though the trail is often too rugged for skiing.

In state parks and forests, dogs should remain under control, and many state lands post signs requiring leashes. Hunting is allowed in season in most state parks and forests. Mountain bikes, cross-country skiing, and snowshoeing are allowed on trails unless otherwise posted.

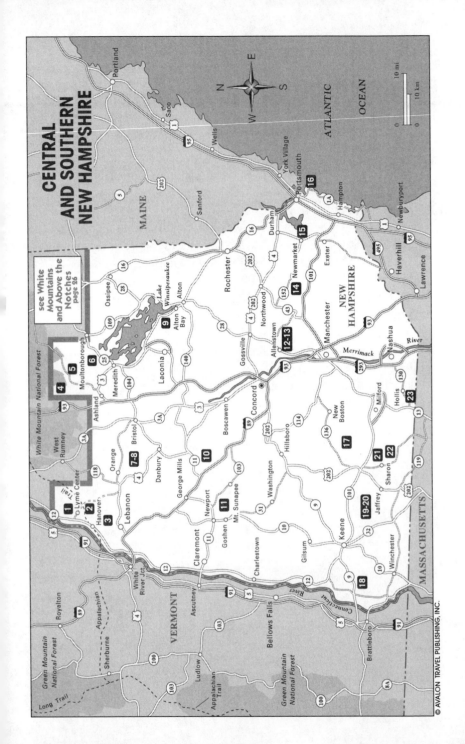

CENTRAL
AND SOUTHERN
NEW HAMPSHIRE

see White
Mountains
and Above the
Notches
page 26

© AVALON TRAVEL PUBLISHING, INC.

Contents

❶ SMARTS MOUNTAIN
in Lyme

Total distance: 7.5 miles round-trip

Hiking time: 4.5 hours

Difficulty: 8

Rating: 9

New England's topography and weather sometimes collaborate to make a smaller peak feel like a bigger mountain. At 3,240 feet, Smarts is one of those peaks. This hike, not to be underestimated, blends nice walks in the woods and along the rocky crest of a ridge with a rigorous final push to the summit through the sort of evergreen forest usually found at higher elevations. A fire tower on the wooded summit offers a magnificent panorama of the upper Connecticut Valley, the Green Mountains, and the Whites on a clear day. The elevation gain is about 2,100 feet.

From the parking lot, pick up the Lambert Ridge Trail (signed), which is also the Appalachian Trail. (The unmarked but wide path at the end of the lot is the Ranger Trail, your route of descent.) Within the first 1.5 miles, the pleasant woods walk is enhanced by several views in various directions atop the rocky Lambert Ridge—itself a nice destination for a short hike. The trail then drops slightly, changes direction a few times—watch for white blazes—and then ascends the relentlessly steep west slope of Smarts, passing the unmarked junction (on the right) with the Ranger Trail 3.5 miles from the parking lot. A half mile farther, a side trail leads right to a tent site where the Smarts tent platform formerly stood. Continuing on the Appalachian Trail about 0.1 mile, watch on the left for a spur trail to the fire tower. Backtrack 0.6 mile and bear left to descend the Ranger Trail 3.5 miles to the trailhead. (The final 1.5 miles of the Ranger Trail, which ascends at a gentle angle, could be skied on an approach in winter, up to an abandoned garage where the trail crosses Grant Brook.)

User Groups
Hikers, snowshoers, and dogs. No wheelchair facilities. This route is not suitable for skis, except for the final 1.5 miles of the Ranger Trail. Bikes, horses, and hunting are prohibited.

Access and Fees
Parking and access are free. The Smarts tent site is located about four miles up the Lambert Ridge/Appalachian Trail and 0.1 mile below the summit.

Maps
A map of the Appalachian Trail between Pomfret, Vermont, and Kinsman Notch, New Hampshire, is available from the Dartmouth Outdoor Programs

Office. This hike is also covered on map 4 in the *Map and Guide to the Appalachian Trail in New Hampshire and Vermont,* an eight-map set and guidebook available for $19.95 ($14.95 for the maps alone) from the Appalachian Trail Conference. For a topographic map of the area, request Smarts Mountain from USGS Map Sales, Federal Center, Box 25286, Denver, CO 80225, 888/ASK-USGS (888/275-8747), website: http://mapping.usgs.gov.

Directions

From Route 10 on the Green in Lyme, take Dorchester Road (at the white church), following signs for the Dartmouth Skiway. Two miles from the Green, you'll pass through the village of Lyme Center. In another 1.3 miles, bear left onto the gravel Lyme-Dorchester Road (across from where the Appalachian Trail emerges from the woods on the right). In another 1.8 miles, just before an iron bridge over Grant Brook, park in a small lot on the left, at the trailhead.

Contact

Appalachian Trail Conference, 799 Washington Street, P.O. Box 807, Harpers Ferry, WV 25425-0807, 304/535-6331, website: www.appalachiantrail.org. Dartmouth Outdoor Programs Office, 119 Robinson Hall, Dartmouth College, Hanover, NH 03755, 603/646-2834, website: www.dartmouth.edu/~doc.

2 HOLT'S LEDGE
in Lyme

Total distance: 2.2 miles round-trip   **Hiking time:** 1.5 hours

Difficulty: 2   **Rating:** 8

Holt's Ledge, at the top of a tall, rugged cliff, lies at the end of a fairly easy walk through the woods along the Appalachian Trail. From Holt's Ledge you can see Smarts Mountain and Mount Cube (beyond and left of Smarts) to the north, Cardigan and Kearsarge to the east, and Ascutney in the distance to the south. Don't venture beyond the weathered fencing on the ledge—the cliff's brink is quite crumbly and peregrine falcons nest below. The ascent gains about 1,000 feet.

From the trailhead, follow the white-blazed Appalachian Trail. At 0.5 mile, it passes a side trail leading 0.2 mile to the Trapper John shelter, where you'll find water and an outhouse. After crossing a stream, the trail climbs a hillside to the cliffs; the Appalachian Trail swings right, and a side trail leads left to the open ledges. Return the same way; or from the ledges, turn left and descend the alpine ski trail.

User Groups

Hikers, snowshoers, and dogs. No wheelchair facilities. This trail is not suitable for cross-country skis. Bikes, horses, and hunting are prohibited.

Access and Fees

Parking and access are free. The Trapper John lean-to shelter is located 0.2 mile down a side path off the Appalachian Trail, 0.5 mile south of this hike's start.

Maps

A map of the Appalachian Trail between Pomfret, VT, and Kinsman Notch, NH, is available from the Dartmouth Outdoor Programs Office. This hike is also covered on map 4 in the *Map and Guide to the Appalachian Trail in New Hampshire and Vermont,* an eight-map set and guidebook available for $19.95 ($14.95 for the maps alone) from the Appalachian Trail Conference. For a topographic map of the area, request Smarts Mountain from USGS Map Sales, Federal Center, Box 25286, Denver, CO 80225, 888/ASK-USGS (888/275-8747), website: http://mapping.usgs.gov.

Directions

From Route 10 on the Green in Lyme, take Dorchester Road (at the white church), following signs for the Dartmouth Skiway. Two miles from the Green, you pass through the village of Lyme Center. In another 1.3 miles, across from the gravel Lyme-Dorchester Road, the Appalachian Trail emerges from the woods on the right. Park either at the roadside or a short distance farther in the dirt lot for the Dartmouth Skiway.

Contact

Appalachian Trail Conference, 799 Washington Street, P.O. Box 807, Harpers Ferry, WV 25425-0807, 304/535-6331, website: www.appalachiantrail.org. Dartmouth Outdoor Programs Office, 119 Robinson Hall, Dartmouth College, Hanover, NH 03755, 603/646-2834, website: www.dartmouth.edu/~doc.

3 MOOSE MOUNTAIN
in Hanover

Total distance: 4.1 miles round-trip

Difficulty: 4

Hiking time: 3 hours

Rating: 7

This loop, incorporating a stretch of the Appalachian Trail, passes over the south summit of Moose Mountain (2,290 feet), where a plane crashed in 1968. The ensuing rescue effort included a bulldozer clearing a route to the summit. The result is a lasting view east and southeast, taking in Goose Pond (in the foreground) and Clark Pond (in the distance) in the town of Canaan, and Mounts Cardigan and Kearsarge even farther in the distance. The hike climbs almost 1,000 feet.

From the parking area, cross the road to the east, following the white-blazed Appalachian Trail northbound. The trail crosses a brook, then the wide, two-track Harris Trail at 0.4 mile. It then begins the ascent of Moose Mountain, climbing at a moderate angle at first, leveling somewhat, then climbing again to the south summit at 1.8 miles. Continue north across the clearing, following the white blazes another half mile to a junction with the Clark Pond Loop. To the right, the Clark Pond Loop leads 0.2 mile to the Moose Mountain shelter. For this hike, turn left (west) onto the Clark Loop and descend 0.7 mile. Follow the gravel road to the left for about 50 feet, turn left (south) onto the Harris Trail, and follow it 0.7 mile to the Appalachian Trail. Turn right and walk the Appalachian Trail 0.4 mile back to Three Mile Road.

User Groups

Hikers, snowshoers, and dogs. No wheelchair facilities. This trail is not suitable for skis. Bikes, horses, and hunting are prohibited.

Access and Fees

Parking and access are free. The Moose Mountain shelter is located 0.2 mile off this loop, 2.3 miles into the hike.

Maps

This hike is covered on map 4 in the *Map and Guide to the Appalachian Trail in New Hampshire and Vermont,* an eight-map set and guidebook available for $19.95 ($14.95 for the maps alone) from the Appalachian Trail Conference. A map of the Appalachian Trail between Pomfret, VT, and Kinsman Notch, NH, is available from the Dartmouth Outing Club. For topographic area maps, request Hanover and Canaan from USGS Map Sales, Federal Center, Box 25286, Denver, CO 80225, 888/ASK-USGS (888/275-8747), website: http://mapping.usgs.gov.

Directions

From I-91, take Exit 13 in Norwich, VT. Head east, crossing the Connecticut River and driving up a long hill to the center of Hanover. Drive straight through the traffic lights (the Dartmouth College Green is to your left) onto East Wheelock Street and follow it 4.3 miles into the Hanover village of Etna. Turn left onto Etna Road, proceed 0.8 mile, and then turn right onto Ruddsboro Road. Continue 1.5 miles and then turn left onto Three Mile Road. Drive another 1.3 miles to a turnout on the left, where the white-blazed Appalachian Trail crosses the road.

Contact

Appalachian Trail Conference, 799 Washington Street, P.O. Box 807, Harpers Ferry, WV 25425-0807, 304/535-6331, website: www.appalachiantrail.org. Outdoor Programs Office, 119 Robinson Hall, Dartmouth College, Hanover, NH 03755, 603/646-2834, website: www.dartmouth.edu/~doc.

4 SQUAM MOUNTAINS
between Holderness and Center Sandwich

Total distance: 5.1 miles round-trip   **Hiking time:** 3 hours

Difficulty: 7   **Rating:** 9

This very popular hike leads to views of Squam Lake and massive Lake Winnipesaukee from the low peaks of the Squam Mountains range. A friend and I made this loop on a sunny Saturday, the first weekend of October, when the fall foliage was at its peak. This is a fairly easy hike with only one short, difficult section—the cliffs on the Mount Morgan Trail—which can be avoided. The vertical ascent is about 1,400 feet.

From the parking lot, walk around the gate onto the Mount Morgan Trail. It ascends gently for more than a mile, then steepens somewhat. At 1.7 miles, the Crawford-Ridgepole Trail enters from the left and coincides with the Mount Morgan Trail for 0.2 mile. Where they split again, the Crawford-Ridgepole bears right for an easier route up Mount Morgan. This hike turns left with the Mount Morgan Trail, immediately scaling low cliffs on a wooden ladder, after which you crawl through a cavelike passage through rocks and emerge atop the cliffs with an excellent view of the big lakes to the south. Follow the blazes up the slabs to Morgan's open summit and extensive views south. Pick up the Crawford-Ridgepole Trail eastward along the Squam Mountains Ridge—with occasional views, including the distinctive horned summit of Mount Chocorua (see the White Mountains and Above the Notches chapter)—another 0.8 mile to the open summit of Mount Percival, which also has excellent views of the lakes. There are two options for descending off the summit of Percival. You can turn right and descend the Mount Percival Trail to the southeast (look for a small trail sign nailed to a tree at the base of the summit slabs). Or descend to the southwest on a path that passes through another boulder cave and rejoins the Mount Percival Trail in 0.1 mile. After a relatively easy descent of 1.9 miles to Route 113, turn right and walk the road for 0.3 mile back to the parking area.

Special note: Some hikers will find that hiking this loop in the opposite direction—and going up the steep section just below the summit of Mount Percival, rather than down it—will be easier on the knees.

User Groups
Hikers, snowshoers, and dogs. No wheelchair facilities. This trail is not suitable for bikes, horses, or skis. Hunting is allowed in season.

Access and Fees
Parking and access are free.

Maps
The Squam Lakes Association, which maintains 50 miles of trails in the area, sells a trail map that covers this hike for $6. Or get the *Crawford Notch-Sandwich Range/Moosilauke-Kinsman* map, $7.95 in waterproof Tyvek, which is available in many stores and from the Appalachian Mountain Club, 800/262-4455, website: www.outdoors.org. For a topographic area map, request Squam Mountains from USGS Map Sales, Federal Center, Box 25286, Denver, CO 80225, 888/ASK-USGS (888/275-8747), website: http://mapping.usgs.gov.

Directions
The trailhead parking lot is on Route 113, about 5.5 miles east of the junction of U.S. 3 and Route 113, and 6.3 miles west of the junction of Routes 109 and 113.

Contact
Squam Lakes Association, P.O. Box 204, Holderness, NH 03245, 603/968-7336, website: www.squamlakes.org.

5 WEST RATTLESNAKE

between Holderness and Center Sandwich

Total distance: 1.8 miles round-trip **Hiking time:** 1 hour

Difficulty: 2 **Rating:** 9

This easy hike, a good one for young children, follows a wide trail that rises gently for 0.9 mile to cliff-top views from several hundred feet above Squam Lake. From the parking area for the Mount Morgan Trail, cross Route 113 and walk west about 100 feet to the Old Bridle Path. Continue on the Old Bridle Path for 0.9 mile; where the main trail turns left, follow a side path to the right about 100 feet to the cliffs. At the summit, you may notice rock barriers surrounding Douglas' Knotweed, a threatened plant; avoid walking on the vegetation. Return the way you came.

User Groups

Hikers, snowshoers, and dogs. No wheelchair facilities. This trail is not suitable for bikes, horses, or skis. Hunting is allowed in season.

Access and Fees

Parking and access are free.

Maps

The Squam Lakes Association sells a trail map that covers this hike for $6. Or get the *Crawford Notch–Sandwich Range/Moosilauke–Kinsman* map, $7.95 in waterproof Tyvek, which is available in many stores and from the Appalachian Mountain Club, 800/262-4455, website: www.outdoors.org. For a topographic area map, request Squam Mountains from USGS Map Sales, Federal Center, Box 25286, Denver, CO 80225, 888/ASK-USGS (888/275-8747), website: http://mapping.usgs.gov.

Directions

The trailhead parking lot is on Route 113, 5.6 miles east of the junction of U.S. 3 and Route 113, and 6.3 miles west of the junction of Routes 109 and 113.

Contact

Squam Lakes Association, P.O. Box 204, Holderness, NH 03245, 603/968-7336, website: www.squamlakes.org.

6 EAGLE CLIFF

north of Center Harbor

Total distance: 1.2 miles round-trip

Hiking time: 0.75 hour

Difficulty: 2

Rating: 9

A few steps off the road and along the unmarked trail, you pass a small sign reading Eagle Cliff Trail. Rising moderately for much of its 0.6-mile climb, the trail grows steep for the final 0.2 mile (and should be avoided in icy conditions). Near the top, turn left to reach open ledges with a dramatic view from high above Squam Lake. Across the water rises the low ridge of the Squam Mountains. To the north lie the southern White Mountains; the most readily identifiable is the horn of Mount Chocorua to the northeast. Hike back along the same route, or descend the Teedie Trail from Eagle Cliff. The Teedie Trail is a much less steep ascent or descent, so it's the recommended route if the ground is wet; or if you want to do a loop hike in dry conditions, the Teedie is a preferable descent route so hike up the Eagle Cliff Trail. The Teedie Trail will bring you back to Bean Road, next to a private tennis court at the Sandwich-Moltonborough town line, 0.4 mile from where you parked.

User Groups

Hikers, snowshoers, and dogs. No wheelchair facilities. This trail is not suitable for bikes, horses, or skis. Hunting is allowed in season.

Access and Fees

Parking and access are free.

Maps

The Squam Lakes Association sells a trail map that covers this hike for $6. Or get the *Crawford Notch–Sandwich Range/Moosilauke–Kinsman* map, $7.95 in waterproof Tyvek, which is available in many stores and from the Appalachian Mountain Club, 800/262-4455, website: www.outdoors.org. For a topographic area map, request Squam Mountains from USGS Map Sales, Federal Center, Box 25286, Denver, CO 80225, 888/ASK-USGS (888/275-8747), website: http://mapping.usgs.gov.

Directions

In Center Harbor, immediately east of the junction of Routes 25 and 25B, turn north off Route 25 onto Bean Road. Follow it five miles. At 0.4 mile beyond the Sandwich-Moltonborough town line—where the road becomes

Squam Lakes Road—look for roadside parking. The trail is marked by a small sign downhill from the road and not visible until you start down the path. The trail enters the woods across the road from a "Traffic turning and entering" sign (for southbound traffic).

Contact

Squam Lakes Association, P.O. Box 204, Holderness, NH 03245, 603/968-7336, website: www.squamlakes.org.

7 MOUNT CARDIGAN: WEST SIDE LOOP

in Cardigan State Park east of Canaan

Total distance: 3.5 miles round-trip   **Hiking time:** 2 hours

Difficulty: 4   **Rating:** 10

This loop, much easier than the Mount Cardigan East Side Loop, is probably the most popular route up this locally popular mountain. See the trail notes for the next hike for more description about Mount Cardigan. While living nearby for four years, I enjoyed trail running this loop many times. The vertical ascent from this trailhead to the 3,121-foot summit is about 1,200 feet.

From the parking area, the orange blazes of the West Ridge Trail lead immediately uphill, climbing steadily on a wide, well-maintained, if sometimes rocky footpath. At 0.5 mile, the South Ridge Trail enters from the right; you will eventually descend on this trail. Stay to the left on the West Ridge Trail, crossing a small brook on a wooden footbridge and passing a junction with the Skyland Trail. More than a mile from the trailhead, the West Ridge Trail emerges onto the nearly barren upper cone of Mount Cardigan, climbing steep slabs to the summit at 1.5 miles, where there is a fire tower. Turn around and descend about 100 feet on the West Ridge Trail, then turn left and follow the white blazes of the Clark Trail, which is marked by a sign. It descends the rock slabs generally southward, but watch carefully for the blazes, because it's easy to lose this trail above tree line. The trail becomes briefly quite steep on slabs that can be a bit hazardous when wet, reaching the tiny warden's cabin 0.2 mile past Cardigan's summit. Turn right and follow the orange blazes of the South Ridge Trail past the cabin, moving in and out of low trees for 0.3 mile to South Peak, with good views to the south and west of the hills of central/western New Hampshire. The South Ridge Trail enters the forest and continues descending, very steeply in spots, for another mile to the West Ridge Trail. Turn left and descend another half mile to the parking lot.

User Groups

Hikers and dogs. Dogs must be leashed. No wheelchair facilities. Snow-shoeing is possible at lower elevations but may be difficult above tree line due to ice and harsh weather. This trail is not suitable for bikes, horses, or skis. Hunting is allowed in season unless otherwise posted.

Access and Fees

Parking and access are free. The access road is maintained in winter only to a parking area about 0.6 mile before the summer parking lot.

Maps

A free, basic map of trails is available at the trailhead parking lot. Or get the *Monadnock/Cardigan* map, $7.95 in waterproof Tyvek, from the Appalachian Mountain Club, 800/262-4455, website: www.outdoors.org. For topographic area maps, request Mount Cardigan from USGS Map Sales, Federal Center, Box 25286, Denver, CO 80225, 888/ASK-USGS (888/275-8747), website: http://mapping.usgs.gov.

Directions

From the junction of Routes 4 and 118 in Canaan, drive north on 118 for 0.6 mile and then turn right at a sign for Cardigan State Park. Follow that road for 4.1 miles to a large dirt parking lot. The trail begins beside the parking lot.

Contact

New Hampshire Division of Parks and Recreation, P.O. Box 1856, Concord, NH 03302-1856, 603/271-3254. Trails on Mount Cardigan are maintained by the Cardigan Highlanders, P.O. Box 104, Enfield Center, NH 03749, 603/632-5640.

8 MOUNT CARDIGAN: EAST SIDE LOOP
in Cardigan State Park west of Alexandria

Total distance: 5.2 miles round-trip   **Hiking time:** 3.5 hours

Difficulty: 7   **Rating:** 10

Left bare by a fire in 1855, the 3,121-foot crown of Mount Cardigan affords long views in a 360-degree panorama of the Green and White Mountains, and prominent hills to the south such as Mounts Ascutney and Sunapee. It's a popular hike: Hundreds of people, many of them children, will climb Cardigan on sunny weekends during the warm months. This steep hike up the east side of Cardigan provided quite a big-mountain adventure for my two nephews and niece, ages six to nine at the time of our climb on a sunny, blustery September Saturday. As we scaled the mountain's upper slabs to the summit, they called out comments like, "Wow, this is steep!" and "Wow, look how high we are!" The upper portion of the trail does grow quite steep, involving exposed scrambling on open slabs that become dangerous when wet or icy—and on which I watched the kids closely even though the rock was dry. The vertical ascent on this loop hike is about 1,800 feet.

From the parking area, the Holt Trail at first follows a wide, nearly flat woods road for almost a mile. At 1.1 miles, the trail crosses Bailey Brook, then follows the brook (other trails

the author's wife on Mount Cardigan's East Side Loop

branch left and right from the Holt). Growing steeper, the trail leaves the brook and ascends very steep, exposed rock slabs for the final 0.3 mile to the open summit, 2.2 miles from the parking area. Turn right (north) onto the Mowglis Trail and follow it off the summit, dropping sharply into the saddle between the main summit and Firescrew Mountain, a shoulder of Cardigan. The Mowglis Trail then climbs to the open top of Firescrew, with more long views, 0.6 mile from Cardigan's summit. Turn right (east) and follow the Manning Trail, descending steadily with good views for about 0.2 mile, then reentering the woods and reaching the Holt Trail nearly three miles from Cardigan's summit. Turn left and walk back to the parking lot.

User Groups

Hikers and dogs. Dogs must be leashed. No wheelchair facilities. This trail may be difficult to snowshoe, in part because of severe winter weather, and is not suitable for bikes, horses, or skis. Hunting is allowed in season unless otherwise posted.

Access and Fees

Parking and access are free. The access road is maintained in winter.

Maps

Get the *Monadnock/Cardigan* map, $7.95 in waterproof Tyvek, from the Appalachian Mountain Club, 800/262-4455, website: www.outdoors.org. For topographic area maps, request Mount Cardigan and Newfound Lake from USGS Map Sales, Federal Center, Box 25286, Denver, CO 80225, 888/ASK-USGS (888/275-8747), website: http://mapping.usgs.gov.

Directions

From the junction of Routes 3A and 104 in Bristol, drive north on Route 3A for 2.1 miles and turn left onto West Shore Road at a stone church at the south end of Newfound Lake. Continue 1.9 miles and proceed straight through a crossroads. Reaching a fork in 1.2 miles, bear right onto Fowler River Road, and then turn left 3.2 miles farther onto Brook Road. Continue another 1.1 miles and turn right onto the dirt Shem Valley Road; just 0.1 mile farther, bear right at a red schoolhouse. Drive 1.4 miles to the end of that road, where parking is available near the Appalachian Mountain Club's Cardigan Lodge. (At intersections along these roads, there are signs indicating the direction to the Cardigan Lodge.)

Contact

New Hampshire Division of Parks and Recreation, P.O. Box 1856, Concord, NH 03302-1856, 603/271-3254. Trails on Mount Cardigan are maintained by the Cardigan Highlanders, P.O. Box 104, Enfield Center, NH 03749, 603/632-5640.

9 MOUNT MAJOR
between West Alton and Alton Bay

Total distance: 3 miles round-trip

Hiking time: 1.5 hours

Difficulty: 4

Rating: 9

Perhaps the most popular hike in the lakes region, especially among families with young children, Mount Major has a bare summit that affords breathtaking views of Lake Winnipesaukee and north to the White Mountains on a clear day. From the parking lot, follow the wide, stone-littered trail climbing 1.5 miles and 1,100 feet to Major's summit. Descend the same way.

User Groups

Hikers, snowshoers, and dogs. Dogs must be leashed. No wheelchair facilities. This trail is not suitable for bikes, horses, or skis. Hunting is allowed in season.

Access and Fees

Parking and access are free. The state owns the summit area and maintains the parking lot, but the trail crosses private property.

Maps

For a topographic area map, request Squam Mountains from USGS Map Sales, Federal Center, Box 25286, Denver, CO 80225, 888/ASK-USGS (888/275-8747), website: http://mapping.usgs.gov.

Directions

The Mount Major Trail begins from a large parking area on Route 11, 2.4 miles south of the intersection of Routes 11 and 11A in West Alton, and 4.2 miles north of the junction of Routes 11 and 28A in Alton Bay.

Contact

New Hampshire Division of Parks and Recreation, P.O. Box 1856, 172 Pembroke Road, Concord, NH 03302, 603/271-3556, camping reservations 603/271-3628, website: www.nhstateparks.org.

10 MOUNT KEARSARGE
in Winslow State Park in Wilmot

Total distance: 2.8 miles round-trip

Hiking time: 2 hours

Difficulty: 4

Rating: 10

The barren, 2,937-foot summit of Mount Kearsarge, offering views of the White Mountains, Green Mountains, and southern New Hampshire, makes this one of the finest short hikes in New England—and while steep, a great adventure for children. Previous editions of this book described the hike ascending and descending the Winslow Trail. But the state park has since opened a new trail, the Barlow Trail, which offers a less-steep descent route that's easier on the knees than the Winslow Trail. This hike climbs about 1,100 feet in elevation.

Walk to the upper end of the parking lot in Winslow State Park and pick up the red-blazed Winslow Trail. The wide, well-beaten path rises quite steeply and relentlessly, and grows even more rugged the higher you go. At 0.8 mile, a large boulder on the left gives a good view north. A short distance farther, you break out of the trees onto the bald summit, with views in every direction, including Mount Sunapee and Lake Sunapee to the southwest, Mount Cardigan to the northwest, the Green Mountains to the west, and the White Mountains to the north. This is also a wonderful hike during the height of the fall foliage colors. A fire tower stands at the summit, and nearby are a pair of picnic tables—although on windy days it can be hard to linger up here for very long. Hike back along the same route.

Special note: In October 1997, the state allowed the construction of a 180-foot communications tower on the summit, something that offended many locals and prompted an effort to have the tower dismantled. Unfortunately, a Merrimack County Superior Court judge ruled in May 2000 that the tower does not violate any deed restriction for the property, as had been claimed by the land's previous owner, the Society for the Protection of New Hampshire Forests.

User Groups

Hikers and dogs. Dogs must be leashed. No wheelchair facilities. This trail may be difficult to snowshoe, in part because of severe winter weather, and is not suitable for bikes, horses, or skis. Hunting is allowed in season.

Access and Fees

Winslow State Park is open 9 A.M.–8 P.M. from May 1 to mid-November. There is a $3-per-person park entrance fee levied daily during the open season; children under 12 and New Hampshire residents 65 and older enter free. The last 0.6 mile of the entrance road is not maintained in winter (beyond the fork at the dead end sign).

Maps

A basic trail map of Winslow State Park is available at the park or from the New Hampshire Division of Parks and Recreation. For topographic area maps, request New London, Andover, Bradford, and Warner from USGS Map Sales, Federal Center, Box 25286, Denver, CO 80225, 888/ASK-USGS (888/275-8747), website: http://mapping.usgs.gov.

Directions

Take I-89 to Exit 10 and follow the signs to Winslow State Park. From the tollbooth at the state park entrance, drive to the dirt parking lot at the end of the road.

Contact

Winslow State Park, P.O. Box 295, Newbury, NH 03255, 603/526-6168. New Hampshire Division of Parks and Recreation, P.O. Box 1856, 172 Pembroke Road, Concord, NH 03302, 603/271-3556, camping reservations 603/271-3628, website: www.nhstateparks.org.

11 MOUNT SUNAPEE

in Mount Sunapee State Park in Newbury

Total distance: 4 miles round-trip　　　　　　**Hiking time:** 2.5 hours

Difficulty: 5　　　　　　　　　　　　　　　　　**Rating:** 9

The Summit Trail up central New Hampshire's popular Mount Sunapee offers a fairly easy, four-mile round-trip route from the ski area parking lot to the 2,743-foot summit. Many hikers will be satisfied with that. But this description also covers the Monadnock-Sunapee Greenway Trail from Sunapee's summit to Lucia's Lookout on Sunapee's long southern ridge—an ambitious round-trip from the parking lot at 12.8 miles and about seven hours, but well worth the effort for the views along the ridge, particularly overlooking Lake Solitude. I walked this trail with an organizer of the Monadnock-Sunapee Greenway Trail Club one September afternoon, and we spotted several moose tracks. The climb to Sunapee's summit is about 1,300 feet.

From the parking lot, walk behind the North Peak Lodge about 100 feet to where two ski trails merge, and look to the right for a sign for the Summit Trail, marked by red blazes. Ascending easily but steadily through the woods for two miles, the trail emerges onto an open meadow, where to the right (south) you get a view toward Mount Monadnock. Turn left and walk to the summit lodge a short distance ahead. Some of the best views on the mountain are from the decks at the lodge, with Mount Ascutney and the Green Mountains visible to the west, and Mounts Cardigan and Moosilauke and Franconia Ridge to the north. To complete this four-mile hike, return the way you came. To lengthen it with a walk along the somewhat rugged Sunapee Ridge, from where the trail emerges from the woods at the summit, trend right along the edge of the woods, behind the ski lift, then turn left and drop downhill a short distance, and turn right, looking for a sign and white blazes marking where the Monadnock-Sunapee Trail (which is also the trail to Lake Solitude) enters the woods off the ski trail.

After reentering the woods 0.2 mile from the summit, the greenway reaches the open White Ledges 0.9 mile from the summit; the trail swings left, but walking to the right will lead you to an open ledge with an excellent view of beautiful Lake Solitude, a small tarn tucked into the mountain's shoulder. Mount Monadnock is visible beyond the lake. Continuing south (left) on the greenway, you skirt the lake's shore within 0.2 mile. The trail passes over an open ledge 2.7 miles from the Sunapee summit before reaching Lucia's Lookout, 4.2 miles from the summit. Here, the views take in Mount Monadnock and Lovewell Mountain to the south, the Green

Mountains to the west, and Mount Kearsarge and the White Mountains to the north. Hike back the way you came.

Special note: Future expansion at the Mount Sunapee ski area could affect access to the Summit Trail. Check with Mount Sunapee State Park or the New Hampshire Division of Parks and Recreation.

User Groups

Hikers, snowshoers, and dogs. Dogs must be leashed. No wheelchair facilities. This trail is not suitable for bikes, horses, or skis. Hunting is allowed in season unless otherwise posted.

Access and Fees

Parking and access are free.

Maps

A free map of trails is available at the state park or from the New Hampshire Division of Parks and Recreation. A tear-proof, waterproof map of the entire Monadnock-Sunapee Greenway, a trail stretching 50 miles from Mount Monadnock to Mount Sunapee, costs $6, and The Greenway Trail Guide, which includes the map, costs $14; both can be purchased from the Monadnock-Sunapee Greenway Trail Club (MSGTC) or from area stores listed at the MSGTC website. For a topographic area map, request Newport from USGS Map Sales, Federal Center, Box 25286, Denver, CO 80225, 888/ASK-USGS (888/275-8747), website: http://mapping.usgs.gov.

Directions

From I-89 southbound, take Exit 12A. Turn right, drive about 0.6 mile, and turn right onto Route 11 west. Continue 3.5 miles and turn left onto Route 103B. (Or from I-89 northbound, take Exit 12, turn left, and follow Route 11 until turning left onto Route 103B.) Drive another 3.5 miles on Route 103B, go halfway around a traffic circle, and bear right at a sign for the state park. Continue to the end of the road and a large parking area at the base of the ski area.

Contact

Mount Sunapee State Park, P.O. Box 2021, Mount Sunapee, NH 03255, 603/763-3149. New Hampshire Division of Parks and Recreation, P.O. Box 1856, 172 Pembroke Road, Concord, NH 03302, 603/271-3556, camping reservations 603/271-3628, website: www.nhstateparks.org. Monadnock-Sunapee Greenway Trail Club (MSGTC), P.O. Box 164, Marlow, NH 03456, website: www.msgtc.org.

12 CATAMOUNT HILL
in Bear Brook State Park in Allenstown

Total distance: 2.2 miles round-trip   **Hiking time:** 1.5 hours

Difficulty: 2   **Rating:** 6

This 2.2-mile hike ascends a few hundred feet to one of the park's highest points, 721-foot Catamount Hill, where a mostly wooded ridge offers limited views of the state park's rambling forest. From the parking lot, cross Deerfield Road and follow it briefly back toward Route 28. About 100 feet past the tollbooth, a trail marked One Mile Road enters the woods. Follow it for 0.2 mile, bearing left where another dirt road enters from the right. In 0.1 mile from that junction, turn right onto the Catamount Hill Trail, which is marked by a sign. The trail climbs steadily, reaching the first lookout about 0.6 mile past the dirt road, just below the summit. Continue another 0.2 mile to the summit ridge, where another view is partially obscured by low trees. Return the way you came. At the bottom of the Catamount Hill Trail, turn left on One Mile Road; do not take the first trail on the right, which leads to a footbridge over Bear Brook. At the second junction, bear right to return to the tollbooth area.

User Groups
Hikers, snowshoers, and dogs. No wheelchair facilities. This trail is not suitable for bikes, horses, or skis. Hunting is allowed in season.

Access and Fees
An entrance fee of $3 per person is collected at the state park entrance. Children under 12 and New Hampshire residents 65 and older enter state parks free.

Maps
A free trail map is available at the park entrance and several other points within the park. For topographic area maps, request Suncook and Gossville from USGS Map Sales, Federal Center, Box 25286, Denver, CO 80225, 888/ASK-USGS (888/275-8747), website: http://mapping.usgs.gov.

Directions
The entrance to Bear Brook State Park is on Deerfield Road, off Route 28 in Allenstown, three miles north of the junction of Route 28 and U.S. 3. Turn left into a parking lot just past the entrance tollbooth on Deerfield Road.

Contact

Bear Brook State Park, 157 Deerfield Road, Allenstown, NH 03275, 603/485-9874. New Hampshire Division of Parks and Recreation, P.O. Box 1856, 172 Pembroke Road, Concord, NH 03302, 603/271-3556, camping reservations 603/271-3628, website: www.nhstateparks.org.

13 BEAR BROOK STATE PARK BIKE RACE LOOP
in Bear Brook State Park in Allenstown

Total distance: 12 miles round-trip

Hiking time: 6 hours

Difficulty: 8

Rating: 8

Bear Brook—the largest developed state park in New Hampshire—comprises nearly 10,000 acres and 40 miles of trails. The mostly moderate terrain makes for excellent mountain biking and cross-country skiing, and the difficulty ranges from relatively easy gravel roads to technically demanding single-track trails.

This loop—originally mapped out for a mountain bike race the park hosted, but also excellent for skiing—provides a good introduction to Bear Brook's varied offerings. Trails and roads are generally well marked with signs at intersections. Biking the somewhat hilly 12-mile trail takes about three hours.

From the parking lot, head across Podunk Road onto the narrow, winding Pitch Pine Trail. In a little more than a mile, the trail crosses the paved Campground Road. About a quarter mile farther, merge straight onto the Broken Boulder Trail (entering from the right). It passes a side path to a shelter at Smith Pond, then crosses the gravel Spruce Pond Road 0.5 mile past Smith Pond. Continue nearly another mile on the Broken Boulder Trail, then take a sharp right and run straight onto Podunk Road, which is gravel here. Follow the gravel road about a mile, turn right onto the gravel Spruce Road, and then take an immediate left onto the Chipmunk Trail.

The Chipmunk Trail winds through the woods for nearly a mile, then you'll bear left onto the Bobcat Trail. Cross Podunk Road (gravel) and Hayes Field; bear left at a fork onto the Carr Ridge Trail. Cross two trails within 0.5 mile, then bear right about a mile beyond the second trail, crossing onto the Cascade Trail. Reaching a junction in less than 0.25 mile, turn right on the Lane Trail, following it over rough ground along Bear Brook. It eventually turns away from the brook and a mile farther reaches a junction with the Hayes Farm Trail; turn left, then left again within 0.5 mile (before reaching the gravel Podunk Road) on the Little Bear Trail, which leads a mile back to the parking lot.

User Groups
Hikers, bikers, dogs, horses, skiers, and snowshoers. No wheelchair facilities. Hunting is allowed in season.

Access and Fees
An entrance fee of $3 per person is collected at the state park entrance. Children under 12 and New Hampshire residents 65 and older enter state parks free.

Maps
A free trail map is available in a box in the parking lot at the start of this hike and at other points in the park. For topographic area maps, request Suncook and Gossville from USGS Map Sales, Federal Center, Box 25286, Denver, CO 80225, 888/ASK-USGS (888/275-8747), website: http://mapping.usgs.gov.

Directions
The entrance to Bear Brook State Park is on Deerfield Road, off Route 28 in Allenstown, three miles north of the junction of Route 28 and U.S. 3. From the entrance tollbooth on Deerfield Road, drive another 2.2 miles and turn right on Podunk Road (at signs for the Public Camping Area). Continue another 0.3 mile and turn right into a parking lot for hikers and mountain bikers.

Contact
Bear Brook State Park, 157 Deerfield Road, Allenstown, NH 03275, 603/485-9874. New Hampshire Division of Parks and Recreation, P.O. Box 1856, 172 Pembroke Road, Concord, NH 03302, 603/271-3556, camping reservations 603/271-3628, website: www.nhstateparks.org.

14 PAWTUCKAWAY STATE PARK
in Raymond

Total distance: 7 miles round-trip   **Hiking time:** 3.5 hours

Difficulty: 8   **Rating:** 8

Pawtuckaway is far and away the most diverse natural area in southeastern New Hampshire. Many of its trails are ideal for hiking, mountain biking, or cross-country skiing, and you might be surprised by the extensive views from the ledges and fire tower atop South Mountain, though it rises less than 1,000 feet above sea level. Besides this hike, there are numerous trails to explore—try stretching this hike into a 12-mile loop by combining Tower Road with the Shaw and Fundy Trails.

From the parking lot, follow the paved road around to the right for about a quarter mile. After passing a pond on your left, turn left at a sign onto the Mountain Trail. Where it forks, stay right. Almost three miles from the pond, you will reach junction 5 (marked by a sign); turn right and ascend the trail to the summit of South Mountain. (This trail is passable on bikes or skis until the steep final stretch.) Check out the views from the ledges to the left and right of the trail just below the summit; the east-facing trails to the right will be warmer on a sunny day when the breeze is cool.

User Groups

Hikers, bikers, skiers, and snowshoers. No wheelchair facilities. Trails are closed to bikes during mud season, usually for the month of April. Dogs and horses are prohibited. Hunting is allowed in season.

Access and Fees

The parking lot opens at 10 A.M. Monday–Thursday and at 9 A.M. Friday–Sunday. A daily $3 entrance fee is charged to people age 12 and older at the park entrance from mid-June to Labor Day, except for New Hampshire residents 65 and older, who enter free. There is no fee the rest of the year.

Maps

A noncontour map of park trails is available at the park's main entrance. For a topographic area map, request Mount Pawtuckaway from USGS Map Sales, Federal Center, Box 25286, Denver, CO 80225, 888/ASK-USGS (888/275-8747), website: http://mapping.usgs.gov.

Directions

From Route 101, take Exit 5 for Raymond (there is a sign for Pawtuckaway). Follow Route 156 north and turn left onto Mountain Road at the sign for Pawtuckaway State Park. Follow the road two miles to the state park entrance and a parking lot on the left.

Contact

Pawtuckaway State Park, 128 Mountain Road, Nottingham, NH 03290, 603/895-3031. New Hampshire Division of Parks and Recreation, P.O. Box 1856, 172 Pembroke Road, Concord, NH 03302, 603/271-3556, camping reservations 603/271-3628, website: www.nhstateparks.org.

15 GREAT BAY NATIONAL ESTUARINE RESEARCH RESERVE: SANDY POINT TRAIL

in Stratham

Total distance: 1 mile round-trip

Hiking time: 0.75 hour

Difficulty: 1

Rating: 8

The Great Bay National Estuarine Research Reserve comprises a 4,500-acre tidal estuary and 800 acres of coastal land that provide a refuge for 23 species of endangered or threatened plant and animal species. Bald eagles winter here, osprey nest, and cormorants and great blue herons, among other birds, can be seen. Ecosystems range from salt marshes to upland forests and mud flats to tidal creeks, and three rivers empty into the bay. Great Bay also consistently has some of the finest sunsets I've ever seen. The Sandy Point Trail is one of two self-guided interpretive trails in the reserve; Adams Point in Durham, across the bay, also has an eagle-viewing platform. This trail largely follows a boardwalk for easy walking.

User Groups
Hikers only. The boardwalk is wheelchair accessible. This trail is not suitable for bikes, dogs, horses, skis, or snowshoes. Hunting is prohibited.

Access and Fees
Parking and access are free. Sandy Point Discovery Center is open to the public Wednesday–Sunday, 10 A.M.–4 P.M., May 1 to September 30, and on weekends in October. The grounds are open daylight hours throughout the year.

Maps
An interpretive trail pamphlet available at the Sandy Point Discovery Center guides visitors along a boardwalk at the estuary's edge and offers information about natural history and the local environment. The pamphlet and other information can also be obtained through the Great Bay Reserve Manager. For topographic area maps, request Newmarket and Portsmouth from USGS Map Sales, Federal Center, Box 25286, Denver, CO 80225, 888/ASK-USGS (888/275-8747), website: http://mapping.usgs.gov.

Directions
From the Stratham traffic circle at the junction of Routes 108 and 33, drive 1.4 miles north on Route 33 and turn left onto Depot Road at a sign for the Sandy Point Discovery Center. At the end of Depot Road, turn left

on Tidewater Farm Road. The Discovery Center is at the end of the road, and the trail begins behind the center.

Contact

Great Bay Reserve Manager, New Hampshire Fish and Game Department, Marine Fisheries Division, 225 Main Street, Durham, NH 03824, 603/868-1095, website: www.greatbay.org. New Hampshire Division of Parks and Recreation, P.O. Box 1856, 172 Pembroke Road, Concord, NH 03302, 603/271-3556, camping reservations 603/271-3628, website: www.nhstateparks.org.

16 ODIORNE POINT STATE PARK
in Rye

Total distance: 2 miles round-trip

Hiking time: 1 hour

Difficulty: 1

Rating: 7

A relatively small park at 330 acres, Odiorne is still the largest tract of undeveloped land along New Hampshire's 18-mile shoreline. It has a rich history: Beginning about 400 years ago, the Pennacook and Abenaki tribes frequented the area. Later, several generations of descendants of settler John Odiorne farmed and fished here, and during World War II, the military acquired the property for the construction of Fort Dearborn. Ever since it became a state park in 1961, the point has offered the public a rugged shore and a great place to catch an ocean sunrise or watch storm-fattened waves crash against the rocks.

Head to the far end of the parking lot and pick up the paved walkway; bear right where it forks. You'll walk past the small grove of low trees known as the Sunken Forest on your right, and continue out to Odiorne Point and a picnic area. The paved walkway leads through the picnic area to form a loop leading back to the parking lot. From the picnic area, walk the rocky shore or a path just above the beach to the Seacoast Science Center; a paved path leads left back to the parking lot. Or continue on either the beach or a trail past the center all the way out to the jetty at Frost Point for a broad shoreline view. Turn inland again along a wide trail. Turn left in front of a high military bunker, bear right onto a trail around a freshwater marsh, and follow the shoreline trail back to the science center and the parking lot.

User Groups

Hikers, bikers, skiers, and snowshoers. A portion of the trail is wheelchair accessible. Dogs, horses, and hunting are prohibited.

Access and Fees

The park is open daily year-round. There is a $3-per-person park entrance fee levied daily from early May to late October and on weekends the rest of the year; children under 12 and New Hampshire residents 65 and older enter free. Admission to the park's Seacoast Science Center is $1 per person.

Maps

For a map with historical and natural information about Odiorne, contact the New Hampshire Division of Parks and Recreation. For a topographic area map, request Kittery from USGS Map Sales, Federal Center, Box 25286, Denver, CO 80225, 888/ASK-USGS (888/275-8747), website: http://mapping.usgs.gov.

Directions

The main entrance to Odiorne is on Route 1A, 1.6 miles north of Wallis Sands State Beach and three miles south of Portsmouth. Park in the lot to the right beyond the entrance gatehouse.

Contact

The New Hampshire Division of Parks and Recreation, East Region Office, 603/436-1552. The Seacoast Science Center, Audubon Society of New Hampshire, 603/436-8043. New Hampshire Division of Parks and Recreation, P.O. Box 1856, 172 Pembroke Road, Concord, NH 03302, 603/271-3556, camping reservations 603/271-3628, website: www.nhstateparks.org.

17 NORTH PACK MONADNOCK
in Greenfield

Total distance: 3.2 miles round-trip   **Hiking time:** 2 hours

Difficulty: 3   **Rating:** 8

My nephews Stephen and Nicholas and niece Brittany were three, six, and four years old when I took them on this fairly easy 3.2-mile hike, which ascends less than 1,000 feet in elevation to the top of North Pack Monadnock. They gorged on the ripe blueberries along the trail, and celebrated like mountaineers when they reached the summit, with its view west to Mount Monadnock.

From the parking area, walk south into the woods, following the yellow triangle blazes of the Wapack Trail. It ascends at an easy grade through the Wapack National Wildlife Refuge for a mile, then climbs steep ledges and passes over one open ledge with a view east before reaching the summit at 1.6 miles. From the 2,276-foot summit, the views of southern New

Hampshire's wooded hills and valleys are excellent, especially to the west and north. Return the way you came.

User Groups

Hikers, snowshoers, and dogs. No wheelchair facilities. This trail is not suitable for bikes, horses, or skis. Hunting is allowed in season.

Access and Fees

Parking and access are free. Camping is allowed only at designated sites along the entire 21-mile Wapack Trail, but not along this hike. Fires are prohibited.

Maps

An excellent contour map of the Wapack Trail is available for $4 (including postage) from the Friends of the Wapack; the organization also sells a detailed guidebook to the entire trail for $11 (including postage). The *Guide to the Wapack Trail in Massachusetts & New Hampshire* three-color map costs $3.95 from New England Cartographics, 413/549-4124 or toll-free 888/995-6277, website: www.necartographics.com. For topographic area maps, request Peterborough South, Peterborough North, Greenfield, and Greenville from USGS Map Sales, Federal Center, Box 25286, Denver, CO 80225, 888/ASK-USGS (888/275-8747), website: http://mapping.usgs.gov.

Directions

The Wapack Trail begins at a parking area on Old Mountain Road in Greenfield, 2.6 miles west of Route 31 and 4.3 miles east of U.S. 202 in Peterborough (via Sand Hill Road).

Contact

Friends of the Wapack, Box 115, West Peterborough, NH 03468, website: www.wapack.org. New Hampshire Division of Parks and Recreation, P.O. Box 1856, 172 Pembroke Road, Concord, NH 03302, 603/271-3556, camping reservations 603/271-3628, website: www.nhstateparks.org.

18 MOUNT PISGAH

in Pisgah State Park between Chesterfield and Hinsdale

Total distance: 5 miles round-trip   **Hiking time:** 3 hours

Difficulty: 6   **Rating:** 8

Tucked away in the state's rural southwest corner, New Hampshire's largest state park includes this big hill called Mount Pisgah, where open summit ledges afford nice views of rolling countryside and Mount Monadnock to the east, and toward Massachusetts and Vermont to the southwest. Key trail junctions are marked with signs, and there's just a few hundred feet of uphill. From the trailhead, follow the Kilburn Road Trail, bearing left at junctions with the Kilburn Loop Trail, eventually turning onto the Pisgah Mountain Trail. Double back from the summit on the same trails. This is a wonderful intermediate ski tour, though you may have to carry skis up the steep stretch of trail below the summit. Though mountain bikes are permitted in much of the park, they are prohibited on these trails.

Special note: Want a little added adventure? For a challenging ski tour, continue over the summit of Mount Pisgah, following the sporadically blazed Pisgah Mountain Trail to the Reservoir Trail (which sees snowmobile use). Turn left (north) and keep bearing left at trail junctions until you reach a sign that reads "to Baker Trail." Turn left and follow the Davis Hill Trail past the Baker Trail and Baker Pond on the left; it eventually winds southwest to your starting point, completing a loop of about 10 miles. Bear in mind that snowmobilers use the Reservoir Trail and other paths in the park during winter, as do hunters in late fall.

User Groups
Hikers, snowshoers, and dogs. Dogs must be leashed. No wheelchair facilities. This trail may be difficult to snowshoe, in part because of severe winter weather, and difficult to ski due to the terrain's steepness. It is not suitable for bikes or horses. Hunting is allowed in season.

Access and Fees
Parking and access are free.

Maps
For a map of park trails, contact the state park or the New Hampshire Division of Parks and Recreation. For topographic area maps, request Winchester and Keene from USGS Map Sales, Federal Center, Box 25286, Denver, CO 80225, 888/ASK-USGS (888/275-8747), website: http://mapping.usgs.gov.

Directions
From I-91 in Brattleboro, VT, take Exit 3 for Route 9 east. At Route 63, turn right (south), pass through Chesterfield, and continue three more miles to an entrance and parking area for Kilburn Road in Pisgah State Park.

Contact
Pisgah State Park, P.O. Box 242, Winchester, NH 03470-0242, 603/239-8153. New Hampshire Division of Parks and Recreation, P.O. Box 1856,

172 Pembroke Road, Concord, NH 03302, 603/271-3556, camping reservations 603/271-3628, website: www.nhstateparks.org.

🔟 MOUNT MONADNOCK: WHITE ARROW TRAIL

in Monadnock State Park in Jaffrey

Total distance: 4.6 miles round-trip

Hiking time: 3 hours

Difficulty: 6

Rating: 10

Long one of my favorite mountains (also see the next listing), Monadnock is a peak I also hiked—via this route—with my niece Brittany and nephew Stephen when they were just six and five years old. They loved scrambling up the rocky trail, and did great on this ascent of 1,600 vertical feet. From the parking lot, walk past the gate onto the old toll road; you can either follow the wide road or immediately bear left onto the Old Halfway House Trail, which parallels the old carriage road for 1.2 miles to the meadow known as the Halfway House site. Cross the meadow to the White Arrow Trail, which ascends a

rock-strewn but wide path for another 1.1 miles to the summit of Mount Monadnock. The final quarter mile is above the mountain's tree line and very exposed to harsh weather. White blazes are painted on the rocks above the trees. Just below the summit, the trail makes a sharp right turn, then ascends slabs to the summit. Hike back the same way.

User Groups

Hikers only. No wheelchair facilities. This trail may be difficult to snowshoe, in part because of severe winter weather, and is not suitable for bikes, horses, or skis. Dogs are prohibited. Hunting is allowed in season, but not near trails.

near the summit of Mount Monadnock

Access and Fees

There is a parking fee of $3 per person, usually from April to November, and the parking lot is not maintained in winter. Children under 12 enter for free.

Maps

A free map of trails is available from the state park or the New Hampshire Division of Parks and Recreation. Or get the *Monadnock/Cardigan* map, $7.95 in waterproof Tyvek, from the Appalachian Mountain Club, 800/262-4455, website: www.outdoors.org. For topographic area maps, request Monadnock Mountain and Marlborough from USGS Map Sales, Federal Center, Box 25286, Denver, CO 80225, 888/ASK-USGS (888/275-8747), website: http://mapping.usgs.gov.

Directions

This hike begins from a parking lot on the north side of Route 124, 7.1 miles east of the junction of Routes 101 and 124 in Marlborough, and 5.4 miles west of the junction of Route 124, Route 137, and U.S. 202 in Jaffrey.

Contact

Monadnock State Park, P.O. Box 181, Jaffrey, NH 03452-0181, 603/532-8862, website: www.nhstateparks.org/ParksPages/Monadnock/Monadnock.html. New Hampshire Division of Parks and Recreation, P.O. Box 1856, 172 Pembroke Road, Concord, NH 03302, 603/271-3556, camping reservations 603/271-3628, website: www.nhstateparks.org.

20 MOUNT MONADNOCK: WHITE DOT–WHITE CROSS LOOP
in Monadnock State Park in Jaffrey

Total distance: 4.2 miles round-trip   **Hiking time:** 3 hours

Difficulty: 6   **Rating:** 10

At 3,165 feet high, majestic Mount Monadnock rises about 2,000 feet above the surrounding countryside of southern New Hampshire, making it prominently visible from many other lower peaks in the region. It was designated a National Natural Landmark in 1987. One of New England's most popular summits, it is said that Monadnock is hiked by more people than any peak in the world except Japan's Mount Fuji—although any ranger in the state park would tell you that's impossible to prove. Growing up not far from here, I soon adopted Monadnock as one of my favorite mountains in New England. I would estimate I've hiked it 50 or 60 times, in every season (conditions can be dangerous above tree line in winter). This can be a very crowded place from spring through fall, and this route may be the most commonly used on the mountain. Nonetheless, it's a scenic and moderately difficult two-mile route to the summit, climbing about 1,700 feet.

From the parking lot, walk up the road past the bathrooms and state park headquarters onto the White Dot Trail. The wide path dips slightly, crosses a brook, then ascends gently. At 0.5 mile, the Spruce Link bears left, leading in 0.3 mile to the White Cross Trail, but stay to the right on the White Dot. At 0.7 mile, the White Cross turns left, leading a short distance to Falcon Spring, a good water source; this hike continues straight ahead on the White Dot. The trail climbs steeply for the next 0.4 mile, with some limited views, until emerging onto open ledges at 1.1 miles. It then follows more level terrain, enters a forest of low evergreens, and ascends again to its upper junction with the White Cross Trail at 1.7 miles. The trail climbs the open, rocky terrain of the upper mountain for the final 0.3 mile to the summit. Descend the same way, except bear right onto the White Cross Trail, which descends steeply, with occasional views, for a mile. Continue straight ahead onto the Spruce Link Trail, which rejoins the White Dot in 0.3 mile. Turn right and walk 0.5 mile back to the trailhead.

User Groups

Hikers only. No wheelchair facilities. This trail may be difficult to snowshoe, in part because of severe winter weather, and is not suitable for bikes, horses, or skis. Dogs are prohibited. Hunting is allowed in season, but not near trails.

Access and Fees

An entrance fee of $3 per person is charged at the state park's main entrance year-round. Children under 12 enter for free.

Maps

A free map of trails is available from the state park or the New Hampshire Division of Parks and Recreation. Or get the *Monadnock/Cardigan* map, $7.95 in waterproof Tyvek, from the Appalachian Mountain Club, 800/262-4455, website: www.outdoors.org. For topographic area maps, request Mount Monadnock and Marlborough from USGS Map Sales, Federal Center, Box 25286, Denver, CO 80225, 888/ASK-USGS (888/275-8747), website: http://mapping.usgs.gov.

Directions

From Route 124, 10.4 miles east of the junction of Routes 101 and 124 in Marlborough, and 2.1 miles west of the junction of Route 124, Route 137, and U.S. 202 in Jaffrey, turn north at a sign for Monadnock State Park. Follow the state park signs to the large parking lot at the park's main entrance.

Contact

Monadnock State Park, P.O. Box 181, Jaffrey, NH 03452-0181, 603/532-8862, website: www.nhstateparks.org/ParksPages/Monadnock/Monadnock.html. New Hampshire Division of Parks and Recreation, P.O. Box 1856, 172 Pembroke Road, Concord, NH 03302, 603/271-3556, camping reservations 603/271-3628, website: www.nhstateparks.org.

21 TEMPLE MOUNTAIN
in Sharon

Total distance: 5.8 miles round-trip

Hiking time: 3.5 hours

Difficulty: 6

Rating: 8

One of the more scenic stretches of the Wapack Ridge Trail, this hike traverses the long ridge of Temple Mountain all the way to the Temple Mountain Ledges, a 5.8-mile round-trip with, all told, more than 1,200 feet of climbing. But there are several nice views along the way that make worthwhile destinations for anyone seeking a shorter hike. I took my seven-year-old niece, Brittany, on this hike: She ran ahead much of the way and loved the wild blueberries on the Sharon Ledges.

From the parking area, cross Temple Road and follow the yellow triangle blazes of the Wapack Trail into the woods. About 0.1 mile from the road, the trail passes a dilapidated old house. At 0.3 mile, it reaches an open area at the start of the Sharon Ledges, and a view of Mount Monadnock. A sign points to an overlook 75 feet to the right with a view toward Mount Watatic. Continuing northeast, the Wapack follows the Sharon Ledges for 0.75 mile, with a series of views eastward toward the hills and woods of southern New Hampshire. The trail enters the woods again and 1.4 miles from the road passes over the wooded subsidiary summit known as Burton Peak. Nearly 0.5 mile farther, a side path leads right to the top of cliffs and an unobstructed view to the east; on a clear day, the Boston skyline can be distinguished on the horizon. A short distance farther north on the Wapack lies an open ledge with a great view west to Monadnock—one of the nicest on this hike. The trail continues north 0.7 mile to the wooded summit of Holt Peak, another significant bump on the ridge. A half mile beyond Holt,

the author's wife and niece on Temple Mountain

watch through the trees on the left for a glimpse of an unusually tall rock cairn, then a side path leading to a flat, broad rock ledge with several tall cairns and good views in almost every direction. You've reached the Temple Mountain Ledges. The Wapack continues over Temple Mountain to Route 101, but this hike returns the same way you came.

User Groups

Hikers, snowshoers, and dogs. No wheelchair facilities. This trail is fairly difficult to ski and is not suitable for bikes or horses. Hunting is allowed in season unless otherwise posted.

Access and Fees

Parking and access are free. Camping is allowed only at designated sites along the entire 21-mile Wapack Trail; there are no designated sites along this hike. Fires are illegal without landowner permission and a permit from the town forest-fire warden.

Maps

An excellent contour map of the Wapack Trail is available for $4 (including postage) from the Friends of the Wapack; the organization also sells a detailed guidebook to the entire trail for $11 (including postage). The *Guide to the Wapack Trail in Massachusetts & New Hampshire* three-color map costs $3.95 from New England Cartographics, 413/549-4124 or toll-free 888/995-6277, website: www.necartographics.com. For topographic area maps, request Peterborough South and Greenville from USGS Map Sales, Federal Center, Box 25286, Denver, CO 80225, 888/ASK-USGS (888/275-8747), website: http://mapping.usgs.gov.

Directions

From the junction of Routes 101 and 123 (west of the Temple Mountain Ski Area), drive south four miles on Route 123 and turn left on Temple Road. Continue another 0.7 mile to a small dirt parking area on the right. Or from the junction where Routes 123 and 124 split, west of New Ipswich, drive north on Route 123 for a mile and turn right on Nashua Road. Continue another 0.6 mile and turn left on Temple Road. Drive 0.3 mile to the dirt parking area on the left.

Contact

Friends of the Wapack, Box 115, West Peterborough, NH 03468, website: www.wapack.org. New Hampshire Division of Parks and Recreation, Bureau of Trails, P.O. Box 1856, Concord, NH 03302-1856, 603/271-3254.

---

22 KIDDER MOUNTAIN

in New Ipswich

Total distance: 3 miles round-trip   **Hiking time:** 2 hours

Difficulty: 3   **Rating:** 8

This easy, three-mile hike gains less than 400 feet in elevation, yet the views from the open meadow atop 1,800-foot Kidder Mountain take in a grand sweep of this rural corner of southern New Hampshire. To the south, the Wapack Range extends to Mount Watatic in Massachusetts; behind Watatic rises Mount Wachusett. Two of us relaxed up here one July afternoon when there was just enough breeze to temper the heat and keep the bugs down, as we munched on the blueberries growing wild all over the meadow.

From the parking area, follow the yellow triangle blazes of the Wapack Trail into the woods, heading north. At 0.3 mile, the trail crosses a clearing and ascends a small hillside to the woods. At 0.6 mile from the road, the Wapack crosses a power line right-of-way. Turn right (east) at a sign onto the Kidder Mountain Trail. The trail follows a jeep road under the power line corridor for 0.1 mile, then turns left, crossing under the lines and entering the woods. It gradually ascends Kidder Mountain, reaching the open summit meadow nearly a mile from the Wapack Trail. Follow the same route back.

User Groups

Hikers, snowshoers, and dogs. No wheelchair facilities. This trail is not suitable for horses or skis. Hunting is allowed in season unless otherwise posted.

Access and Fees

Parking and access are free. Camping is allowed only at designated sites along the entire 21-mile Wapack Trail; there are no designated sites along this hike. Fires are illegal without landowner permission and a permit from the town forest-fire warden.

Maps

An excellent contour map of the Wapack Trail is available for $4 (including postage) from the Friends of the Wapack; the organization also sells a detailed guidebook to the entire trail for $11 (including postage). The *Guide to the Wapack Trail in Massachusetts & New Hampshire* three-color map costs $3.95 from New England Cartographics, 413/549-4124 or toll-free 888/995-6277, website: www.necartographics.com. For topographic area maps, request Peterborough South and Greenville from USGS Map Sales, Federal Center, Box 25286, Denver, CO 80225, 888/ASK-USGS (888/275-8747), website: http://mapping.usgs.gov.

Directions

The trailhead parking area is on the north side of Route 123/124 in New Ipswich, 2.9 miles west of the junction with Route 123A and 0.7 mile east of where Route 123 and Route 124 split.

Contact

Friends of the Wapack, Box 115, West Peterborough, NH 03468, website: www.wapack.org. New Hampshire Division of Parks and Recreation, Bureau of Trails, P.O. Box 1856, Concord, NH 03302-1856, 603/271-3254.

23 BEAVER BROOK
in Hollis

Total distance: 2.5 miles round-trip	**Hiking time:** 1.5 hours
Difficulty: 1	**Rating:** 8

Chartered in 1964 by the state as an educational nonprofit organization, the Beaver Brook Association manages nearly 2,000 acres of land and about 35 miles of trails here at its main campus in Hollis. This place is a local jewel that attracts hikers, snowshoers, cross-country skiers, and mountain bikers from a wide radius. The terrain varies from flat wetlands that cover at least one-third of the land, to abrupt little-forested hills. Many of the trails are ideal for beginning skiers and bikers; some are appropriate for people with intermediate skills. This hike involves some trails that are closed to bikes and horses, but there are about 20 miles of trails here open to those activities. Do not overlook the trails on the north side of Route 130, in the area of Wildlife Pond; the Rocky Ridge and Mary Farley Trails also offer particularly nice hiking opportunities.

From the office, follow the wide woods road called Cow Lane. Turn onto the first trail on your left, Porcupine Trail, and follow it down to the wetlands. Turn right onto the Beaver Brook Trail, which parallels the broad marsh—a good place for bird-watching. Turn left and cross the boardwalk over the marsh, then continue straight onto Jason's Cutoff Trail. Turn right onto the wide forest road called Elkins Road and follow it to a right turn where a woods road crosses Beaver Brook, leading to the Brown Lane barn. Walk Brown Lane a short distance, and turn right onto the Tepee Trail, which leads back to Cow Lane. Turn left to return to your car.

User Groups

Hikers, dogs, skiers, and snowshoers. Dogs must be leashed. No wheelchair facilities. This trail is not suitable for bikes or horses. Hunting is prohibited.

Access and Fees

Parking and access are free.

Maps

A trail map is available at the Beaver Brook Association office. Office hours are weekdays, 9 A.M.–4 P.M. For a topographic area map, request Pepperell from USGS Map Sales, Federal Center, Box 25286, Denver, CO 80225, 888/ASK-USGS (888/275-8747), website: http://mapping.usgs.gov.

Directions

From the junction of Routes 130 and 122 in Hollis, drive south on Route 122 for 0.9 mile and turn right onto Ridge Road. Follow Ridge Road to the Maple Hill Farm and the office of the Beaver Brook Association. Once you become familiar with the trails here, another good access point to the Beaver Brook land is from the parking area off Route 130, west of the town center and across from the Diamond Casting and Machine Company.

Contact

Beaver Brook Association, 117 Ridge Road, Hollis, NH 03049, 603/465-7787, website: www.beaverbrook.org.

© MICHAEL LANZA

Resources

Public Lands Agencies

**New Hampshire Division of
 Parks & Recreation**
P.O. Box 1856
172 Pembroke Road
Concord, NH 03302
603/271-3556, fax 603/271-2629
camping reservations: 603/271-3628
website: www.nhstateparks.org

**White Mountain National
 Forest Supervisor**
719 North Main Street
Laconia, NH 03246
603/528-8721 or
 TDD 603/528-8722
website: www.fs.fed.us/r9/white

Map Sources

DeLorme Publishing Company
800/253-5081
website: www.DeLorme.com

Trails Illustrated
800/962-1643
website: http://maps.national-
 geographic.com/trails

United States Geological Survey
Information Services
Box 25286
Denver, CO 80225
888/ASK-USGS (275-8747),
 fax 303/202-4693
website: http://mapping.usgs.gov

Trail Clubs and Organizations

Appalachian Mountain Club
5 Joy Street
Boston, MA 02108
617/523-0655
website: www.outdoors.org

**Appalachian Mountain Club
 Pinkham Notch Visitor Center**
P.O. Box 298
Gorham, NH 03581
603/466-2721
website: www.outdoors.org

Appalachian Trail Conference
799 Washington Street
P.O. Box 807
Harpers Ferry, WV 25425-0807
304/535-6331
website: www.appalachiantrail.org

Cardigan Highlanders Club
Sanborn, Craig
P.O. Box 104
Enfield Center, NH 03749
603/632-5640

Friends of the Wapack
Box 115
West Peterborough, NH 03468
website: www.wapack.org

**Monadnock-Sunapee Greenway
  Trail Club (MSGTC)**
P.O. Box 164
Marlow, NH 03456
website: www.msgtc.org

Randolph Mountain Club
P.O. Box 279
Randolph, NH 03581
website: www.randolphmountain-
  club.org

Squam Lakes Association
P.O. Box 204
Holderness, NH 03245
603/968-7336
website: www.squamlakes.org

**Wonalancet Out Door Club
  (WODC)**
HCR 64 Box 248
Wonalancet, NH 03897
website: www.wodc.org

Acknowledgments

I want to thank the many people who accompanied me on these trails, in particular my wife and hiking partner, Penny Beach. My parents, Henry and Joanne Lanza, deserve recognition—both for putting up with a son who has shown up at their door a few times since they first got rid of him, and for being good hiking partners. Of the friends who have shared trails with me, Mike Casino warrants special thanks for enduring innumerable miles in my company (and I still hope and pray he will again quit his job and have more free time for hiking). I also want to thank my editors and the rest of the very talented staff at Avalon Travel Publishing.

While I have personally walked every hike described in this book—some of them many times—updating a volume as comprehensive as this one cannot possibly be accomplished without the assistance of many people. To that end, I relied on friends, acquaintances, people active with hiking and conservation groups, and managers of public lands and private reserves to do some on-the-ground "scouting" of trails and send me current reports on the hikes in this book. Much deep appreciation goes out to: Joe Albee, Mike and Rick Baron, Mark Bogacz, Denise Buck, Steve Buck, Peter Cole, Mark Fenton, Anna Garofalo, Marco Garofalo, Larry Gies, Judy Glinder, Kellen Glinder, Betsy Harrison, Ed Hawkins, Joe Kuzneski, Brittany Lanza, Cassidy Lanza, Julie Lanza, Kaylee Lanza, Nicholas Lanza, Stephen Lanza, Marjorie LaPan, Carol Lavoie, Denis Lavoie, Peter Mahr, Diane Mailloux, Pete and Marilyn Mason, Eddie Maxwell, Bill Mistretta, Kim Nilsen, Brion O'Connor, Ed Poyer, Gerry Prutsman, Keith Ratner, Janet Scholl, Roger Scholl, Bob Spoerl, Tim Symonds, Doug Thompson, Rod Venterea, Matt Walsh, and Barbara Wilkins.

There were also many helpful people at various organizations and public agencies, including: Appalachian Mountain Club; Appalachian Trail Conference; Beaver Brook Association; Cardigan Highlanders; Chatham Trails Association; DeLorme Publishing Company; Monadnock-Sunapee Greenway Trail Club; New Hampshire Division of Parks and Recreation; Randolph Mountain Club; Squam Lakes Association; White Mountain National Forest; and Wonalancet Out Door Club.

Index

Notes

Notes

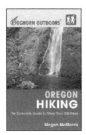
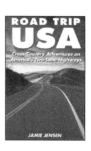